DECADES OF STARS

About the Author

Brendan Fullam is a native of Ardagh, Co. Limerick. From an early age, influenced by the GAA activity in his native parish, he took a keen interest in Gaelic games and particularly in hurling. Strangely enough, his earliest memory is of a football final – when Cork beat Cavan in 1945.

His banking career took him to many parts of Ireland, where he played with the local team: Killorglin, Kilrush, Clifden, Ballyshannon and Wexford. Over the years he has written about almost 300 Gaelic players and has given to posterity a valuable work.

His previous books include *Hurling Giants, Legends of the Ash, Giants of the Ash, Captains of the Ash* and *Lest We Forget.*

DECADES OF STARS

A Collection of Hurling Heroes

BRENDAN FULLAM

Forewords by Liam Griffin and Criostóir Ó Cuana

WOLFHOUND PRESS

Wolfhound Press
33 Fitzwilliam Place
Dublin 2

Tel: +353 1 278 5090
Fax: +353 1 278 4800

www.wolfhoundpress.com

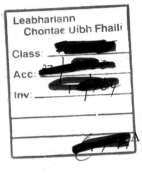

© Brendan Fullam, 2011

ISBN: 978-0-86327-972-0

A catalogue record for this book is available from
the British Library.

Printed in Ireland by Colorman Ltd.

FOREWORD

Many are gone; Brendan Fullam has made sure they will never be forgotten. *Decades of Stars* concentrates on the last fifty years but preserves a link with the past by including a selection of household names from earlier decades.

In my office at home, I have three of Brendan's previous publications close at hand. From time to time, when in need of a necessary uplifting of the spirit, I pick up one of these books and open it – anywhere. Suddenly I am in Thurles or Croke Park. The time of day, the season and even the weather has changed in my mind. On one page I am a boy again. I can even sense my parents beside me as I see once again the great games and great players we once saw together. Change the page – now as a man I am a witness. I turn another page and I'm off again on an emotional hurling journey across the decades. It is in those moments of absolute escapism that I understand why modern sports psychologists extol the virtues and power of visualisation.

Brendan Fullam's books have no beginning and no end. There is no feeling that the story has ended – in fact, the more you read the more you realise that the story is always just beginning. Questions arise; they are bound to. To mention just one – who is the greatest hurler of them all? Now the passions rise and the county loyalties soon become apparent. That debate will rage as long as hurling is played.

A few years ago in Thurles, a small bespectacled oldish Cork man, resplendent with his red and white paper hat, stood in front of me as I walked through that famous match day square towards Tom Semple's field. "Liam Griffin", he shouted in his rich melodious Cork accent, "You are the man who said D.J. Carey was as good a hurler as Christy Ring. Well, that proves you know feck-all about hurling!" The crowd lustily cheered; I enjoyed the moment as much as he and they did. The names between these covers certainly feature prominently in "The Great Debate".

My tuppence worth – great hurlers "would have been great in any era". Their dedication, ambition, background and passion would have seen to that. Read their stories here and make up your own mind. Is hurling better today than in decades past? It's certainly different. It's faster, fairer, safer. All sports have evolved with modern training methods and knowledge. This is no slight on any time or any era, as the sporting evolution has been constant. Hurling is different today in marginal ways, but in the end we are arguing over a shade of difference. One fact is certain though – hurling is without question a truly great, different and unique game. The more time progresses, the more this book actually will illustrate the uniqueness of the hurler in the modern sporting world. Players of the past were rooted in their native parishes and counties. The same applies to the players of today. Club and county loyalties matter as much today as they did in the past. The esteem in which great hurlers are held starts in the local field, and follows the players to the county grounds and to Croke Park. *Decades of Stars* thankfully recognises the greatness of so many.

To those of us who have been lucky enough to master the game to any level, I feel it has changed our vision and appreciation, not just of hurling, but of all sports.

Brendan Fullam's passion for hurling has enhanced our appreciation and understanding by leaving us with an insight into so many greats of the game. We are truly grateful.

Liam Griffin
Retired manager of the Wexford senior hurling team and former player
September 2011

FOREWORD

Is cúis mhór áthais dom na focail seo a leanas a scríobh don leabhar iontach seo a dhéanann cur síos ar roinnt den iománaithe ab fhearr chun ár gcluiche a imirt.

As Uachtarán Chumann Luthchleas Gael, it gives me great pleasure to contribute to this book, *Decades of Stars: A Collection of Hurling Heroes*, which commemorates some of hurling's finest ever players.

Since the GAA was formed in 1884, it has provided a social, cultural and sporting outlet for people all over the country.

Our games have produced many heroes in that time and, although some live on through the memories of our members and supporters, the reality is that a large number of our former players fade from the memory with the passing of time.

This compilation of memoirs and stories from players from all over the country over numerous decades captures the spirit and goodwill that still exists towards so many of these figures in the GAA today.

This book, which mainly focuses on hurlers from the last fifty years, will provide readers with a wonderful insight into so many fascinating characters that the sport has spawned.

It shines a light on the feats and characters of players of the calibre of Brian Cody, Eddie Keher, Ken McGrath, Brendan Cummins and Henry Shefflin, among many others who have served the sport so well as true ambassadors over the years.

It is also a pleasure to see that recent legends like these are to be found alongside recollections of others such as Christy Ring, Lory Meagher, Nicky Rackard and Jack Lynch, all of whom will be forever remembered for their individual contributions to our games.

It's a rare experience for a reader to get an insight into the lives and wonderful minds of so many sporting legends through the prism of one publication.

As our games continue to thrive and captivate the imagination of our people, both here and overseas, I have no doubt that in another hundred years a similar exercise will need to be undertaken.

Until then enjoy this fine publication.

Ar aghaidh len ár gcluichí,

Criostóir Ó Cuana
Uachtarán Chumann Lúthchleas Gael
September 2011

PREFACE

Since the foundation of the GAA in 1884, countless thousands have played the game of hurling. Only a fraction of that figure has played the game at the highest level, and only a fraction of these are remembered as the decades roll on.

It is a pity that so many are forgotten, I thought to myself one day, when I heard of the death of an old-timer. It put me thinking. So, armed with the photographs of the players I had begun cutting from the daily newspapers in the mid 1940s and a large leather-bound journal of 600 pages that technology has now made redundant, I set forth in 1980 on what turned out to be an odyssey – a journey that brought me in contact with the hurling lives of almost 300 players: players I had heard of; players I had read about; players I had seen in action.

The journal contains the signatures and the written contributions of the players, which ranged from a few sentences in some cases to pages in other cases, from John T. Power of Kilkenny (born in 1883) to recently retired modern-day stars such as Ken McGrath (Waterford) and Damien Fitzhenry (Wexford), and players still in action like Brendan Cummins (Tipperary) and Henry Shefflin (Kilkenny).

In my books to date, I have written about almost 300 of our hurlers – just a small number of those who played at the highest level. It keeps their memory alive. Otherwise, some of them would be forgotten – even the great ones of their day. How many now know of Sean Óg Hanly, Jim Kelliher, Mikey Maher, Sean O'Kennedy, Jack Rochford and Mick King? I could go on.

Decades of Stars contains an abridged presentation of a selection of players from all my previous books and concentrates, almost exclusively, on those whose careers belonged to the last fifty years. However, with a view to preserving a link with times past, a selection of household names from earlier decades is also included. The result is an encounter with hurling men from the early days of the GAA right up to the present day – a journey of nostalgia and enjoyment.

I would like to have included many more, among them Gerry O'Malley (Roscommon); John McGrath (Westmeath); Ciaran Barr (Antrim); Jimmy Grey, Mick Daniels and Des Ferguson (Dublin); Matt Nugent, Tom McInerney, Pa "Fowler" McInerney and John Joe Doyle (Clare); Sean Duggan, Mick King, Josie Gallagher, Paddy Gantley and Donal Flynn (Galway); Johnny Ryan, Martin Kennedy, Jimmy Coffey, Jimmy Kennedy, Phil Shanahan, Tony Wall and Jimmy Finn (Tipperary); Johnny Quirke, Con Murphy, Dave Creedon, John Lyons, Willie John Daly and Jim Young (Cork); Jim Ware, Phil Grimes, Séamus Power, John Barron, Christy Moylan, Andy Fleming and Mick Hickey (Waterford); Ned Wheeler, Padge Kehoe, Paddy Kehoe, Nick O'Donnell, Tim Flood, Jim English, Sam Thorpe and Martin Codd (Wexford); John Mackey, Jackie Power, Paddy Clohessy, Dick Stokes, Tommy Quaid, Mickey Cross, Sean Herbert and Timmy Ryan (Limerick); Terry Leahy, Jim Langton, Paddy Buggy, Johnny McGovern, Jack Rochford, Paddy Phelan and Martin White (Kilkenny).

In meeting all the players who featured in my books, one thing in particular stood out. And it was something I hadn't anticipated. Being remembered as the years rolled by was as special and important to them as their successes on the playing field.

I saw the spirits and the well-being of old-timers lift. I saw dying energies come to life as deeds of yore were recounted and relived.

Decades of Stars will hopefully ensure that some who might otherwise be forgotten will be remembered.

I wish to thank Con Collins of The Collins Press for permission to use material from *Lest We Forget*.

Brendan Fullam
October 2011

CONTENTS

1960s

1980s

Contents

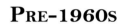

PRE-1960S

KEVIN ARMSTRONG
ANTRIM

Born: 1922
Interviewed: 1985

Kevin (right) reminiscing with Jimmy Doyle,
legendary Tipperary forward of the 1960s.

"I was delighted to have played hurling and football. I got great enjoyment out of the games and they made my life just wonderful. I have played hurling and football against great men of all the provinces. I look back on those days as the greatest days of my life. My boyhood heroes were Mick Mackey and Bobby Beggs."

While I was primarily interested in Kevin the hurler, it was of course impossible to ignore Kevin the footballer – All-Time All-Star award football recipient in 1988. He recalled three special memories from his football days:

• The triumph in Ulster in 1946 that ended thirty-three years of waiting

- His selection for the Ulster Railway Cup team of 1942, when he played with the elite of Ulster that included great names like Jim McCullough (Armagh), Vincent Duffy (Monaghan), John Joe O'Reilly (Cavan), Alf Murray (Armagh) and Big Tom O'Reilly (Cavan). Ulster won the competition and took the trophy to the Northern province for the first time
- Being captain of the Ulster football team of 1947; again they won the trophy and Kevin had the honour of being the first man ever to take the cup across the border. It was Kevin's second of four medals from six final appearances

But let's now turn to Kevin the hurler, whose prowess with the camán enabled him to win a place at left half-forward on the Centenary team of players who never won an All-Ireland medal.

Kevin was part of an Antrim team that, in 1943, surprised Gael-dom with quarter-final and semi-final wins over Galway and Kilkenny respectively. Unfortunately, prospects of All-Ireland glory ended with a heavy defeat at the hands of all-conquering Cork in the All-Ireland final: "a super side – maybe the best ever to leave the Leeside."

Two years later, their second year in the competition, Ulster shocked Leinster in the Railway Cup semi-final by winning 3:1 to 2:3. They fell to Munster in the final, 6:8 to 2:0. But it was no disgrace. Munster was star-laden. Ring was there and also the hero of Kevin's youth, Mick Mackey. At centre-forward for Ulster, Kevin was opposed by Jackie Power. "I felt honoured to have played in such company in 1945."

Dimigh Kevin – fear uasal, macánta – ar shlí na firinne ar an 13 Lúnasa 1992.

Kevin Armstrong

TOMMY DALY
CLARE

Born: 1894

Being carried in triumph following victory over Galway in the 1932 All-Ireland semi-final.

The name Tommy Daly is revered in the hurling homes of Clare where he is remembered as one of the all time great goalkeepers. In his native Tulla, the local pitch is named after him.

He won an All-Ireland junior medal in 1914 with his native Clare. With UCD he won three Fitzgibbon Cup titles in the 1920s and captained the 1922/23 team. He played with his adopted Dublin in six All-Ireland finals and was victorious in 1917, 1920, 1924 and 1927, to become Clare's most decorated All-Ireland medal holder. He was in goal for Leinster when the province won the inaugural Railway Cup competition in 1927. A year later he was chosen on the Tailteann Games team.

He declared for his native Clare in 1928 – having played his last game with Dublin in the All-Ireland semi-final of 1928 against Cork – and won a Munster title in 1932. Later that year, in the All-Ireland semi-final against Galway, at Limerick, he was involved in one of the most dramatic hurling games ever played. Down sixteen points in the second half, and with some of the crowd streaming away, Clare staged a recovery that gave them a final score victory of 9:4 to 4:14. They failed to Kilkenny in the All-Ireland final by 3:3 to 2:3. Munster Railway Cup selectors honoured Tommy in 1933, but the final was lost to Leinster by 4:6 to 3:6.

Tommy was also a prominent referee. He had charge of the memorable All-Ireland final of 1935 between Limerick and Kilkenny.

He died following a fatal car accident at Tuamgraney, in east Clare, in September 1936. He was only forty-two.

"The dirge of Tommy Daly
Goes surging on through Clare."

JOHN DOYLE
TIPPERARY

Born: 1930
Interviewed: 1986

1953 Munster Final (Tipp. v. Cork). John Doyle clears, watched by Mickey Byrne (Tipp.) and Paddy Barry (Cork) on the right. (Photo by Bord Fáilte photographer T. Hayde.)

"From an early age my big ambition was to be on the Tipperary team and nothing was going to stop me. I must say I was fortunate enough to get on a great Tipp. team at the start of my career. I was very lucky when I think of all the great players who never won any major competitions."

John Doyle departed this life on 29 December 2010, a few weeks short of his eighty-first birthday.

In his time he gave much to hurling and gained much from it, too. He won an All-Ireland minor medal in 1947 and two years later entered senior ranks. He remained there until he retired in 1967, following an All-Ireland defeat by Kilkenny.

In between those years, John won fame and renown as a hurling defender. He was daring and dashing rather than stylish and classical. But, above all, he was inspirational.

His career spanned two great Tipperary hurling eras that brought him eight All-Ireland medals to equal the record held by Christy Ring. From 1949 to 1951 he won three in a row. He almost called it a day in 1957 but shrewd Tipperary mentor Paddy Leahy persuaded him otherwise. John won a fourth medal in 1958. That led the way to the second era – the 1960s. He won medals back to back in 1961–1962 and 1964–1965. Kilkenny denied him a ninth in 1967.

All the honours the game had to offer came John's way, including a remarkable eleven National League titles. Personal honours included Hurler of the Year in 1964, entry to the Hall of Fame in 1992 and selection for the Centenary and Millennium teams.

Though gone, his fame lives on.

John Doyle

HARRY GRAY
LAOIS AND DUBLIN

Born: 1915

Harry (left) receiving the Hall of Fame Award from Séamus O'Riain of Tipperary, GAA President 1967–1969.

Few would disagree with the suggestion that the late Harry Gray was one of Laois's greatest hurling sons, and one of the game's finest midfielders. He was chosen at centre half-forward on the Laois team of the Centenary.

He was born in Mill Street, Rathdowney. As a juvenile he was part of a street team known as the "Flourbags" – their togs were made from them. He won a senior hurling title with his native Rathdowney in 1936.

The following year, Harry was lured to Dublin by Tommy Moore, the Kilkenny man who brought many a fine hurler to Dublin and looked after them. Harry won seven county titles with Faughs – the club Tommy Moore was associated with.

His senior hurling career began in 1934 with his native Laois – having played minor with the county in 1933. He retired from inter-county hurling in 1949 after Laois were defeated by Tipperary in the All-Ireland final. Harry, who had declared for his native Laois in 1948, played at centre forward in the All-Ireland final of 1949.

Between the years 1934 and 1949, Harry made his name as a midfielder in the Dublin and Leinster jerseys. He won All-Ireland honours with his adopted Dublin in 1938 and a National League title in 1939 – both teams captained by Tipperary born Mick Daniels.

Harry figured regularly on Leinster Railway Cup selections. He won his only title in 1941 when he was partnered at midfield by Tipperary-born Ned Wade.

Liam O'Neill who partnered Harry at midfield for Laois minors in 1933 described him as a man of powerful physique and a wonderful stylist. As a midfielder, he saw him as being in the mould of the great Jim Hurley of Cork – and in appearance a larger edition of Alan Ladd, the film star.

Canon Sean Collier PP, Borris-in-Ossory, knew Harry well. They played together on the Laois team of 1948. Of Harry he said, "Big in physique – he relied very much on his skill to "read the game" and made maximum use of the least opportunity. His striking accuracy was tops and he could score from any angle. When I visited him in hospital shortly before his death he still had high hopes for Laois hurlers – his witty comment was, "Will they listen to you, Fr Sean?"

Harry died in 1978. But he is not forgotten in his native Laois. His memory is commemorated through the Harry Gray Cup, which is now presented each year to the Laois minor hurling champions.

SEÁN ÓG HANLY
LIMERICK

Born: 1877

Seán Óg Hanly hailed from Kilfinane in Co. Limerick and scaled the hurling heights in the infant years of the GAA.

He was christened Jim, but those who watched him in action were reminded of the physique and athleticism of his grandfather Seán – so they named him Seán Óg – and it stuck.

He was a *ciotóg* – holding his hurley right hand under – and was a natural left hander. He was a man of great strength and weighed about 14 st., but his hurling style was based on speed and art. The length of his clearances was prodigious.

The gate to fame opened when Kilfinane defeated Cappamore by 4:9 to 4:8 in the county final of 1897. In the Munster final of that year, played at Tipperary on 25 September 1898, Limerick overcame Cork by 4:9 to 1:6.

Seán Óg was vice-captain when Limerick defeated Kilkenny by 3:4 to 2:4 in the All-Ireland final, at the same venue, on 20 November 1898. He was the outstanding man on the pitch on both occasions, following which his fame and prowess spread nationwide.

In the Croke Cup final of 1897, played at Thurles on 9 July 1899, with Dr Croke in attendance, Limerick again defeated Kilkenny by 3:8 to 1:4. Seán Óg stood apart.

Having played for Commercials in Dublin in 1899, Seán Óg emigrated to England. He played with London in the All-Ireland final of 1900 against Tipperary. The power of his hurling at full-back kept Tipperary at bay for fully fifty-five minutes of the hour. The score read London 0:6, Tipperary 0:5. Then, two late goals saved Tipperary from a sensational defeat.

He was associated with the London team which shocked Cork in the All-Ireland final of 1901. The game was played at Jones's Road on 2 August 1903. The final score was London 1:5, Cork 0:4. He was a member of the London team of 1903 that lost to Cork by 3:16 to 1:1 in the All-Ireland final, which was played at Jones's Road on 12 November 1905.

Seán Óg died in his fifties and was mourned by the hurling world. He is buried in Kensal Rise Cemetery. The fumes of London town had taken a toll on his health. So great was the esteem in which he was held that the Gaels of Limerick and London subscribed to erect a monument over his grave.

"Carbery", who had seen more than fifty hurling finals, was asked by the *Gaelic Sportsman* to pick a hurling team titled "The Best Men of My Time" in the 1950s.

In selecting Seán Óg at full-back, he wrote: "[He] was the greatest hurler of his day – six foot one and a half inches, powerfully built; his name lives on with Limerick and London Irish – phenomenal length of drive."

JOHN KEANE
WATERFORD

Born: 1917

Munster Captain 1939, with the Railway
Cup. (Photo courtesy of Margaret Curran.)

I can still remember cutting the photograph of John Keane from one of
the daily newspapers during Waterford's All-Ireland campaign of 1948.

I had often heard about John and, in particular, his Herculean performance on the mighty Mick Mackey of Limerick, then at the zenith of his
greatness, in the Munster semi-final at Clonmel in 1937. In a gripping
contest, Waterford went down before the power of Limerick by just two
points: 3:4 to 3:2.

John was born on 18 February 1917, the second youngest of a family
of nine. From his school days at Mount Sion he grew in hurling stature,
winning county minor titles in 1934 and 1935 and playing inter-provincial

colleges with Munster for three successive years from 1933. To those achievements, he added a county junior title in 1934 and an All- Ireland junior medal the same year, playing at full-back. In his prime, he stood 5'10½" and turned the scales at 13½ st. He was always supremely fit, never sparing himself, whether playing for club, county or province.

After Waterford's great performance at Clonmel in 1937, John's thoughts turned to winning an All-Ireland senior hurling title. There would be many disappointments – three in particular. So let's look at them.

In 1938 Waterford won their first Munster senior title. In the All-Ireland final against Dublin, John discarded his boots after ten minutes and played the rest of the game in his stocking feet. Despite inspiring hurling by John at centre half-back and a contribution of four points, Waterford lost by 2:5 to 1:6.

In 1940, after two gripping contests with Limerick, 4:2 to 3:5 and 3:5 to 3:2, Waterford made their exit from the championship. John Keane watched and pondered on what might have been as Limerick went on to win Munster and All-Ireland honours.

The year 1943 came, and to quote, with a slight amendment, William Wordsworth of the beautiful Lake District: "Three years have passed; three summers with the length of three long winters!" – and still there was no sign of an All-Ireland crown. Waterford faced Tipperary in the first round and won by 4:5 to 1:2. Was it John Keane's greatest display? The late Pat Fanning, in an article in *An Deiseach* in 1974, recalled that June afternoon:

> Then came the greatest display of courage and determination and perhaps his greatest personal triumph – his epic display at Dungarvan in 1943 against Tipperary, when with a badly injured ankle he stood at centre back and almost alone broke the back of every Tipperary attack. Well do I remember cutting the boot from his swollen ankle at the end of that excruciating hour. And I recall, too, the old wizened man of Tipperary who pushed his way through the crowd to where John lay, to shake, as he said, "the hand of John Keane, the greatest man in Ireland".

In the Munster semi-final, Waterford faced Limerick. The teams served up another superb spectacle of sport. Two goals directly from frees by John Keane and wonderful goalkeeping by Jim Ware, the captain, saw

Waterford through by one point, 3:7 to 4:3. The Munster final against
Cork was another heart-breaking day for John Keane. Cork won by two
points, 2:13 to 3:8. And one of those Cork goals was deflected in by a
Waterford defender. The loss to Cork assumed much greater proportions
when, in their next game – the final – the Leesiders routed Antrim by 5:16
to 0:4.

Success came, rather unexpectedly, in 1948. A two-point win over
Clare booked them a place in the Munster final against Cork. John Keane,
normally a defender, was now operating at centre-forward, so as to add
punch to the attack.

I was "listening in" to Mícheál O'Hehir's broadcast. I was conscious
that Cork had contested six of the previous seven All-Ireland finals and
won five. My heart was with the underdog and their veteran John Keane.
What has remained in my mind is the eight-point lead Waterford had built
up with a quarter of an hour to go. Cork whittled it down to one. Late
in injury time, Christy Ring got possession about forty yards out. There
was a nudge from defender Mick Hayes, as Christy struck for the equalising point. The ball sailed just barely wide of the upright. The puck-out
brought the final whistle and Waterford's first provincial title in ten years
and their second in all.

They beat Galway in the All-Ireland semi-final and faced Dublin in the
final – a repeat of 1938. This time the result was different. Outfield, John
Keane was the team's general – an inspiring one who scored 3:2. Waterford won by 6:7 to 4:2 and deservedly joined the list of All-Ireland senior
hurling winners. For good measure, John Keane added a Munster junior
football medal to his successes of 1948.

He retired in 1951. He had much to be proud of – a career that included,
as well as those already mentioned, eight county senior hurling titles – the
first in 1938, the last in 1951; seven Railway Cup victories from 1937 to
1949 – captain in 1939; and captain of Waterford in seven championships.

The years rolled by and when the Centenary (1984) and Millennium
teams (2000) were chosen, John was named for centre-back. By that time,
John was no longer with us.

It was 1975. John Keane was unwell and he knew it. In the autumn
of that year he set forth on a final pilgrimage, as if responding to an
urgent inner call. He headed for Kilkenny and spent time with Jim Langton, recalling the past. Back in Waterford, after a night's rest, he set out

for Kinsale to reminisce with the stout-hearted Jack Barrett. His next stop was Tralee, to meet and converse with a hurling friend he greatly admired, Jackie Power of Limerick. The next morning, he took off for Limerick intending to meet Mick Mackey, Timmy Ryan and others of the Limerick team of their era, for whom he had a great grá. He took the route via Listowel and along the Shannon River. He never reached Limerick. He died by the wayside, his journey and mission incomplete. It was Wednesday, 1 October 1975. He was taken to Limerick where all Munster honoured him.

David Smith, in his book *The Unconquerable Keane*, wrote:

I will never forget the enormous crowd that greeted us when we arrived at the hospital. On seeing that huge crowd we realised with a great sense of humility that John belonged not just to Waterford but to the nation. That was also seen as the hearse left the mortuary when former All-Ireland hurlers Mick Mackey, Jack Barrett, Jackie Power, John Mackey and Mick Herbert acted as pallbearers, and present and past players lined the route from the hospital for fully two hundred yards down the street. We took him home to Waterford and Mount Sion...

John Keane

JIM KELLIHER
CORK

Born 1878

The village of Dungourney in Co Cork will always be associated with the name of Jim Kelliher. Jim was a hurler and a horseman. He excelled at both – a horseman supreme; a hurler par excellence.

He has been described as a dapper man, 5'9" in height, wide-shouldered and neatly built from head to ankle. His early life was spent between the plough and the hunt. On Sundays he patronised his favourite camán game. He was always match-fit and throughout his life remained a non-drinker and non-smoker. He had the ideal temperament for competitive sport and his calm disposition and equanimity enabled him to handle victory or defeat with graciousness.

He bred and trained many first-class hunters and won several cross-country trophies. His victory, on a mare called Home Chat, in a point-to-point race (a steeplechase) against many of the leading gentry of the day, was widely acclaimed.

In *A Story of Champions,* written by John P. Power, the following is recorded:

The story of his victory in the open steeplechase at Ceim, near Rathcormac, in the early days of the century, when it was an unheard of thing for a farmer to ride against the "gentlemen" of the country – let alone beat them – sang like a ballad in the hearts of Cork men. For that gruelling six-mile not only did Jamesy Kelliher win a horse race but he also won a kind of freedom for the people.

In the GAA world, he is remembered for his matchless hurling skills. He was one of the outstanding men of his time. He usually played at full-back or centre half-back but in reality he could play anywhere. "Carbery" described him as "perhaps the greatest Roman of them all" and added "Kelliher had brains, skill, stamina and ash-craft in abundance. I saw him play in twenty-six major matches and he never left the field without being the outstanding hurler of the hour." It used to be said that a Cork team without him would have been like Hamlet without the prince.

Jim played in seven All-Ireland finals. The first in 1901 was surprisingly lost to London. The final of 1905 was lost to Kilkenny following an objection and a replay. He was successful in 1902 as captain and again in 1903. The finals of 1904, 1907 and 1912 were all lost to Kilkenny by just one point.

Jim was also captain in 1907. The final was played in Dungarvan on 21 June 1908. It was a classic – a game that became the yardstick by which all subsequent games were measured. It looked like ending in a draw until a clearance by John Anthony was doubled on, on the drop, as it hit the ground and sent sailing over for the winning point.

Of Jim it used be said, "He could call the ball and tell it where to go." When "Carbery" chose his team – "The Best Men of My Time" – in the 1950s, he handed the No. 6 jersey at centre halfback to Jim Kelliher.

And when the Cork Team of the Century was chosen in 1984, Jim was selected at right full-back. Jim died in 1943.

JACK LYNCH
CORK

Born: 1917
Interviewed: 1981

At the launch of *Giants of the Ash* at Croke Park with (from left) former county hurlers Andy Fleming (Waterford), Damien Martin (Offaly) and Paddy Buggy (Kilkenny).

Jack Lynch was a born leader, calm and disciplined, highly respected, a man of the people. In his time he captained his school, club, county and province to top honours. As Taoiseach of his country, his talents and calming influence, served the nation well in difficult political days and challenging times.

He was born on the Feast of the Assumption, 15 August 1917, to Dan and Nora (née O'Donoghue). He was christened John Mary and was the youngest of a family of seven children – five boys and two girls.

From his teenage years, he was involved in competitive hurling and football – brilliant at hurling, good at football. When he finally called it a day on Gaelic fields after the county football final of 1951 he could look back and reflect with immense satisfaction on a sporting career replete with all kinds of honours.

In his minor days, Cork county titles in both hurling and football were won. For three successive years, 1934–1936, he played on the North Mon. senior hurling team that won the Munster Colleges' title and brought home the coveted Harty Cup. Jack was captain in 1936. In 1935 and 1936, he added Munster Colleges' senior football titles to the hurling successes.

He was chosen on the Munster Colleges' interprovincial hurling teams of 1934, 1935 and 1936 as captain, and on the football teams of 1935 and 1936. The hurling selections of 1935 and 1936 were victorious.

Jack won his first of eight in a row senior hurling titles with Glen Rovers in 1934 and he added a further three in the years 1948–1950. When Glen Rovers defeated St Finbarr's in the 1950 county final, Jack was a remaining link with the 1934 team.

Cork senior football titles were won in 1938 and 1941 with St Nicholas, sister club of Glen Rovers. To these was added a Dublin senior football title with Civil Service in 1944. Jack won a Munster senior football title in 1943, playing at right half-back, and repeated the success in 1945, playing at right full-forward – the latter leading to an All-Ireland victory at the expense of Cavan – Cork's third football title and their first since 1911.

Jack made his senior county hurling debut in the National League of 1935 against Limerick and followed with a championship debut against Clare in 1936. He was captain of the county senior hurling team in 1938 (losing to Waterford in the Munster semi-final), in 1939 (losing to Kilkenny in the All-Ireland final) and in 1940 (losing to Limerick in the Munster final replay). It is worth mentioning here, because it isn't widely known, that, as well as being captain of the hurling team in 1939, Jack was also captain of the Cork senior football team, beaten by Tipperary in the second round of the Munster Championship.

I met Jack on three occasions – first in Dáil Éireann, later at an All-Star gathering and in 1991 at the launch of my book *Giants of the Ash*, in which he featured. I recall him telling me that he remembered more facets of the 1939 All-Ireland hurling final against Kilkenny than any other he played. Little wonder really – thunder, lightning, torrential rain, some controversy and a last-minute point from Jimmy Kelly of Carrickshock that spelt defeat for the Leesiders. He also told me that there were times when he used wonder if he would ever win an All-Ireland medal.

Well, we know that he did. It began in 1941, and between then and 1946 he won six in a row – a record for a Gaelic player – five in hurling and a football one in 1945. The seventh in a row final was lost to Kilkenny in 1947, by a last-minute Terry Leahy point in a dramatic finish.

Jack played with and against the greats of his era. Outside of his native Cork, which at the time produced several wonderful exponents of the game of hurling, he had a special *grá* for Harry Gray of Laois and Dublin, Paddy Phelan and Jim Langton of Kilkenny, John Keane and Christy Moylan of Waterford and the Limerick trio Paddy Scanlan, Mick Mackey and Timmy Ryan.

In retirement, further honours awaited Jack – among them an All-Time All- Star in 1981, and being chosen for the Team of the Century in 1984, the Team of the Millennium in 2000 and also the Cork team of the Millennium. He received the Hall of Fame Award under the heading of Gaelic Sport in 1993. He was joining elite company, as the following list of GAA Hall of Fame Award recipients shows:

Hurling
Mick Mackey (Limerick) 1961
Christy Ring (Cork) 1971
John Doyle (Tipperary) 1992

Football
John Joe Sheehy (Kerry) 1963
Larry Stanley (Kildare) 1970
Mick Higgins (Cavan) 1989
Kevin Heffernan (Dublin) 1998

Jack was successful in his personal life too. He was called to the Bar in 1945. In 1948, he was elected to Dáil Éireann. Following a term as Parliamentary Secretary from 1951–1954, between 1957 and 1966 he was at different times Minister for The Gaeltacht, Education, Industry and Commerce, and Finance. He was Taoiseach from 1966 to 1973, and again from 1977 to 1979.

Cork honoured him, a beloved son, in a special way, when they made him a Freeman of Cork on 19 December 1980. The tunnel under the River Lee, the Jack Lynch Tunnel, perpetuates his memory.

Jack died on 20 October 1999 – aged 82.

MICK MACKEY
LIMERICK

Born: 1912
Interviewed: 1980

Mick Mackey, son of John "Tyler" and May (née Carroll), was born on 12 July 1912, the eldest of a family of eight.

Thanks to his ancestry, hurling skills, physical strength, courage and daring coursed through his veins. He had a temperament suited to the game and was the hurling phenomenon of his time.

Mick was eighteen in November 1930 when he played for Limerick in a National League game against Kilkenny and, as he said afterwards, "I didn't exactly set the hurling world on fire."

He played his last game in the green of Limerick when he came on as a sub against Tipperary in the championship of 1947. In 1951, he wore the Ahane jersey for the last time.

Between times, he thrilled and entertained and dazzled tens of thousands of hurling enthusiasts with displays of rare magnificence that became a metaphor for excellence. He added a new dimension to the game and made his name synonymous with it.

In retirement more honours flowed – a Hall of Fame Award in 1961, a Commemorate Tribute from his club in February 1962, in 1980 an All-Time All-Star award, and centre-forward on the Centenary and Millennium teams.

As a hurler Mick was supreme – skilful, daring, dashing and extremely strong. As a personality, he was warm, gregarious, affable and generous hearted. Mick was the laughing cavalier, the Falstaff of the hurling arena. And the stories about his antics on the pitch are many.

Mick's moments of captaincy glory came in 1936. He was magical. It was a year in which he displayed all the power, speed, imagination, vision, composure, flamboyancy and daring that made him an inspirational leader. In the All-Ireland final of that year, Kilkenny went down by 5:6 to 1:5.

Four years later, Mick was leading Limerick around Croke Park again – Kilkenny, reigning All-Ireland champions, led by Jim Langton provided the opposition. That day, Mick roamed the pitch and was the hero of the hour. It ended 3:7 to 1:7 in Limerick's favour. Mick became the seventh captain to lead his county to more than one All-Ireland success.

Mícheál O'Hehir once said, "When I was growing up Mick was my hero…he was a great leader of a Limerick team, a very strong hurler and a great character – there was a charisma about him. The word 'great' is thrown about like snuff at a wake but the Limerick team of the 1930s and the 1940s – they deserved it."

"Carbery" had this to say when he picked the best team of his time in the 1950s: "At centre-forward, Playboy of the Southern world – Munster's pride and Limerick's glory – the one and only Mick Mackey."

Someone else described him as follows – "Probably the most colourful player that ever gripped a camán or graced the green sward of any hurling arena."

Con Houlihan said:

In our part of Kerry we had a special love for Mick Mackey because we looked on Limerick as our hurling county. And we loved him for another reason – because he played with such obvious enjoyment. He took his craft seriously but not solemnly. He could laugh and joke on the field…He gave the world far more than ever it gave him but he didn't worry too much about that…He was a modest broad-minded man who liked honest praise but was embarrassed by adulation.

I met Mick in the autumn of 1980. I found him resting at his home. He was in good spirits and recovering from a stroke. When I asked him if he would make a written contribution to the book I was compiling he said, in true open-hearted fashion, "Of course I will."

Eventually he got around to autographing the book and I suggested he write "a special memory". He gazed silently at the book for some seconds, pensive and reflective, biro in hand, head cast downwards. I wondered what moments were flashing through his mind: perhaps 1933, when Limerick were thwarted by Johnny Dunne's only goal of the game; his first All-Ireland medal after a draw and replay with Dublin in 1934; the Munster final against Tipperary in 1936, when he scored 5:3; 1944 in Thurles and the two epic Munster final games with Cork; or, perhaps, just those many evenings of his youth as he hurled with abandon on the local pitch. And then, without lifting his head, he said in a tone tinged with resignation and, I thought, a little sadness – "It's all memories now."

He walked to the car with me and we stood for a few moments talking in the sunshine. As I bade farewell on that beautiful autumn day I couldn't help feeling that, despite his illness, he still had in his countenance that look of granite that characterised so many of his displays.

Within two years he was dead – 13 September 1982. He was buried like a king. They came from all over Ireland. The funeral cortége was three miles long. The route was lined with mourners. It was the last farewell to a hurling legend.

LORY MEAGHER
KILKENNY

Born: 1899

Reaping a harvest in a different field.

In the eyes of many a friend, foe and follower, Lory the hurler was "The King".

In 1935, eleven years after his county debut against Dublin at Portlaoise, Lory, with the big wide shoulders and very long back and arms, was thirty-six years of age – an age when most hurlers would have retired from inter-county fare. On Sunday, 1 September he led Kilkenny onto the pitch at Croke Park and gave a display in the All-Ireland final, against a great Limerick team, that came to be regarded as his greatest hour in the black and amber.

A hurling classic was in prospect. A record crowd of 46,591 thronged Croke Park. The rain came down in torrents. It fell during the entire game. Despite the awful conditions, the teams served up an epic contest.

Lory, wily old warrior that he was, had done his homework well. Prior to going onto the pitch he said to his men, with reference to the sliotar, "Keep it on the ground, pull first time, keep it moving." He was a hurling strategist. He knew that those tactics, coupled with the wretched conditions, would benefit Kilkenny.

He brought to bear on his display that day at midfield all the cunning and craft and artistry of a lifetime devoted to hurling. His matchless ball control and myriad of skills were invaluable to Kilkenny as he directed operations from midfield and, like a magician, did the ground work for vital scores as he guided the sodden sliotar over the rain-drenched pitch, sending intelligent and beautifully placed passes to his forwards. Kilkenny won by 2:5 to 2:4.

Lory from Tullaroan was born in 1899 and christened Lorenzo Ignatius. The hurley was an extension of himself and he gave expression to all that was delightful in hurling with his displays at midfield where, so often, he reigned supreme. He could steal a score from far out in days when scores were hard to come by and a point from midfield could be worth a king's ransom. There were occasions when the hurley in Lory's grasp seemed to have an intelligence of its own.

It was no wonder, then, that the young generation of Kilkenny men that succeeded Lory used to proudly chant, "Over the bar said Lory Meagher."

In private life Lory was shy and retiring. He never married. He avoided the limelight and was known to give journalists the slip from time to time. Fame, when linked to publicity, weighed heavily upon him. He was, however, always at ease with the camán. The game of hurling remained very dear to his heart. So, when an over-forty game was arranged between a Tullaroan selection and a Kilkenny selection, it was no real surprise to learn that Lory togged out with another great stylist Paddy Phelan for the occasion.

So as to learn a little more about Lory, I visited his nephew Dan Hogan in Tullaroan. According to Dan: "My greatest memory of Lory was his intense interest in the formative or early days of the Association. He had a fascination with those days in Thurles, to my mind to the total exclusion of his own deeds. He was a Nationalist at heart. Memories of his childhood made him an ardent supporter of the 'Ban'. He never lost the hurling artistry. I can remember when my brother and myself used visit him in our early teens, Lory would take down the hurley and ball, hit the ball straight up into the clouds – or so it seemed to us – and the ball would come back down and land at his feet. He would repeat this several times. The skill, the artistry and the hurling were still there at sixty. Only the youth was gone."

When Lory died, Pádraig Puirséal described the funeral of this shy hurling star thus:

And, on a spring evening in 1973, Kilkenny gave him a funeral befitting a prince. As the steel blue clouds spread like a mourning pall across the evening sky, hundreds, young and old, filed through the mortuary chapel of St Luke's Hospital for a last glimpse of one of the greatest craftsmen of the camán. Then, the heavens themselves wept without restraint, and the funeral procession wound its slow way through the narrow streets of Irishtown, old world streets silent now, but streets that had so often re-echoed the thundering cheers of victory for returning heroes garlanded with hurling glory.

> *"Goodbye and farewell to a friend and a neighbour;*
> *The last final whistle has parted our ways;*
> *The game is all over and the crowds are dispersing,*
> *And I can't help remembering those happier days."*
>
> *(Paddy Fitzpatrick)*

Lorenzo Meagher

THE RACKARDS
WEXFORD

Born: Nicky – 1922; Bobby – 1927; Billy – 1931
Interviewed: 1981 (Billy); 1988 (Bobby)

Nicky (right) with Jim English, Wexford captain, following the 1956 All-Ireland win.

In the Spring of 1918, Bob Rackard and Stasia Doran – daughter of James and Esther (née Keating) – married in Davidstown parish church. There was a seventeen-year age difference.

The marriage was blessed with nine children – five boys and four girls. Nicky, Bobby and Billy became the high-profile members of the family, because of their prowess in the world of Gaelic games. All three were also talented horsemen, a talent inherited from their father who was a great judge of bloodstock.

In 1956, Nicky, Bobby and Billy created a family record in hurling which will never again be equalled. All three played on the Leinster team that won the Railway Cup and on the Wexford team that won Leinster, National League and All-Ireland titles.

Nicky and Bobby were chosen on the Centenary hurling team of 1984.

I saw Nicky in action, only through the eyes and golden voices of Mícheál O'Hehir and Mícheál Ó Muircheartaigh. His 21-yard frees were known as Rackard specials. The net usually bulged. His path to stardom began at St Kieran's College, Kilkenny in 1938 where he won Leinster Colleges' titles and was chosen for the Leinster Colleges' team.

By 1942, he had made his debut on both the Wexford county senior hurling and football teams. Nicky was strong, dashing and inspirational. In every year from 1943 to 1957 he was selected for the Leinster hurling team. He won his Railway Cup medals in 1954 as a substitute and as a team member in 1956, when he scored 2:6 of Leinster's 5:11.

Nicky was selected for the Railway Cup football teams of 1946 and 1950 – both finals were lost. He won a Leinster football title in 1945. He also won Oireachtas titles, Leinster titles and a National League in hurling. And then, well into the autumn of his playing days, came the crowning glory – All-Ireland hurling titles in 1955 and again in 1956 when he was in his thirty-fifth year.

His scoring feats were exceptional. He scored 7:7 against Antrim in the All-Ireland semi-final of 1954. He was top scorer in the 1955 All-Ireland Championship; likewise in 1956, with a tally of 12:15 in four games. In the All-Ireland semi-final of that year, against Galway, Nicky accounted for 5:4 of Wexford's total of 5:13. In the 1956 season, in nineteen games, he recorded 35:50.

Side by side, however, with all the glory of Gaelic fields there was a cross that weighed heavily on himself and on his family. In *Hurling Giants,* I wrote, "the Apollo-like Nicky had a big heart and a gregarious personality. He had great strength, but he had a weakness too. Alcoholism caused him much suffering. He eventually triumphed over it and crusaded against it."

In the same book, I quoted his brother Billy as saying, "It looked that in his late forties he had finally sorted his life out. He was a member of AA and, as we know, was doing heroic work for people in all walks of life who had drink problems…I met him one day in summer and he was wearing a scarf around his neck. He dismissed my obvious question…He was in fact condemned to death with one year to live. Nobody knew. He still didn't complain and eventually he died in Vincent's – a decimated human being, a victim of that awful scourge we all know so well…His funeral cortége was akin to a state funeral …flowers from friends he had helped, especially those with drink problems, came from every county in Ireland…Nicky was finally at peace." He was born on 28 April 1922. He died on 10 April 1976.

I got to know Bobby – a gentleman, reserved and private – when I was writing *Giants of the Ash.* I asked him to write some memories of his hurling days in the large leatherbound journal in which all the hurling men I had met had written. He agreed, but said that he would like to reflect on it. That didn't surprise me. I knew he possessed an innate pride that would cause him to aim for perfection in everything he did.

"A study in total concentration": Bobby Rackard with Captain Christy Ring (Cork) (left) and Art Foley (Wexford goalkeeper) on right. (Photo by Bord Fáilte photographer T. Hayde.)

Weeks later, he came to my home and filled four pages of the journal – written in beautiful script. It was all so typical of Bobby.

His approach to the game of hurling was no different. He pondered deeply on the game, made a study of it. In advance of a game, he would always make a study of his opponent. He said that Christy Ring was no different to any other player on the field when he hadn't got the ball. The late Martin Codd recalled a game Wexford played against Cork at the Polo Grounds, New York in 1957: " I particularly remember that day the way Bobby Rackard contained Ring. The field had no corner flags then, because the shape was oval. Any time Ring got possession out near the flags, Bobby used to stalk and shadow and dispossess him." It wasn't, of course, the first time that Bobby had performed with distinction on the Maestro.

Bobby won all the honours the game of hurling had to offer. Only once was he spoken to by a referee. By nature he was very quiet. He told me that in one particular inter-county game his opponent persisted in jabbing and niggling and generally annoying him. Patience exhausted and unable to tolerate any more, Bobby grabbed his opponent by the shoulders and began to shake him. The referee arrived on the scene. "Get a grip on your-self," he said to Bobby. That was all. No name taken. The referee probably knew the opponent's form.

Bobby probably gave his greatest display in the All-Ireland final of 1954 against Cork, when he moved from centre half-back to full-back to replace the injured Nick O'Donnell. He proceeded to give an exhibition of defensive play – awesome really – as he cleared ball after ball that descended on the Wexford goal. And to think that illness had kept him from doing any worthwhile training for the game.

A farm accident in 1957, ten years after he came on the county scene, cut short his hurling career at county level. He was thirty years of age and probably playing the best hurling of his career. He continued to play some games for his club Rathnure. One of these was the 1961 county final against St Aidan's of Enniscorthy. Playing at full-forward, he was facing former county colleague Nick O'Donnell. "How did you fare?" I queried. "I had the sympathy of the crowd," said Bobby. What he didn't tell me was that he scored two goals in a title-winning contest.

In 1992, Bobby, jointly with his brother Billy, was honoured with the Bank of Ireland All-Time All-Star award – richly deserved. Bobby, who was born on 6 January 1927, died on 19 October 1996.

I knew Billy well – a sociable and gregarious personality. A nine-year spell in Wexford town began for me in December 1957. On arrival, one of the first things I did was to go in search of Billy Rackard's drapery shop and meet the man himself – his name then a household word in hurling circles. Some time later, I bought a suit of clothes from him. It cost £8. Emblazoned on the inside pocket of the coat was the message "Let your next suit be a Rackard special" – a reminder of the prowess of his brother Nicky when it came to taking 21-yard frees.

At the time I met Billy, his triumphs on the hurling field were many – medals for county, provincial, National League, Railway Cup and

Oireachtas titles. Wexford had adorned the Oireachtas competition. For seven years from 1950, the county contested every final – each a hurling thriller – and won four. He once described his hurling days to me as "a parcel of moments".

Billy was a useful footballer too. Not many realise that he played at senior level for the county and in 1953 they only lost the Leinster final to Louth by 1:7 to 0:7.

Billy Rackard. (Photo courtesy of the Rackard family).

He wasn't an instant success at county level in senior hurling. It took him some time to find his feet. Billy loved to tell the story associated with the 1950 Leinster hurling final at Nowlan Park, against Kilkenny. He was playing at corner-back and, while he felt he wasn't playing badly, it seemed he didn't impress the selectors. In the dressing-room at half time, the County Chairman Sean Browne was delegated to tell Billy to lie down and feign injury at the earliest opportunity in the second half. Those were the days when you could only be replaced if you were injured. Having received the instruction, Billy simply nodded his head. The second half resumed and Billy was preparing himself mentally for his "injury". Three times in rapid succession the ball came between him and his marker Liam Reidy. Each time, Billy made a spectacular clearance. Then came a lull. Down went Billy holding his ankle. He looked to the sideline and prepared for what would be an assisted limping-off. Sean Browne rushed in. "Get up, get up," he said. "You're fine." It was sweet music to Billy's ears. Great days and wonderful displays lay ahead.

In later years, when writing my books, I had two very pleasant meetings with Billy when I enjoyed the hospitality of his household and his warm help and co-operation. And as was the case with his brother Bobby, his written contribution in the "Journal of the Giants" is a treasured piece.

Billy's senior hurling career at county level lasted from 1949 to the end of the 1964 season. I will never forget his display in the Leinster final of 1960 against Kilkenny. He was magnificent. According to Joe Sherwood of the *Evening Press*: "He strode the scene like a Greek colossus." He was born on 14 April 1930. He died a few weeks before his seventy-ninth birthday, on 23 March 2009.

All three are now gone "to a bourne in Paradise where all the hurlers go."

But the memory remains, still vivid, of three outstanding sportsmen – never to be forgotten by those of us who were privileged to have seen them in action on the hurling field.

Solas na bhFlaitheas go bhfeicidh an triúr acu.

Bobbie Rackard   *Billy Rackard*

TONY REDDIN
TIPPERARY

Born: 1919
Interviewed: 1988

No place for handymen as Tony emerges from his goal ably protected
by defender Mickey Byrne, in the 1950 All-Ireland final v. Kilkenny.

"I started my career in 1940 with Galway against Cork in junior; played
Galway senior in 1943–1944. I went to Tipperary in 1947; played for ten
years with Tipperary – won three All-Irelands, five Railway Cups, six
National Leagues, three Munster medals. I enjoyed my hurling career, and
have many memories of great games."

As Tony Reddin entered his thirtieth year, it was unlikely that he had
All-Ireland medals on his mind. After all, it was an age when many would
be contemplating retiring. But great things lay ahead.

This native of Mullagh, Co. Galway got his baptism of fire to championship hurling in the fury of the exchanges between Tipperary and Cork

in 1949 at Limerick – a draw, a replay and extra time. One hundred and fifty minutes of exchanges that at times bordered on warfare.

It was an era when forwards, legitimately, could bundle the goalkeeper into the net. I asked Tony if such a prospect ever bothered him: "No. I always kept my eye on the ball. I never blocked a ball down in the goal; I either caught it or deadened it, and I was good at the side step. The forward coming in never really bothered me. I felt I could anticipate every situation and instinctively do the right thing." I was able to detect in Tony exceptional powers of concentration and anticipation. Add to this his cross-country training, his fearlessness, his deft side-step and his ability to clear left and right, and you have a goalkeeper of tremendous mental alertness and physical agility.

In retirement, it sometimes happens that an opportunity arises to relive the excitement and the ecstasy of the playing days. This happened for Tony when the Centenary hurling team was selected and announced in 1984. It was the day after his daughter's wedding, and he was drinking a cup of tea before going to Mass. People started calling and congratulating him. He thought it was about the wedding. Then someone said, "Did you hear about it? You got it: You're top goalkeeper." According to Tony: "I couldn't believe it. I didn't think I could get it – not with Tommy Daly of Clare and Paddy Scanlon of Limerick and Ollie Walsh and Noel Skehan of Kilkenny in the running. I walked up and down the kitchen. I was filled with excitement. I wasn't able to finish the breakfast. I set off for Mass. Everyone in Banagher was congratulating me – pulling my coat and slapping me on the back and shaking hands with me. I said no prayers at all at Mass that Sunday – the distraction was too great." It was the ultimate honour for Tony.

He closed his eyes and his mind went back to the past: to Limerick, to Killarney, to Croke Park. He stood between the posts again; beneath the crossbar. He heard the strains of "Amhran na bhFiann"; the hurley was firmly gripped; he was standing on the goal line, to quote Oliver Goldsmith, "the very spot, where many a time he triumphed."

Tony Reddin

CHRISTY RING
CORK

Born: 1920

Opponents united in retirement (left to right): Johnny Ryan (Tipp.), Christy Ring (Cork), Mick Mackey (Limerick). (Photo courtesy of Ed O'Shea, Thurles.)

"Toscanini for good music
Kathy Barry for crubeens
– and Ringey for goals"

"I had fierce determination going for a ball. I would go through a stone wall to get a 50/50 ball. I would stop at nothing. My strength was largely hidden....I only used my strength when needed. I had it automatically, and I'd say it was in the mind. Seventy-five per cent of everything is in the mind, and it's the mind that counts."

Christy Ring, son of Nicholas and Mary, one of a family of three boys and two girls, grew up in Cloyne, close to where he was born on 12

October 1920. His youth was spent playing hurling in Cloyne and in 1941 he joined the Glen Rovers Club in Cork City.

He succeeded Limerick's Mick Mackey as the High King of hurling. His reign lasted longer. He was Cork's greatest hurler. The game absorbed his entire thought process. His remarkable high level of fitness the whole year round contributed in no small way to his greatness.

Christy's career is dotted with records and achievements of all kinds: eighteen Railway Cups; third captain to lead his county to three All-Ireland successes, following in the footsteps of Mikey Maher (Tipperary) and Dick Walsh (Kilkenny); first hurler to win eight All-Ireland medals, subsequently equalled by John Doyle (Tipperary) in 1965, and the Kilkenny trio Henry Shefflin, Noel Hickey and Eddie Brennan in 2011; Hall of Fame Award 1971; and the No. 10 jersey on the Centenary and Millennium teams.

As a hurler, Christy was always supremely confident – dedicated and skilful, fanatical and intense, powered with a burning passion; a never-ending threat to all defenders. As a person he could be very shy and reserved, remote and retiring, but as a friend his loyalty and generosity knew no limits. Like us all he had more than one persona. Two of them contrasted starkly. In social situations, he was shy. In the hurling arena, he was a phenomenon – assertive, determined and hortative.

Kevin Cashman summed it up well in an outstanding article on the maestro in the *Sunday Independent* on 31 December 1995: "He would have been 75 years old in this year of tremendous hurling happiness. His would have been the most profound – and most reserved – happiness; for, except among truest friends, the immensity of his generosity and intellect remained well wadded in reticence. "I'm not much good at speeches," he told the spellbound thousands who welcomed him and the MacCarthy Cup home to Cloyne, in 1946 – and proved it by shutting up four sentences later. That changed utterly at every throw-in of a sliotar. He would exhort and goad his own, and seek to disconcert and down-face the other lot, with trenchant wit and colour."

He played his first game for his native Cork in a league match against Kilkenny in 1939. His last game with Cork was in 1962, with Munster in 1963 and with his club in 1967. When he died on 2 March 1979 at the relatively young age of fifty-eight, the hurling world was stunned.

At his graveside, many a friend and foe shed a silent tear and no doubt recalled again some dazzling deeds of yore:

- Perhaps his dramatic goal after a fine solo run in the closing stages of the replayed Munster final of 1944 against Limerick that denied the Shannon-siders another draw

- Or his solo run coming up to half time in the All-Ireland final against Kilkenny in 1946 that split their defence and finished with the ball in the net

- Or the last quarter of the Munster final of 1956 when Limerick were two goals clear and were looking good, and Christy, who was getting no freedom from Donal Broderick, scored three goals and one point in less than ten minutes

- Or that day in November 1959, aged thirty-nine, when he scored six goals and four points against Wexford at the Athletic Grounds in Cork

- Or his three goals in the last quarter in the County semi-final of 1962 against Imokilly – aged forty-two – that paved the way to victory

- Or… or …or …

I called on his brother Willie John at Cloyne. When I asked him what was Christy's greatest era, this is what he said about a brother he idolised: "He didn't really have one as such. He played for over a span of twenty years and was always as fit as he could humanly make himself. He was liable to hit a peak and rise to great heights at any time in his career." Then he said, "He had a heart of gold. He regularly visited patients in hospital. He was a religious man and Mass played a big part in his life."

In Cork City there is a bridge over the River Lee called the Christy Ring bridge. There is also a Gaelic grounds named after him in the city. And in Cloyne, his native place, a nine-foot high bronze statue honours him – "[It] will stand in his native town for hundreds and hundreds of years, an eternal and everlasting tribute to this great hurler" (sculptor Yann Goulet).

JOE SALMON
GALWAY

Born: 1931
Interviewed: 1986

Seán O'Siocháin presenting Joe with a magnificent Galway Crystal Trophy, following his being chosen as Galway Hurler of the Century in 1984.

"We are blessed with the most wonderful field game in the world. No sport is more skilful, more graceful, more revealing of those who play it, and nobody who has seen hurling played by its greatest exponents can be in any doubt about what beauty is, or graciousness or courtesy either.

"There is something else that is innate to hurling: the spirit in which the game is played. You can hurt, maim or even kill a man with a blow from a camán. You can intimidate an opponent more persistently and to more effect in hurling than in any other game. The camán can be a skilful instrument or a bloody weapon; that traditionally it has been the former

39

rather than the latter is something to be proud of – something to be properly cherished and nurtured.

"Without a certain decency of spirit hurling would be rendered ugly. Decency in this sense is, like the game itself, distinctly Irish."

"What age are you?" said Vin Baston of Waterford to Joe Salmon in the closing stages of a Railway Cup semi-final in the early 1950s.

"I'm twenty," said Joe.

"You'll be great," replied Vin. It was a prophecy that came true.

Joe's father was a great hurling enthusiast and followed his son's hurling career with deep interest. After a particularly good performance Joe would test his father for reaction, and he often remembers being told, "You're not as good as Timmy Ryan yet." In Joe's father's eyes, Timmy Ryan of Limerick was the complete midfielder.

In 1984 the Galway County Board set about finding the Galway Hurler of the Century. A very professional approach was adopted to meet a very difficult task; the chosen player would have to be a man of many skills and in many ways a man apart. The honour fell to Joe Salmon, and he was presented with a magnificent Galway Crystal trophy by Seán O'Siocháin.

Joe's boyhood heroes were John Killeen and "Inky" Flaherty of his native Galway, and Christy Ring. He played his first game in Croke Park in 1947 when Galway minors were heavily defeated by Tipperary. He watched Ring in the senior final; little did he think then that he would one day be Ring's colleague and team-mate in the Glen Rovers jersey, with whom he would win five county titles.

Joe always enjoyed playing against Kilkenny and Cork. These counties played the fast-flowing type of game that suited his style of open hurling, where you kept the ball moving and let it do the work.

He found Theo English a difficult opponent to handle. Ned Wheeler of Wexford was difficult too, but in a different way. Ned had strength and enthusiasm; Theo played it tight and first-time. But the midfielder he admired most was Phil Shanahan of Tipperary. "He was great under a dropping ball. Standing over six feet tall, he was strong and would double first time. He was the best I played on at midfield."

Joe was on the losing side in three All-Ireland finals: 1953 v. Cork – "it might have been won"; 1955 v. Wexford; and 1958 v. Tipp.

In a career (1949–1964) dotted with many wonderful displays, Joe's rewards at county level were rather meagre – one National League and three Oireachtas titles. However, he was honoured in the Centenary Year 1984, when selected at midfield on the team of hurlers who never won an All-Ireland senior title.

There is one aspect of the evolving game that bothers Joe. A player puts his hand up for the sliothar; the opponent pulls on the ball and hits the hand as well, and has a free given against him. "[It's] not cricket," says Joe. "Hurling is about pulling on the flying ball. I learned that in my early years. I was nineteen playing for Erin's Hope against Castlegar. I soloed in from midfield and, as I reached for a return pass to grab the ball, Stephen Connor, the Castlegar full-back – a big, hefty fellow – connected first time and cleared the ball up-field. I shook my bleeding hand – the cut looked nasty. The full-back took a look at it. 'It will be alright; don't put it up again, a mhic,' he said. I never forgot it." *Is fearr ciall ceannuig ná dhá chiall a múintear.*

On 23 July 1991 Joe went to "a bourne in Paradise where all the hurlers go".

Joe Salmon.

JIMMY SMYTH
CLARE

Born: 1931
Interviewed: 1981; 2011

Memory lane reflections (left to right): Jimmy Smyth (Clare), Dan McInerney (Clare) and John Doyle (Tipp.). (Photo courtesy of Jimmy Symth.)

Jimmy Smyth arrived in this world on 1 Jan 1931 weighing 12lbs. At fourteen years of age he was match fit at almost 13 st. And in his playing days, fit, he weighed 15½ st.

He was a true hurling artist. His prowess with a camán demonstrated itself very early on. He went to school to that great hurling nursery St Flannan's of Ennis, and had the rare distinction of winning three successive All-Ireland college titles in 1945, 1946 and 1947. It was at St Flannan's that he met former Clare star Tull Considine. "He was my inspiration. He was Ireland's greatest mentor. I never had the pleasure of seeing him play."

At fourteen years of age Jimmy was selected for the county minor team and played for five seasons, thus creating a record in this grade that may never be equalled. He made his senior debut in 1948 at the age of seventeen and continued to adorn the hurling scene for a further nineteen years.

"I had the pleasure of playing with Christy Ring for ten years in the Railway Cup. It would be interesting to see if many Cork men, and how many, have played beside him for so long. My most important memories are of winning five championships with my own parish, Ruan."

In 1949 he captained the Clare junior team. They were beaten in the final at Ennis by London by one point. A great hurler and captain knew disappointment. In the Centenary year (1984), Jimmy was chosen on the team of players who had never won an All-Ireland senior title. Worthy recognition for a true artist of the game.

"No matter how good a player is, he has really lost if he doesn't play the game. It is vital that he can approach his opponent after a game to shake his hand; it gets more important as the years roll onward."

Recently I asked Jimmy, now eighty years of age, to reflect on hurling from that vantage point. He did so under the title: The Broc, Ground Play, Air Play and Eighty years of Hurling.

"I have seen and played a lot of hurling since I was four years old. In our parish, Ruan, the game was not called 'Hurling' when played by children. It was a pre-hurling activity called 'Broc' [pronounced 'Bruck']. We always asked, 'Will you come for a Broc?' Hurling was a game for adults. Unfortunately, nowadays, the game of hurling reverts more often than not to the Broc, a group of adults following a ball all over a field, with continuous shuffling, tipping, tapping and jostling. This type of play was, and should now be, unacceptable for adult hurling. It has eliminated ground play and air play – both have now almost vanished.

"Ground hurling is a skill of the past. Possession seems to be the target of present day players. There is no opportunity for the genius to stick an unexpected ground ball to the net. Ring in his hey-day got most of his goals from inside the twenty yards line by fast ground strokes from his left or right hand side. The urge for possession, through the Broc, has taken the real excitement, the sting and the beauty from the game of hurling. This urge leaves our great hurling talent and energy in the wilderness."

"Carbery", writing about the 1934 All-Ireland final replay between Limerick and Dublin, had this to say: "In the thirty five hurling finals I have seen, never a one approached last Sunday's in uniform thrill, in speed, in magnificent ground play….What struck me most about this game, as compared with the great finals of the past was the great quality of the ground hurling…it was a finish for the gods."

This is a paragraph that would not, and could not, be written nowadays. The ground skills are gone. We have to try and revive the old combination of air and ground hurling which made it "a game for the gods". Hurling is a game that has a thousand skills for a talented player but the Broc has eliminated many skills. The game goes beyond talent. It also includes the fire and excitement generated by the player when he responds immediately to the unexpected speed and twists of a ground ball. This kind of ball challenges the real greatness of players. It was loved by the people.

The big questions are, will hurling continue to consume the hearts of the Irish people as it has done from the beginning? Is this going to last without the great fire that ground and air hurling have brought, and would continue to bring, into the game? Are we going to allow the Broc to dominate and extinguish the ancient art of ground hurling and air hurling?

PAT STAKELUM
TIPPERARY

Born: 1927
Interviewed: 1986

On parade, prior to Munster final of 1949 v.
Limerick. (Photo courtesy of his son Pauric.)

"As one of a family of ten with modest means, growing up in the depression of the thirties, I do not know what I would have done without the great happiness which I experienced from playing hurling. My father, who is the finest man I ever met, encouraged us all to play hurling. There was always a feeling that we were safe and involved in a healthy activity when we were hurling. We made our own hurleys, and hurleys were handed down from the oldest to the youngest. I remember one Christmas when my Uncle sent three hurleys for the 'chislers'. I was fourth in line and had to settle for a hand-me-down.

"Hurling was the most topical conversation in our house. People who made the parish team were our heroes. The one, Dinny Gorman, who made the county team – he was God in our youthful eyes. I would say that I learnt to read from studying the Monday reports from 'Carbery', 'Greenflag', etc. I was never in Dublin until I played a minor All-Ireland in 1945.

"The Limerick and Cork games of the late thirties and early forties were the greatest games of hurling I ever saw. Mackey, Scanlon, Timmy Ryan, Clohessy, Power, Donovan, Lynch, Ring, Quirke, Lotty – they were all great."

"I was only a garsún," Pat said to me, "as I watched the drawn and replayed Munster final of 1940 between Limerick and Cork in Thurles. I was there again in 1944 watching another draw and replay between the same counties. Those were the greatest games I have seen. They were super teams – they were mighty men. They had a major influence on my game. Hurling reached a pinnacle then that has not since been equalled. After those games, we used to go home and go out hurling, all ten of us – even the girls in our house played hurling – and we were all Mick Mackeys and Paddy Clohessys and Johnny Quirkes."

Pat remembers the day in 1947 that they went down to play Tullaroan in a friendly and Lory Meagher refereed the game, and they all felt honoured to be in his presence. It was a milestone in Pat's hurling life.

The most dramatic scene Pat ever witnessed in a dressing-room during his hurling career was in Limerick in 1949, after the replay between Cork and Tipperary had ended in another draw. "As we headed for the dressing-room I was beside Paddy Leahy. Reddin was limping. "Don't limp," said Leahy – the psychological battle was now on. Passing by Jack Lynch, Leahy said, "Isn't it great stuff, Jack? How will we decide on it at all?" "I don't know," said Jack, "but I have enough of it." On hearing this comment, Leahy put a spring in his step and made haste for the dressing-room.

"The question now was would extra time be played or not. The dressing-room was crowded. It included two priests – Fr Barry, a Passionist, and Fr Dwyer. In the normal way these priests would be vying with each other before a game as to who should bless the ball. Now they were united: there would be no extra time; it would be immoral to demand any more of the boys. It was then that Paddy Leahy spoke. 'This is a moment of crisis,' he said. 'All out except the players.' 'Aye, Aye,' said the two priests. 'Sorry, but that includes you, Father, and you, Father, too,' said Leahy."

It was now time to move out again under the evening sun. Some got stuck in the doorway as they charged out. Within the hour they returned bearing victory: "It was the greatest moment of my career."

"Back in Thurles I collected my bicycle and headed for Holycross with my boots and socks on the handlebars. And, would you believe it, the Munster senior hurling cup, too, was taken on the bike after the victory over Limerick in the final. I have the bike still – I got it done up. I'm mad about that ould bike."

Pat retired in 1957 but made a one-game comeback in 1959 – losing to Waterford. He had much success to reflect on six National Leagues, five Railway Cups, one Oireachtas, three county titles, three Munster titles and three All-Irelands. In 1993 he would be honoured with the All-Time All-Star award.

Reflecting on our meeting as we parted, Pat said, "You have brought back many memories. God be with those who are gone and God speed the camán in the future." And then he added:

> *"May the Great Referee when he calls my name*
> *Say, you hurled like a man – you played the game."*

The Great Referee called Pat's name on 4 April 2008.

Pat Stakelum:

1960s

TED CARROLL
KILKENNY

Born: 1939
Interviewed: 1982

"Hurling is a game that I have got great enjoyment from and at the same time has been very good to me. Like every youngster, I had an ambition to win a medal at the game. After what seemed ages, I achieved my goal at sixteen years of age when I won a Leinster Colleges' junior medal with St Kieran's.

"After making the breakthrough, I was lucky enough to win an All-Ireland Colleges' medal. On making the Kilkenny Senior panel, I had one great wish: to win an All-Ireland medal with Kilkenny.

"The win over Waterford in 1963 was my greatest thrill, but the sweetest win for me was the 1967 victory over Tipperary. The reasons were:

- Tipperary were the best team in my era

- Kilkenny were waiting so long for this victory

- My next-door neighbour, the late Bill Kenny, had played on the 1922 Kilkenny team

51

"My greatest regret in hurling was not winning a Senior Championship medal with Lisdowney.

"The county players I admired most in my time were Liam Devaney, Donie Nealon and Babs Keating of Tipperary. Ray Cummins of Cork was a great forward to get possession."

Drama attended the early moments of my meeting with Ted Carroll at his home in Kilkenny. We were just settling down to a pleasant chat when a large window-pane was badly shattered. When the initial shock passed, the message dawned. Ted's son, who had been playing in the back garden, had hit the wrong target with the sliotar.

Ted hurried out, it seemed, with drastic action in mind. However, by the time he reached the back garden his mind had travelled back to his own youth, and similar misdeeds were recalled. I don't think that even a yellow card was shown.

Club success at county level is very special to all players. Even though Ted failed to win a county title with his native Lisdowney, he had the compensation of winning a county title with University College Dublin (UCD) in 1961.

All other honours the game of hurling had to offer came Ted's way. He played in five All-Ireland finals – losing in 1964 to Tipperary and in 1966, rather surprisingly, to an unfancied Cork team. The wins came in 1963 v. Waterford, 1967 v. Tipperary and 1969 v. Cork. Playing at right full-back in the 1969 final, Ted had an outstanding hour. He made a major contribution to victory and collected his third of three All-Ireland medals. His display in 1969 saw him honoured with the Texaco Hurler of the Year Award.

Ted, who died on 22 December 1995, will always be associated with two defensive positions: centre-back and right full-back. He filled both with distinction for county and province.

Ted Carroll

TOM CHEASTY
WATERFORD

Born: 1934
Interviewed: 1995

"I was born in Ballyduff, Lower, Co. Waterford, in 1934. My father, Geof-frey, was a native of the parish. My mother, Kathleen (Walsh), was from Mooncoin in south Kilkenny. At about the age of four I went to live with my mother's aunt and uncle, who were from south Kilkenny. They had bought a farm about a mile from my father's place. As with most Kilkenny people, there was always talk about hurling – mostly the old Mooncoin team, the Doyles and 'Drug' Walsh. Mick Doyle was a personal friend of my mother's family. They lived on hurling.

"I started to play minor hurling when I was fifteen years old. I played for the Waterford minors the year after at wing half-forward. I played full-back for the minor footballers. I don't think I was very skilful but I was fairly strong and a fast runner.

"As a young fellow, working on a fairly big mixed farm in the late forties and early fifties, there was still a lot of manual work to be done; physical strength was an asset, whether you were at a threshing, in a hayfield or a cornfield. Strong, hardy men were what was wanted. As a man of 5'8" plus and around 13 st., I was able to hold my own with most of them. You need to be strong, fit and tough to survive playing with a middling junior club.

"Looking back now on all the years of hard training with club and county, and many disappointments, I often wonder whether it was worth it or not. At times you think maybe it was: you meet people and make friends, have something to have a bit of a chat about. I wasn't really that happy with my life on the land, so hurling, football and a bit of running – this was my life. That's about it.

"In the days of my youth the men I looked up to were John Keane, Mick Hickey, Christy Moylan, Mick Hayes, Andy Fleming, Charlie Ware, Éamon Moynihan – a close friend and neighbour, a man I looked up to who won a junior All-Ireland with Westmeath in 1936 – and Fad Browne, whose grandson Tony is now a very good inter-county hurler; and the Foran family, who live near us in Knockaderry and played with Ballyduff in the forties and early fifties."

The circumstances surrounding Tom's debut in the Waterford jersey can only be described as akin to something you would read in a novel or see in a film. "It was the autumn of 1954. I was standing on the embankment of Walsh Park, awaiting a league game between Waterford and Kilkenny. Waterford were short – stuck for players. I was approached to play, given a loan of a hurley and boots, and togged out."

Thus started the senior county career of a player destined to make his mark at centre-forward. Strong, fit and fast, uncompromising in exchanges, he held his own with the leading centre half-backs of the day. Unorthodox in style, he would gain possession, surge forward, and scoop the ball ahead or over the bar.

An indestructible hurler was Tom. He was always exceptionally fit; he won 100-yard competitions and cross-country races, and worked on the farm at home. "I can remember opening up the headland with a scythe in preparation for the harvesting. I'd be sent out picking turnips and would take the hurley and boots with me. I'd do a quick job on the turnips – wouldn't be as good as my father would like. I would then do a few rounds of the field, go on a few solo runs and then puck around for a while with Mick Power, the workman. That would be when the evenings were short and I wouldn't have time to go to the field." No wonder he had speed and stamina and was as hard as nails!

In 1956, Waterford were on the threshold of a great era, which was to bring an All-Ireland title in 1959, Munster titles in 1957, 1959 and 1963, Oireachtas victory in 1962 and National League honours in 1963. And yet Tom wasn't happy. "I now look back with a sense of overriding disappointment. Only one All-Ireland. We lost 1957 by one point; we lost 1963 by one goal after scoring 6:8 – each time to Kilkenny. I feel we could have won both; tradition, I suppose, won it for Kilkenny. Yes, I'm disappointed."

Tom looks on 1959 as being Waterford's best hurling year of that era. And no wonder. "We trounced the All-Ireland champions, Tipp. – revenge for a sixteen-point defeat the previous year. We beat Cork in a pulsating Munster final at Thurles, 3:9 to 2:9. A draw with Kilkenny in the final and victory in the replay by a margin of eight points sealed our greatness in 1959. Very few can claim to have beaten the 'Big Three' on the way to All-Ireland success."

After the drawn game with Kilkenny, Tom and Ollie Walsh were joint Sports Stars of the Week, and in the replay Tom recalls scoring a personal tally of 2:2 from play. He sees the year ending in September 1963 as probably their most successful twelve months. "It began with the winning of the Oireachtas in the Autumn of 1962 with a good win over Tipp. We beat them again in the home final of the league. I probably played my best-ever game for Waterford that day. It was one of the few days I got the better of Tony Wall. It brought me a Sports Star of the Week award.

"I wasn't on the team for the drawn game and the victorious replay against New York. There is a story behind that. I went to a soccer dance in the Olympia and got suspended. I got no league medal. If they offered it to me now I don't think I'd take it.

"We beat Tipp. in the Munster final. That was our fourth major victory over Tipp. – and, remember, they were a very good team. We beat them in the championship of 1959; the Oireachtas of 1962; the league of 1963; the Munster final of 1963. We felt confident for the All-Ireland final of 1963. Going onto Croke Park that day I felt fitter than in 1959. But I didn't have a good game on Ted Carroll. We nullified each other. Kilkenny dominated at midfield. I regret I didn't switch to midfield – I played mainly there for my club. Sometimes now, when I look back, I regret I didn't spend my career hurling in defence at county level. I think the half-back line would have suited me best, given my physique, temperament and style of play."

Tom then reminisced and mused about great hurlers. "I played on one of the Hennessys in New York – both good hurlers. They came from the Kerry Ballyduff. Ollie Walsh was a magnificent goalkeeper; there was great style about him. Jack Lynch was one of the nicest men I ever met – a gentleman; never forgot his hurling roots; always willing to attend a function. I always found Paddy Barry of Cork hard to mark: he was elusive. Philly Grimes would be my outstanding man of that era: he had a great turn of speed – more effective in the loose than in the tight. John Horgan of Cork was a marvellous corner-back – great to read a game and clear from the full-back line. Jimmy Doyle could do anything he liked with the ball; I think I'd put him after Mackey and Ring."

Tom played senior hurling for his club into his early forties. In 1982 he was asked to train the Ballyduff junior team. He agreed, and jokingly added, "And I'll play with them next year." Well, play he did, and a couple of months before his fiftieth birthday he won the county junior title with his native Ballyduff – operating, would you believe, at centre-forward, and nursing a broken bone in his hand from an earlier game.

Pat Fanning, president of the GAA, 1970 to 1973, in a tribute to Tom wrote:

No man in Waterford's hurling story symbolises the spirit and the style of Decies hurling at its best than does Tom Cheasty of Ballyduff/Portlaw. His distinctive style marked him apart as, in turn, he jinked and weaved his way through the tightest defence, or burst through for a decisive score, seemingly impervious to personal danger. He was as brave as he was strong, and he was happiest when the battle was at its fiercest. A man of tremendous physical strength, he was, nevertheless, a ball player, who spearheaded a Waterford attack noted for its teamwork.

Déag Tom ar 10 Lúnasa 2007.

SÉAMUS CLEERE
KILKENNY

Born: 1940
Interviewed: 1996

Five victorious Kilkenny captains (from left): Noel Skehan (1972),
Mickey Kelly (1957), Séamus Cleere (1963), Jim Treacy (1967), and
(inset) the late Dan Kennedy (1947).

"Growing up in Bennettsbridge in the late forties and fifties, it was every
young boy's ambition to wear the green and gold of his native club.

"In the early sixties I started playing for Kilkenny, and for almost ten
years I was privileged to wear the black and amber. 1963 would probably be the highlight of my hurling career, when I had the honour of
captaining Kilkenny to a glorious win over Waterford in the All-Ireland
final. In the same year I won the Caltex Award. It gives me a great sense
of pride to have taken part in our national game at county level for ten
years. I enjoyed every minute of it – on the field and also the great social

gatherings afterwards. During that time I made many friends – friendships that have endured over the years."

Séamus belonged to a wonderful club, with which he won six county titles. Between 1947 and 1972, five Bennettsbridge men captained Kilkenny to All-Ireland success: Dan Kennedy (1947), Michael Kelly (1957), Séamus Cleere (1963) – when his displays earned him Hurler of the Year Award – Jim Treacy (1967) and Noel Skehan (1972).

When it came to travelling up North to play Antrim in a league game in 1959, Paddy Grace sent a taxi for Johnny McGovern and Liam Cleere with instructions to collect whoever they could around Bennettsbridge. Thus did Séamus make his debut in the black and amber. "I was handed boots in the dressing-room, and we played the game in sleet and snow."

He was a sub on the Kilkenny minor team that lost to Galway at the semi-final stage in 1958. "I was mad to get in, to play beside Keher; instead I found myself in the goal. Anything I learned as a young lad about the game came from Johnny McGovern. He had great heart as a player and always encouraged young lads."

Séamus made his Railway Cup debut in 1963 and for six successive years, from 1963 to 1968, he "owned" the right-half back position on the Leinster team – a tribute to his consistency and brilliance in that position. He won medals in 1964 (captain), 1965 and 1967.

Séamus was involved in five All-Ireland final days and was successful on three occasions – 1963 with victory over Waterford; 1967 with victory over Tipperary for the first time since 1922 in a final; and 1969 when injury kept him among the subs in the final against Cork. He was on the losing side in 1964 and 1966 to Tipperary and Cork respectively.

The 1964 result of Tipperary 5:13, Kilkenny 2:8, probably does an injustice to Kilkenny from the point of view of out-field exchanges. The Kilkenny selectors took the strange option of moving Séamus from right half-back to right half-forward for the game. Why? "I hurled centre half-back for my club and used to nip up-field and get a few scores. Maybe they thought it would add scoring power to the attack. I started the game on Tipp's captain, Michael Murphy, and finished up on Mick Lonergan, who came on as a sub. I remember in the first half I collected a ball; went on a solo run; seemed to be clear, when I ran into a shoulder from Michael Maher, the Tipp. full-back. It was like running into a fireplace. I was looking at stars for the remaining fifteen minutes or so of that half."

All-Ireland final day 1966 was a very disappointing one for Kilkenny. They were favourites. They wanted to atone for 1964; they didn't want two losses in a row. But that's how it turned out. "We had a good team, and Cork had been struggling for quite a while to make an impact. We prepared well, but things didn't work out. Colm Sheehan got three goals for Cork. We missed sitters." Kilkenny were back again for final day in Croke Park in 1967 and faced their arch-rivals, Tipperary. "We had to do something about beating Tipp. It was a needle affair. For us it was a good day but it wasn't a great match. It was tough, rugged and close marking. Looking back, I didn't get a lot of the ball. I started off on Donie Nealon; then McKenna; after that Jimmy Doyle; and I think Devaney was on me for a while. That can upset you." The final score was Kilkenny 3:8, Tipperary 2:7. The jubilant Kilkenny captain, Jim Treacy, collected the MacCarthy Cup to record their first All-Ireland win over Tipperary since 1922.

In 1968 Séamus damaged a ligament in his knee. "After the 1969 Leinster final and All-Ireland semi-final against London, the knee was in a bad way." As a sub, Séamus collected his third All-Ireland medal. Later that year he retired from the inter-county fray.

Séamus was a classical hurler: "poetry in motion" is an expression that aptly describes him. His displays epitomised all that is graceful and gracious in the ancient game. This great hurler and sportsman came to be acknowledged as one of the outstanding exponents and gentlemen of the game.

MARTIN COOGAN
KILKENNY

Born: 1940
Interviewed: 1992

"I am proud to be a Comer man. I was born there in a place called The Spike in 1940.

"Whenever Kilkenny won we replayed the match that evening on the (Spike) road, pretending we were the Kilkenny heroes of that day. Another reason why I am proud of our road is for the honour and fame brought to it by my great friend and neighbour Mick Dowling, the boxer. Mick was a good hurler too.

"Like every chap in Comer at that time I too went down the pit and spent two years mining anthracite. It was a tough life.

"Again, like every chap born in Kilkenny, I had a longing in my heart to wear the black and amber and play for Kilkenny. I always felt I would fulfil that ambition. I was overjoyed when I got my first call. I was on a Kilkenny team to play against a Kilkenny All-Star selection.

"In the years that followed, I trained with the county team in Nowlan Park, came home, togged out again and went to the Prince grounds in Castlecomer and continued training until I was satisfied that I was fit. I also practised the skills and my own favourite – the lift and strike without handling the ball. I spent hours every evening at that.

"The Kilkenny selectors saw something in me and I played with Kilkenny from 1960 until 1972 – two years at centre-field and the rest at left half-back. I am a natural left-handed hurler and I played right hand below. This made it difficult for opponents to hook me or block down the ball. In my years with Kilkenny I played against almost every hurling county in Ireland and I felt honoured to have played with some of the greatest hurlers and teams that Kilkenny ever produced.

"I feel that the umpires and linesmen should take more action and help the referee with his difficult task. I also think that no player should be penalised as a result of what is seen later on video. There are enough officials watching to take action during the game. No player at country level should get himself sent off. He should be able to discipline himself at that level and always put his team first. In my day the pressure was a bit less. We all headed off with the boots stuffed with stockings and togs and tied to the hurl. I liked that."

Martin Coogan was a right-hand-under natural left-handed hurler. He arrived on the scene in 1961 and played against Wexford in a Walsh Cup game. After the 1969 All-Ireland victory over Cork, he received the "Man of the Match" award. This was followed in 1971 by his selection for the first-ever All-Star team.

Martin always placed tremendous emphasis on fitness and good sportsmanship. In this regard he was a shining example to youth. The disciplines he placed upon himself were quite remarkable – extra running after coming home from a training session, bed at 9.30 p.m. from the Wednesday night before an important match, no change in food patterns for days before a big match, meticulous attention to the basics of the game, and total dedication to practice and training. He was surely a coach's dream.

His heart was in hurling and he loved to train. Self-effacing and modest, it seemed to me that in some respects playing the game and training for it meant more to him than medals won. These were hidden away in a box until a Tipperary friend called to see his collection. Taken aback by the way they were stored, he returned one month later with a beautiful show-case in which Martin now displays the medals.

He made hurling look easy but he put countless hours into develop-ing the skills and correcting the faults that manifested themselves during matches. He is a great admirer of overhead striking and loves to see play-ers lift and strike in the one movement without handling the ball – "It's terrific – I love watching it." He believes in letting the ball do the work and loves to see players getting rid of it quickly.

Martin also excelled at other games – squash, tennis, handball and golf. It wasn't surprising then that in 1980 the Castlecomer Tennis Club presented Martin with a magnificent "This is Your Life" book. Here are two excerpts from the book:

As a youngster in Castlecomer, his enthusiasm saw him train by candle-light for the game of hurling he loved. Later his efforts in the dark were to be rewarded when he received national acclaim, and when he eventually decided to step down from the inter-county scene, he left to cries of a "lost gentleman from hurling".

The curtain came down on his magnificent inter-county hurling career in 1973 but he left memories that will stand the test of time and be forever among the best.

Martin Coogan

LIAM DEVANEY
TIPPERARY

Born: 1935
Interviewed: 1986

"To win is great and a proud moment. So my great joy was to win a county final with my club Borris-o-leigh, at nineteen years of age, in the year 1953. I won a lot of games and lost a lot of games, but hurling to me was a joy to play – and the friends I made on and off the field.

"My second joy was to play for Munster with Christy Ring, Jimmy Doyle and the stars. As I look back and recall fond memories of past games, I realise that the memories become more important as I get older. I always believe in good sportsmanship on and off the field, and in my hurling days it was always my wish to aim at high standards and a spirit of give and take."

Versatility was one of Liam's hallmarks. In his time he played in defence, midfield and attack. Let's look briefly at the eight All-Ireland finals in which Liam played: 1958 v. Galway – full-forward – won; 1960 v. Wexford – centre-forward – lost; 1961 v. Dublin – left half-forward – won; 1962 v. Wexford – centre field – won; 1964 v. Kilkenny – second-half sub – forward – won; 1965 v. Wexford – left half-forward – won; 1967 v. Kilkenny – left half-forward – lost; 1968 v. Wexford – left full-forward – lost.

63

I look upon his display in the 1961 final as perhaps his greatest. In a second-half switch, Liam was brought back to centre half-back. He steadied a Tipperary defence that was under great pressure. He hurled with confidence and authority. His normal style had panache about it, but in the final of 1961, as he stood supreme at centre-back, there was an added exuberance to his performance that made him stand apart. It was his day. He won the Caltex Hurler of the Year award and was also the journalists' choice as Hurler of the Year.

He regards the 1964–1965 Tipperary combination as an excellent one, and the best he played on. They made a clean sweep of titles in those years, winning Munster, All-Ireland, National League and Oireachtas honours.

He remembers training in Thurles for the 1964 All-Ireland final. At the last training session Paddy Leahy called Liam and Larry Kiely to the back of the stand. "We are going down to pick the team. The two of ye are hurling terrible well – but we can't play the two of ye; ye will get half an hour apiece." And so it was.

Liam had great praise for Paddy Leahy, "who could motivate players in training, lift their spirits from the sideline, and inspire them to great deeds in the dressing-room at half time." Speaking of players, Paddy Kenny was his choice as a top-class corner-forward; he had special words of praise for goalkeeper John O'Donoghue. Of the 1964–65 forward line-up, he had this to say: "I look upon Jimmy Doyle as a hurling genius and comparable to Ring in many respects; McKenna and McLoughlin brought those around them into the game, and didn't always get the recognition they deserved; Keating and Kiely fitted into the Tipperary forward line like a glove." It all added up to a forward combination that fired on all cylinders, moved with a deadly precision and devastated many an opposition.

His admiration for hurling artists is such that he would have settled for fewer honours to see players like Kevin Armstrong (Antrim), "Jobber" McGrath (Westmeath), Joe Salmon (Galway), and Jimmy Murray and Christy O'Brien (Laois) win some major national title – a lovely sentiment and a reflection of the sporting personality of Liam.

Liam Devaney

PA DILLON
KILKENNY

Born: 1938
Interviewed: 1997

Pa the hurler with his daughter Gillian, who excelled at camogie for Kilkenny. (Photo courtesy of the Dillon family.)

"From the first time I caught a hurl and started to puck around, I loved hurling. From listening to Mícheál O'Hehir in the mid-forties and onwards, broadcasting about the stars of the day, we young fellas imagined ourselves as those great hurlers."

He remembers his early days. "Our team won under-14, 16 and minor in a few years and progressed to the local junior team. At that time, junior hurling was pretty tough going. It was badly organised: bad pitches, bad referees, no training; and almost every junior team in the county was illegal. You would often see fellas of forty-plus playing, the togs down to their knees, the wellie turned down; and usually the big full-back or full-forward wore the cap with the peak on the back – and during the game was given a lift with a Baby Power or two.

"In 1960 I got my first call-up for Kilkenny. I was absolutely thrilled. The prize was a trip to Wembley, which we won. I wasn't great that day, as the speed of the Waterford forwards bearing down on goal and the speed of Ollie coming off the goal line, dodging the incoming forwards, left me dazzled. It was a big step up in class.

"I was glad to be a sub on a great Kilkenny team which beat Waterford in the final of 1963. The highlight of that great win was an invite to New York the following spring. We were three weeks out between New York and Chicago.

"I became a regular on the Kilkenny team in 1964, but we were beaten badly by a great Tipp. team in the All-Ireland.

"I retained my position in 1965 at full-back on the team and was also selected full-back for Leinster. We defeated Munster in a great game. A few years previous to that, my club were playing Moycarkey in a challenge. After the game, we were having a drink in the local and I was talking to this man who I did not know at the time. He had a beautiful medal on a chain in his lapel. I asked him about the medal, to be told it was a Railway Cup medal. He was none other than the great Johnny Leahy. So it was a wish come true to win my own.

"Having lost to Cork, who were classed as no-hopers, in the All-Ireland final of 1966, I began to wonder would I ever win an All-Ireland. In 1967 we faced Tipperary in the final. I was at full-back again. We were well on top in the first half against the wind, and Ollie was brilliant. We lost our two best forwards, Tom Walsh and Eddie Keher; and although we were on top we weren't showing it on the scoreboard. We won it. It was my first All-Ireland win. I could not describe the feeling, it was just great.

"1969 was another great year. We won the Leinster final against Offaly. It was Cork in the final. This was the beginning of a great Kilkenny team. It was a thrill to beat Cork.

"In 1972 Cork looked to have it in the bag with twenty-five minutes to go. Keher was switched to half-forward. Martin Coogan came on. Kilkenny were transformed, and we won another All-Ireland. I was a sub the following year and decided to finish my hurling years with my club, St Lactain's — about ten more years. Due to hurling I had the pleasure of playing in Wembley Stadium, New York, Chicago, San Francisco."

Pa was a goalkeeper's dream. He played in the days when the rules allowed the inrushing forwards to bundle the goalkeeper into the back of the net. He saw to it that such activity was kept to a minimum: those who chose to indulge in it had to deal with Pa – if not on the way in, certainly on the way out.

Pa was tall and spare and physically strong. "I never missed a night's training or a match, and hurling never caused me to miss a day's work." He was a versatile performer, a rock-solid defender, who saw no danger and feared no opponent.

Pa has a room that displays a wide range of trophies, medals, and photographs. They range from the humble competition to the pinnacle of success. Prominent in their midst is a silver-plated trophy that holds a special place in Pa's hurling world. "I won it when I was seventeen – a seven-a-side hurling competition; clubs from all over the county. Some of the teams had seven brothers on them – some very tough games; I shed tears and sweat and blood winning that." And that from a man who togged out for eight All-Ireland finals – twice as a sub, in 1963 and 1973 – and won four All-Ireland medals, three on the field and one as a sub.

Father Time, however, catches up with all mortals, even the very trim and fit-looking Pa. Yet he was still playing junior hurling at forty-six. It was against Muckalee: "A high ball came in. I went up for it, still thinking I was twenty-one. I got a belt of a hurl in the forehead, blood everywhere. After the game I was taken to hospital, into casualty. The nurse was filling a form and asked what age I was and what happened. I told her but I didn't want to say forty-six, so I said, 'Put down "Over 40".' As she walked away, I heard her say to another nurse, 'They never get sense, do they?' I felt then it was time to retire."

Pa Dillon

JIMMY DOYLE
TIPPERARY

Born: 1940
Interviewed: 1993

Jimmy (right) with Mick Mackey, a hero of earlier times.

I met Jimmy Doyle of Thurles town in the Summer of 1993. He was a gentleman, shy and retiring. A hurling master, the hurley in his hand was like a magic wand and how he used it was a reflection of his personality.

His array of medals and awards, in excess of 120, is quite staggering – Hurler of the Year 1965; a treasured street league silver medal won in his youth; Harty Cup and Munster Colleges' medals; multiple honours in Munster, All-Ireland, Railway Cup, Oireachtas and National League titles. They represent the power and the glory of Jimmy Doyle and Tipperary hurling.

But they were won at a price – a broken collarbone; a double fracture of the ankle; a broken thumb; broken knuckles; discs put out fourteen times; broken fingers; a litany of sundry "softeners"; and now the threat of arthritis from the myriad of knocks he took as he played the game he loved and breathed from his very early youth. Regrets? "None – I would do it all over again."

What a panorama unfolds as one examines the career of Jimmy Doyle. A brilliant hurling career began when he played in goal for Tipperary minors in 1954 at the age of fourteen. They lost to Dublin in the final but the three succeeding years brought All-Ireland honours. His potency as a forward was heralded in the finals of 1955 and 1956 when he scored 2:8 and 2:3 against Galway and Kilkenny respectively. He confirmed this form at senior level in the All-Ireland semi-final against Kilkenny in 1958 when he contributed 1:8 to a Tipperary total of 1:13.

Hurling followers associate certain teams with specific decades. In the case of Tipperary, the sixties belonged to them. In the years 1961, 1964 and 1965 they made a clean sweep of Munster, All-Ireland, National League and Oireachtas titles. Jimmy added a county title to each of those years. In 1961 he also won a Railway Cup medal and in 1965 he received the Texaco Hurler of the Year award. "In my estimation the best team we had in that era was the 1964 team, captained by Michael Murphy."

Among the highlights of Jimmy's career were the trips to America, and he had several of these. "It was lovely to go. Each one was special but the first at the age of seventeen after winning the National League was the thrill of a lifetime."

Because 1958 was his first All-Ireland win it will always stand out as special. There was a touch of nostalgia about the 1971 win. Despite injury he came on in the last ten minutes and won his sixth All-Ireland medal. But the All-Ireland final of greatest personal drama was 1961 against Dublin.

"In the Munster final against Cork my ankle suffered a double fracture. At the time I didn't realise it and played for the entire game." Jimmy was told by Surgeon O'Donnell at Nenagh Hospital, who put his leg in plaster, that he wouldn't make the final. On the Friday before the final when he couldn't do a sprint, he was told he wouldn't make it. He sat by the sideline and cried – still determined to play.

"Dr Herlihy called to the house to console me. 'I'm sorry, Jimmy, but if you play you're gambling your leg. I can give you injections to deaden your leg but it must be your decision – your responsibility.' My father and mother were there as we talked and Dr Herlihy said he would go away and let the three of us talk about it and come back to hear the decision. There was no way I was going to miss that All-Ireland final and, when Dr Herlihy returned, my father told him I was going to take the field in Croke Park.

"I travelled by car on Sunday morning to Dublin. Three or four minutes before the match I was given three injections – it numbed my leg from the knee down.

"At half time I was given three more. When the final whistle blew we had won by one point – 0:16 to 1:12 for Dublin – and we were lucky to win. I shouldn't really have played. I was back in a plaster for six months after the game."

In his playing days, he stood out as a hurling craftsman of the highest order – a player of rare class, a superb marksman. This was a result of countless hours spent fine-tuning and studying and perfecting – insofar as it is possible to perfect – every skill and swing and swerve and motion associated with the artistry that sets the sublime hurler apart from the useful and the good.

Hurling was in the genes. His father Gerry and his uncle Tommy both played with Tipperary. In many ways, and particularly in sportsmanship, Jimmy was a shining example to youth. No greater sportsman ever graced the hurling fields of Ireland. He had a vast range of hurling skills and his repertoire matched that of Mackey and Ring. He was a virtuoso. He drew from the crowd a different kind of admiration than the two supremos. An Antrim enthusiast who wrote to me echoed the feelings of many when he said "Doyle won All-Irelands in the 1950s, 1960s and 1970s and gave more pleasure to me than any other hurler."

Jimmy called it a day and officially hung up his hurley after the Munster final of 1973 against Limerick when he was a sub. His last inter-county match was in goal against Waterford in the Munster Championship of that year. "I let in two but we still won." So a great career finished as it had started in 1954 – in goal.

AUSTIN FLYNN
WATERFORD

Born: 1933
Interviewed: 1994

"I think that anybody who got as much out of hurling in Waterford as I did would be a fool not to acknowledge the good luck to be playing at a time when a magnificent bunch of hurlers was emerging in Waterford. Coupled with this was the fact that a small band of extraordinary people had the vision, the dream and the courage to suggest that maybe these hurlers could win an All-Ireland title for Waterford.

"For the 1957 championship the panel was brought together in Dungarvan for collective training under John Keane as trainer and selector. Also present that evening were the other selectors, Jackie Good, Mickey Feeney, Seamus O'Brien and the Chairman Pat Fanning who made a famous address to the players which, for me, was the actual night it all started.

"I remember the way he spelt out his firm belief in the capacity of this group to win an All-Ireland for Waterford, the efforts the county board would make towards this goal and the total commitment, dedication and pride in the county that would be expected from the players. I didn't know most of the other players at that time and I remember thinking, 'This is serious stuff' and I remember looking across at Séamus Power and Philly Grimes and thinking, 'My God am I out of my depth here – could I be in the same league as these fellows?' Well, in the years that followed lifelong friendships were forged between all present that night as well as all the replacements over the next seven or so glorious years.

"Waterford played in the 1957, 1959 and 1963 All-Irelands. We won in 1959 in the replay and many think we should have won more but we also won Oireachtas and National League titles. Many of us were in the Munster and Rest of Ireland teams. We travelled to New York as a team in 1960 and it was amazing how the visit brought so many Waterford people together in New York. During the visit, Pat Fanning addressed what would be the equivalent of a county convention in Ireland. He made us all feel proud – he made you feel proud of being from Waterford. He was a wonderful ambassador for the game.

"In 1966 I was picked with Christy Ring, Bernie Hartigan, John Doyle and Pat Dunney to travel to New York for the Cardinal Cushing games. We played in New York and Chicago and had a visit to Robert Kennedy in his office in Washington. I became friendly with Christy during this visit and he often called to my house afterwards.

"Looking back now, the team I admired most was the mighty Wexford team. The best hurler was Christy Ring. The club I admired most was Mount Sion with whom Abbeyside did battle on four occasions for the senior hurling final of Waterford, but we never won.

"The nicest hurler to watch, I thought, was Philly Grimes – to see him in full flight. For determination, true grit and never-say-die attitude – the man who personified all this for me has to be Séamus Power. And for everybody's No. 1 gentleman – John Barron."

In the full-back position at county and inter-provincial level, Austin set high standards in clean play and good sportsmanship. Snippets from his hurling career unfold in no particular order as you talk to him. A vein of humour runs through many.

"I was a 'stupid' hurler, you know – I could only play at full-back. I never missed a match once I established myself – I was afraid they might find someone better.

"I played on Nicky Rackard a few times towards the end of his career. I was always pleased with my performance. I never tried to hurl him close. I learned that lesson about big fellows in my schooldays.

"I remember the day before our championship match with reigning All-Ireland champions Tipp. in 1959. I had been out boating and as I came ashore two hurling fans approached me and enquired, 'How we would fare against Tipp?' To keep the discussion short, I said we would beat the sugar out of them – end of conversation. We played with the wind in the first half and before long scored a goal. Devaney, who was marking me, let a swear out of him and looked at me but I said nothing. Then we got a second and third goal. Devaney kept watching me for a reaction but I looked straight ahead as if it was to be expected. We were about eight goals up at half time and walked the match. The fans I met at the Harbour thought I was a prophet.

"Looking back now I got a great deal out of hurling but more impor-tant than any medals or trophies are the treasured memories and life-long friendships with extraordinary people that could never have happened without the game of hurling."

DES FOLEY
DUBLIN

Born: 1940
Interviewed: 1981

"I regret not having won an All-Ireland hurling medal. I loved the game and all the friends I made from it. Special memories would be the 1961 All-Ireland and all the Dublin championships, hurling and football, with my club St Vincent's, which came first for me, and the comradeship while playing the game for Dublin, which lasted into later life.

"Having failed to win the 1961 All-Ireland, there was compensation by winning the two Railway Cups on St Patrick's Day in 1962, where it was a joy to be associated with the greats of Dublin, Wexford (for whom I had a great grá) and Kilkenny.

"More time should be spent on the basic skills of hurling, which I feel are vital to the game."

As I talked with this great Gaelic sportsman at his home in Kinsealy in North Co. Dublin, it was very evident that Des was in no doubt that the Dublin hurling team of 1961 was a good one. They had beaten the All-Ireland champions, Wexford, in the Leinster final by 7:5 to 4:8. In the Railway Cup final of 1962, Leinster selectors fielded eight of the Dublin team, including the entire full-back line of Des Ferguson, Noel Drumgoole and Lar Foley. They defeated Munster by 1:11 to 1:9 and it is interesting to recall the Munster full-forward line: Jimmy Smyth, Christy Ring and Séamus Power.

Turning to personalities, Des talked in glowing terms of Jimmy Doyle of Tipperary – his immense hurling skills and his great sportsmanship; and the superb artistry and hurling skills of Eddie Keher, which were clearly evident even in his college days, when he played against him in the Leinster Schools' Championship. He had a special admiration for the Wexford hurling teams of the 1950s and 1960s. Ned Wheeler's sportsmanship and hurling style made a particular impression on Des, as did the great hurling prowess of Billy Rackard.

Des was also an outstanding footballer and won an All-Ireland title in 1963 with a 1:9 to 0:10 victory over a Galway team on the threshold of a historic three-in-a-row of All-Ireland titles. I got the feeling a hurling medal would have meant more to Des than a football one.

His brother Lar was also a great dual player – winning All-Ireland football titles in 1958 and 1963. He was left full-back on the hurling team of 1961. He won Railway Cup hurling medals in 1962 and 1964 in the company of his brother Des, who went on to win a third medal in 1965.

Des departed this life, at the relatively young age of fifty-five, on 6 February 1995.

Des Foley

BRENDAN HENNESSY
KERRY

Born: 1938
Interviewed: 1993

Brendan Hennessy, hurler, footballer, athlete, turning the scales in his prime at 13½ st., was a formidable handful for any opponent. In his youth he was North Munster 880 yards and 440 yards champion. He won a National Football League medal in 1964 when New York beat Dublin by 2:12 to 1:13 in New York. He played in six National Hurling League finals with New York but no medal came his way. He played with and against the cream of the hurling world and was at ease in their company.

Brendan hailed from Ballyduff in North Kerry – hurling country. He was educated at St Flannan's College, Ennis – hurling territory. He emigrated to the US on 2 February 1958 – accompanied by five of the Ballyduff team, including his brother Michael. In New York, he hurled for Kilkenny and for New York All-Star selections. He played at midfield and excelled.

A hurling career that began in his youth in Ballyduff ended in New York in 1974, leaving Brendan with many memorable recollections.

"I remember one time when eleven of us (juveniles) piled into Mr Carbery's little car (Morris Minor) going to play a game.

"I remember the day of Confirmation in Ballyduff. After we were confirmed, Richie McCarthy and myself went to Ignatius O'Brien's field

76

in Rattoo to practise. That's all we thought about – practise – practise – practise.

"As juveniles, we had the brown sliotar and when it ripped, up to Stephen Sullivan the harness maker to have it stitched. That sliotar must have had a hundred stitches.

"In 1955, at the age of sixteen, I came onto the Ballyduff senior hurling team and played at midfield. We won the Kerry County Championship for the first time since 1891. The celebrations lasted for a week.

"I won a Munster junior title with Kerry in 1956 and we were beaten by Kilkenny in the All-Ireland final.

"We played against Galway in the National League of 1957. Michael and myself played at midfield. I was on Joe Salmon – that's when I came of age. Joe was full of compliments to me after the match.

"I am happy and proud to say that I played on three Harty Cup teams. We beat North Mon. in the final in 1957 and Kieran's beat us in the All-Ireland Colleges' Final. A team-mate said, 'We didn't win – we didn't lose either – we just gave it away. Leading by eleven points at half time we shouldn't have lost.' But they had Eddie Keher and he got three late goals."

Brendan has never forgotten the St Brendan's Cup game against reigning National League champions Wexford in September 1958. "In the pre-game write-up some of the writers wrote that the Hennessy brothers wouldn't have the experience to play on men like Ned Wheeler and Jim Morrissey. But I guess we proved them wrong – the record speaks for itself. We were sports stars for the week for that game. It was the greatest birthday present I ever got. I was twenty years old the following day. I was on Ned Wheeler that day – a great hurler, a true sportsman – but I guess on the day he got a surprise. Kerry men were not supposed to hurl like we did. Michael and myself were perfect partners – we knew each other's moves."

Then there was that day in 1959 in New York when New York played Tipperary in a challenge game. The late John D. Hickey wrote, "[The] star of the victorious side was Brendan Hennessy who gave an inspired display at centre-back. Not since Pat Stakelum was in his prime have I seen a better exhibition in the berth."

Brendan Hennessy

MICHAEL KEATING
TIPPERARY

Born: 1944
Interviewed: 1994

"How are you Michael?" I enquired as he answered our pre-arranged phone call of Sunday night, 29 May 1994. "I have often felt better," he replied. I understood. His fancied forces – recently crowned league champions – had fallen to the men of Clare. It was unexpected. Tipperary were among the favourites for the 1994 All-Ireland crown and Michael was plotting and planning with that in mind. "That's sport," he said as we ended our conversation and arranged a meeting.

Michael hails from Ballybacon-Grange in South Tipperary – a football stronghold. "I found it easier to play football than hurling. I had to train to play hurling but not football. I felt more confident at football. I was at it from my youth. As I went for the cows I would grab a football and kick it up the fields – from buachalán to buachalán as a test of judgement. I didn't prefer one above the other but looking back now I have to say there is no game in the world like hurling." For ten years he was part of the Munster Railway Cup football panel and won a medal in 1972 when

Munster won the trophy for the first time in twenty-three years, after a replay. Football, of course, was in the blood. His granduncle Tommy Ryan – later to become lieutenant colonel in the Irish Army – played football with Tipperary. He was playing in Croke Park on Bloody Sunday, 21 November 1920 and helped remove Michael Hogan from the pitch after he had been shot by the Black and Tans.

It is, however, as a hurler that Michael will be remembered in the years and decades ahead. He arrived on the inter-county scene in the early sixties. For Michael, success came immediately. An intermediate title was won in 1963. The following year he played under-21 and senior and Tipperary won both titles. In senior ranks he was in the company of one of Tipperary's finest ever combinations and his presence in the forward line made that division a potent sector. He thought that in decades to come he would look back on 1964 as perhaps his most memorable year. He was only twenty and found himself Sports Star of the Week after the National League final, the Munster final and the All-Ireland final. Did he appreciate it all then? "Perhaps it came too young."

If Michael chose 1964, others might have chosen 1971 for him to remember. He was in devastating form. In the National League semi-final against Cork, he scored 1:9. Against Galway in the All Ireland semi-final at Birr he amassed 2:12 – "I got points that day from impossible angles including one from the end line." He had seven points to his credit against Kilkenny in the All-Ireland final. In the Munster final against Limerick at Killarney he left a lasting imprint. It was one of the great southern deciders. Limerick were ahead by two goals at half time and it could have been more. But fortunes changed in the second half, following a display of *comhacht agus fuinneamh agus gaiscíocht* from Michael Keating. He scored three goals following precision clearances from Mick Roche. He finished the game with a personal tally of 3:4. In a game that ended 4:16 to 3:18 Michael Keating was the difference – the big difference. Little wonder that he was nominated Hurler of the Year in 1971. He retired after defeat by Clare in the championship of 1974. In that game he broke his jaw in three places. The evidence is still there.

But he was back the following year and in the semi-final replay against Limerick he demonstrated – especially in the first half – his repertoire of skills and forceful forward play that suggested he might do a 1971 all over again and defeat Limerick on his own. But it wasn't to be.

In 1979 he coached Galway and lost to Kilkenny in the final. When he took over at the helm in Tipperary in 1986, Tipperary hurling was experiencing its longest-ever barren period. Since the All-Ireland victory of 1971, only a National League title in 1979 helped to ease the pain of loss and the hurt of pride.

In taking office, Michael cast the net far and wide. In came players of youth and skill and potential. The building and renewal had begun. Time would add depth to the panel and depth would create a winning blend.

With Michael Keating, sportsmanship and clean play were paramount. And he demanded this side by side with a style of hurling that he wanted played with speed, skill, passion and aggression. In training he preached the five Ss – "Speed and Stamina, Style and Skill, from which should emerge Scores."

During Michael's time with Tipperary he guided them to five Munster titles – three in a row from 1987 to 1989, two All-Ireland crowns and two National Leagues. It was a good return in the space of eight years. "I changed the face of hurling. I treated players well and gave them what they deserve. You must treat players well nowadays. To win an All-Ireland it takes special ingredients – especially courage to play before sixty thousand people. You put on the jersey first for yourself and your family, next for the 'little village', lastly for your county. And when the game is over you must be able to say good luck – thanks."

When Tipperary fell to Clare in the first round of the 1994 Munster Championship, Michael Keating immediately called it a day. The sudden parting was unexpected. He had contributed much. He strove unceasingly and with great intensity for hurling perfection, especially in forward play. He led Tipperary out of the desert. He restored their pride. He would be missed.

Michael Keating

EDDIE KEHER
KILKENNY

Born 1941
Interviewed: 1982

Eddie (right) chatting with John T. Power of Piltown,
star Kilkenny goalkeeper of the 1907–1913 era.

"It is impossible to describe in words the enjoyment I have got and still get
from the game of hurling. It seems only yesterday that I started collect-
ing the photographs of great players and pasting them carefully into a
book which I used read out loud twenty times a day. The great Waterford
team of 1948 is my longest memory, though I never saw them playing. I
remember my mother bringing me over to shake the hand of Jim Ware in
Tramore one day and boasting about it for years afterwards."

Eddie was captain in 1969, when Kilkenny faced Cork in the All-Ireland
final as underdogs. There was a buzz in the Kilkenny camp from early in
the year.

"We were very fortunate against Offaly in the Leinster final. Paddy
Molloy played a stormer that day for Offaly. For most of the game we
were playing catch-up. Only for Pat Delaney we would have lost. He got

our three goals – he palmed the third to the net to give us the lead towards the very end.

"There was panic in our dressing-room before the All-Ireland final when we learned that our midfielder Paddy Moran had the flu. He wouldn't last the hour. He was replaced by Mick Lawler who played a blinder. We won by 2:15 to 2:9."

Eddie was Kilkenny's top scorer with a contribution of eight points. I asked him what made the day special for him.

"There were a number of things: the prematch parade, leading the team; being presented with the Cup and holding it up to delighted supporters; the fact that four players from my club, the Rower-Inistioge, took part in the win – Billy Murphy, Fr Tommy Murphy, Pat Kavanagh and myself; the celebrations when we returned to Kilkenny and especially when we took the Cup to our parish."

When Eddie reflects on a hurling career that stretched at county senior level from 1959 to 1977, three All-Ireland day occasions stand out: "1963 against Waterford when I won my first medal; 1969 against Cork when I was captain; 1972 against Cork because it was such a great game to play in."

Fleeting moments from games listened to and watched tend to stay in one's mind. When I think of Eddie Keher, four such memories from finals remain etched in my mind.

First, there was the 1959 replay against Waterford. In the second half of the game I scanned my programme as I watched a youthful figure come on as a sub – Eddie Keher, still a minor. Little did any of us realise that day in Croke Park that we were witnessing the entry to senior ranks of a player who would make a lasting impact on the hurling scene and join the all-time immortals of the game.

I will never forget his scoring performance in 1963 against Waterford – fourteen points (ten from frees). He scored from all angles and distances: a flawless performance. It was neither a freak nor a once-off. It was the product of patient and painstaking practice. It was attention to detail – "all these trifles lead to perfection." It was the hand of a master at work.

His goal in the 1972 All-Ireland final in the second half from a high probing shot from the Hogan Stand side, about fifty yards out near the sideline, that deceived Paddy Barry in the Cork goal, is as vivid in my mind now as the moment it happened. Eddie was again top scorer of the day with 2:9 to his credit. Eddie recalled: "That was an eighty minute final and I remember feeling drained after it." Later that year he received the Texaco Hurler of the Year Award.

Finally, there was 1975 against Galway. It was shortly after the second half started. A Kilkenny movement saw Eddie drift unmarked to the left. A perfect pass from Mick Crotty and you knew the minute Eddie grabbed the sliotar that it had "goal" written all over it. Again, he was top scorer of the day, with 2:7.

Eddie had a phenomenal scoring record right through his career and, with the exception of 1961, was at all times among the leading scorers – heading the charts in 1965, 1966, 1968 and 1970–1976 inclusive.

He played in an era when Kilkenny contested eleven All-Ireland finals. He participated in ten of those and was successful on six occasions. He has won every honour in the game, including five successive All-Stars in 1971–1975.

Where did the hurling brilliance come from? Not particularly from his antecedents. His mother was a Kilkenny woman, but no strong evidence of hurling existed on her side. His father hailed from Co. Roscommon. He played football with Garda teams and also played football with Kilkenny decades ago. Still, there is nothing in any of that to suggest that great hurling was in the genes. So that brings us back to his college, St Kieran's; his county, Kikenny; the example of so many outstanding county men; and probably most likely and important of all, his own extraordinary levels of fitness, commitment, dedication, diligence and remarkable attention to detail.

Eddie Keher

JUSTIN McCARTHY
CORK

Born: 1945
Interviewed: 1997

Justin (right) in 1967 with Jim Barry, the famous Cork trainer.

"My whole life is centred around hurling, and I'm told by my parents that at eleven months old I had a hurley in my hand. Fifty-two years later I still have that hurley in my hand and get as excited now as I probably did then. It's really a love affair, and I can safely say I have never fallen out with hurling and I am still learning about it. The friends that I made and discipline that hurling has given me have moulded my life for the better.

"My dream was always to play in the red and white of Cork, and that vision never left me. When I was growing up I got the opportunity to play minor in 1963 and then in 1964 I played under-21, intermediate and senior on the championship teams. Thankfully we made the big break-through in 1966, and it was a special year bringing the MacCarthy Cup back to the city by the Lee after twelve years out of the limelight. We also won the under-21 title for the first time, and to cap it all I was chosen as Caltex Hurler of the Year." The celebration took place in the Gresham Hotel. Justin still has the menu.

When Bord na nÓg was formed in Cork in the fifties, Justin took part in under-14, under-15 and under-16 competitions. "Father Roch, a Kilkenny man, taught me a lot about hurling. 'Play your own position,' he would say, 'know it: be in command.'" The same hurling philosophy was preached by Billy Campbell, Jim O'Regan, Johnny Quirke and Dinny Barry Murphy.

In 1955 he wore the Cork jersey for the first time. It was a very proud moment. "Father Roch arranged for the altar boys from Cork to play the altar boys from Kilkenny in Nowlan Park. Everything was laid on for us. We all felt so proud wearing the red jersey and marching behind the band. The Kilkenny boys wore the black-and-amber jersey. We won."

Justin's hurling came from his mother's side. "My father was a west Cork man. My mother's brothers, my uncles Batt O'Mahony and Ger O'Mahony, played with Young Irelands of Boston and won the American Championship of 1934. Batt was captain."

It took three games with Wexford to decide the 1966 under-21 final. "The third meeting took place on 13 November. Jack Lynch threw in the ball. The final score read Cork 9:9, Wexford 5:9." The *Free Press* reported on the game: "Leading the way for the Southerners was Justin McCarthy, a player with a wonderful future before him in the game. He strode the midfield with such class and power that one at times wondered where the Wexford man had gone."

A distinguished hurling career, which seemed destined for greater heights, was abruptly interrupted before the All-Ireland final of 1969. "My hurling world fell apart when, on my way to training for the All-Ireland final, I was involved in a motorbike accident and broke my leg in three places and was out of the game for over two years, missing the 1969 and 1970 finals. I watched the 1969 final from a wheelchair on the sideline. I tell you it wasn't nice sitting there. I was twenty-four – coming into my prime; getting stronger; more experienced; and in really good form. The 1969 team was one of the best I played with.

"My new goal was to win back my place, and I can remember my first game against Dublin in the National League. It was great to be back. Winning a National League medal in 1972 gave me great satisfaction, and a Munster medal that year, but losing the 1972 All-Ireland was a nightmare. My last game was against Waterford in the 1974 Munster Championship, when the Decies beat us."

Justin always had a keen interest in the coaching side of the game. In 1970 he went to Antrim and Antrim won the Intermediate All-Ireland crown. He was coaching Clare when they won successive league titles in 1977 and 1978 with wins over Kilkenny. He was coach to Cork when they won the Centenary title in 1984. He spent six years with Cashel King Cormacs and guided them to a first county title against Holycross in 1991. That paved the way for a Munster title. "They had great players in the Bonnars and Pat Fitzelle – as brilliant a hurler as I have seen."

When I phoned Justin to arrange our meeting he was "out at the back pucking a ball around." He had played his last competitive game with Passage in October 1991, when he won a City Divisional Junior League. On arrival, I was able to identify his house by two hurleys shaped from wrought iron in the gate. In his scrapbook were two little plastic bags. One contained a sample of clay from the Bilboa Stadium in San Francisco, where he played at centre-back against Tipperary as an All-Star replacement in April 1972 and at the same time visited his sister out there. The second bag had a piece of the sod from Wembley, which Justin took as a souvenir after a Monaghan cup final there. These bear witness to a life, blessed with good health and energy, that has been immersed and engrossed in the game of hurling in one form or another from his juvenile days in the fifties right up to the present moment.

Justin McCarthy

OLIVER McGRATH
WEXFORD

Born 1938
Interviewed: 1993

Oliver McGrath, affectionately known as "Hopper" to hurling fans, was the first hurler of prominence to come out of Wexford town. This thinking player on the pitch "can never recall the reason I took such an interest in hurling. I seemed to always have my precious hurl with me."

His background lay in football. His granduncle Tom played in goal in five All-Ireland finals for the Wexford team of the 1914–18 era – losing to Kerry after a replay in 1914 and winning four thereafter. His father played at junior level for the Model County. Hopper could play football too. In 1960, he won a county senior football title with Faythe Harriers. This, together with a senior hurling medal, completed a rare double in Wexford GAA history.

"My early introduction to the GAA was, as I remember, my late father visiting his relations and parents in Hill St, Wexford. I was usually brought with him on Sunday mornings. I shall always remember the thrill of seeing the array of medals at my great uncle's, Tom McGrath.

"There was, of course, at that time no hurling to speak of in Wexford town. I can remember going to the county football final of 1945 on the bar of my father's bicycle."

"Hopper" played minor for Wexford and came on as a sub in the never-to-be-forgotten National League final classic against Limerick in 1958, which Wexford won by 5:7 to 4:8. I saw him in action again in the 1960 All-Ireland final. He had a great game. All his class and potency and elusiveness as a forward were on display. He sent over a point in the opening half minute. He went through for a goal in the early stages of the second half.

I can still see him as he seemed to drift through the Tipperary defence. Both were key scores at key moments. It was probably Hopper's finest day in the purple and gold. The result was a shock: Wexford 2:15; Tipperary 0:11. "The 1960 final was a special day – of that there is no doubt. Arriving back in town and being the first native to achieve the distinction of having won an All-Ireland senior hurling medal was great."

He would like to see the following changes to the game: "I think the square needs to be made smaller. Since the rule change regarding the tackling of the goal man in the square, the scoring of goals has suffered. Too many frees for square infringements. I think that linesmen and umpires should have more input into the game. The 'sin bin' should be brought into play. Referees are reluctant to send off players. If they could send them off for ten minutes I think it would be of greater benefit. If the penalty was defined it would eliminate lobbying for leniency and canvassing the disciplinary officials to intercede on certain players' behalf.

"Players who are regularly sent off and known as hard men have no place in the game. I would like to see a record of their sending off offences referred to and more stringent action taken against them and their clubs. I would like to see the time-keeping in our games looked after some other way. I think the referee should not have this extra responsibility."

This player of skill and flair, scrupulously clean and sporting, departed the hurling scene somewhat prematurely. He trained with the panel in the early stages of the 1968 championship and played a tournament game against Cork. Later he was dropped. He feels he was unlucky to have been dropped. "I was very disappointed. I felt I still had something to contribute. I was only thirty." To add to his disappointment, Wexford went on to win the All-Ireland hurling title of 1968.

Oliver McGrath

MICHAEL MAHER
TIPPERARY

Born: 1930
Interviewed: 1986

Michael (left) under pressure from Wexford full-forward John
Kennedy, in a game against Wexford at New Ross in 1960.

Michael Maher of Holycross was a big, strong and very commanding
full-back. In winning five All-Ireland titles, in 1958, 1961, 1962, 1964 and
1965, he followed in the footsteps of his Uncle Mikey Maher of Tubbera-
dora who captained Tipperary to three All-Ireland titles in 1895, 1896
and 1898, before adding two more in 1899 and 1900.

Michael first wore the senior county jersey in a challenge game against
Wexford in 1952. He was playing on Nicky Rackard and came away feeling he had done quite well. However, it took a little longer to establish
himself permanently in the full-back berth.

"Hurling was the standard topic of conversation amongst the people with
whom I spent my boyhood. It did not require, therefore, divine inspiration

to become involved in playing hurling. The environment was correct, the encouragement was forthcoming, many willing people provided the leadership, and the counter-attractions were not that plentiful.

"Many played hurling in my native parish of Holycross, and I was one fortunate enough to meet with much success. I took part in winning three senior hurling county finals, seven National Leagues, four Railway Cups, and five senior All-lrelands. My first All-Ireland win against Galway in 1958 was probably the sweetest, but the final against Wexford in 1962 was the most memorable. Ned Wheeler played full-forward for Wexford on that day. It was a great hour's hurling. Winning an All-Ireland outshines any other achievements in the playing field, and that includes trips to America, etc."

He recalled having marked Christy Ring on a few occasions, and was particularly taken by his artistry, his strength, and his mad anxiety to win. "His desire for victory was incredible. Every match had to be won. When playing on him you had to hold your concentration for every minute of the game. I can remember him in the 1960 Munster final. I have great memories of that game; it's a win I cherish. There was a great finish to what had been a fierce contest. We were hanging on. Ring was running wild; he was challenging all of us in the Tipperary full-back line. It was a tactic – an attempt to unnerve and unsettle us. But we held the fort and won the day – just – 4:13 to 4:11.

"I remember, too, the 1957 meeting between Cork and Tipperary in Limerick. I hit Ring with a well-timed solid shoulder. He fell awkwardly, and had to retire with a broken wrist. I sent him a get-well card; he appreciated it."

Michael always believed that, as far as Ring was concerned, Glen Rovers came first, Cork second, and the GAA third. He considered that "Jimmy Doyle possessed as much artistry as Ring. However, he wasn't physically as strong. Neither had he the same fanatical approach to the game, nor the same killer instinct."

Michael held many key posts in the GAA at club, county, and Central Council level. He saw it as giving something back in appreciation of the joy the organisation and its games gave him.

Micheál Ó Meachair

PADDY MOLLOY
OFFALY

Born: 1934
Interviewed: 1996

Paddy Molloy (right) with Wexford stalwart defender
Tom Neville at Gaelic Park, New York, 1965.

"I used to listen to Mícheál O'Hehir broadcasting the matches when I was a youngster. There were only two wirelesses in our neighbourhood. A crowd used to gather around Guinan's in the village of Killyon.

"Mícheál O'Hehir made a great impression on me, and I used to imitate him for days after with my own commentary, with the help of a bucket over my face. The excitement that O'Hehir could bring to the air waves was immense and made a great impression on my young mind. He brought the thrills of the game into the kitchen, and as a result I had a dream. It was this: that one day, when I grew up, he would sing my praises on the radio and I would be selling the dummies, side-stepping my man and crashing the ball to the net, and taking frees slap-bang in front of the goal, and sending them over the bar. How often did I hear him say, 'He bends, lifts, and strikes, and sends it over the bar'? It took me a long time to achieve my goal, but luckily I made it, near the end of my playing days."

Paddy made his county debut in goal in 1952 on the Offaly minor team. He was a sub on the junior team that won the Leinster title in 1953 but failed to Tipperary in the home final. By 1955 he had progressed to the senior team and was a regular thereon for the next sixteen years.

He made his name early on as a goalie and defender, but as time passed his versatility was such that he played for Offaly in every position except full-back. "I was a certain kind of disciplinarian – never said no: would play wherever the selectors wanted me."

He was a gifted hurler with exceptional ability, one of Offaly's greatest. In defence, he was resolute and played first-time, no-nonsense hurling. Breaking hurleys was a feature of his game. He always carried at least three, and sees it as vital to have a hurley with which you are familiar. As a forward, Paddy was lethal. Some of his scoring feats were extraordinary: in 1965 in two championship games he scored 4:12; in 1966 in twelve games he scored 11:63; in 1969 in three championship games he scored 8:15; in the Offaly senior hurling final of 1966 he was the top scorer, with 3:3. His performance in that championship won him the Offaly Sports Star of the Year award. "The ferocity of club hurling in my time in Offaly was unbelievable. They used to come to the county final from the surrounding counties to see the action." Paddy was further honoured in 1966 with an Ireland jersey – a forerunner of the All-Stars – at a reception in Dublin.

Unfortunately during Paddy's hurling era, the balance of power had not swung Offaly's way. Lack of success brings its own problems – financial and otherwise. He remembers a league game against Westmeath in the early sixties when Offaly had only thirteen players and had to get two from the gate to make up the numbers. And he remembers well a National League division 2 final when the only fare on offer was bread and raspberry jam. They asked whether they would "have to hurl on that stuff" and were told, "It'll have to do – it's not even paid for." For Paddy it contrasted starkly with the Railway Cup games, when Martin O'Neill would ask, "What will you have, Paddy, chicken, beef, or ham?"

A particular game he remembers? Beating Tipperary in a league game in 1966: "I have great memories of that game, and good reason to remember it. It was played about the end of October. I had three acres of beet ready for drawing out. On the Friday night before the match, my brother told me that if I wanted the tractor I could have it for Saturday; after that he needed it. Without any help, I loaded and unloaded seven trailers – no heeling the load; all thrown in by hand and unloaded by hand. On Sunday morning, I couldn't lift my hands. How can I face hurling [against] Tipperary? I said to myself. I went to Mass; came home; felt a bit better. I went out and picked up an axe and swung it on a block several times; after that, the hurley felt light in my hands. We hammered Tipp. It was a great thrill. I got a lot of congratulations after that game."

For nine successive years he featured on the Leinster selections, beginning as a sub in 1963 and ending similarly in 1971. The Railway Cup victory of 1965 over Munster, 3:11 to 0:9, was a very special day for Paddy and for Offaly: it was the first time an Offaly man had won a Railway Cup hurling medal.

"I had the great honour of meeting Christy Ring during the Cardinal Cushing games of 1965 in the US. Four hurlers were invited: Jimmy Duggan (Galway), Tom Neville (Wexford), Christy Ring (Cork), and myself. In the game between Offaly (New York) and Cork (New York), Tom Neville and myself were guest players with Offaly, and Jimmy Duggan and Christy Ring were guest players with Cork. Ring scored 3:2, at forty-five years of age. We then travelled to Boston to play a Tipperary team. I was marking a fellow called Joe Carey – wasn't taking the game too seriously; was chatting to him. Ring had scored a couple of points. He came over to me and said, 'Lift your game; stop talking – you can talk to him all you like when it's finished. Don't you know we're playing Tipperary? We have to beat them.' The ball hopped nicely in front of goal and I stuck it in the net. I looked at Ring. 'Keep it up: put three or four more with it,' he said. Every year after that, I got a Christmas card from him. I regret now I didn't keep them. One day my daughter ran out to me in the yard and said, 'Your friend is dead – your friend Christy Ring.' I don't mind admitting I shed a few tears.

"I quit inter-county hurling in 1971. After a league game I went to Pat Henderson and said, 'I won't worry you again.' 'Hold on,' he said, 'and we'll win another Railway Cup.' But I knew the legs wouldn't go. You don't give hurling up: it gives you up."

Paddy Molloy

DENIS MURPHY
CORK

Born: 1939
Interviewed: 1993

"I came from a farming family in Donoughmore with no hurling tradition. Went to St Coleman's College, Fermoy where I learned the skills. I was lucky to make corner-forward in my Leaving Cert year 1956, on their Harty Cup team.

"I won a Fitzgibbon Cup medal with University College Cork (UCC) in 1958 and a mid-Cork junior hurling medal with Grenagh that year also. I was now working and living in the city and joined St Finbarr's. I won two county medals in 1965 and 1968; won one All-Ireland in 1966; one National League (captain) in 1969; two Munster Championships in 1966 and 1969; two Railway Cup medals in 1966 and 1969; and the All-Ireland Longpuck in l965 (approx.).

"Christy Ring was the best player I ever played with or against. His dedication and love of the game, which was so evident in the training field, was tremendous. I used to travel with him in his car to the matches for about five years up to his retirement.

"We ran up against some great Tipperary teams in the Munster finals in the sixties and were often humiliated. Our year was 1966– we got the breaks in Killarney against Limerick in the Munster semi-final.

"We were very much underdogs in the All-Ireland against Kilkenny, but, from the moment Colm Sheehan drove home the first goal from a save from a 21-yard free from Fr Seanie Barry, there was no stopping us. The hunger and will to win was so evident in that display.

"The year 1969 was the big disappointment. We beat Tipperary in the Munster final – the first time in the sixties this happened. In the final against Kilkenny we were very hot favourites. About ten days beforehand, Justin McCarthy, our centre-back, was pillion passenger on Joe Murphy's motor-cycle – one of our subs – on the way to training. A car reversed out of an avenue on the Rochestown Road and broke Justin's kneecap. Willie Walsh was moved back to centre-back in his place and gave an exhibition there on Pat Delaney, but it weakened our forward line and this injury, I believe, cost us the match."

This most modest and gentlemanly of players wore the number 4 jersey with rare distinction. He played hurling in the spirit that it should be played, and sportsmanship and consistency were the hallmarks of his illustrious career. He was a calm, thinking and unobtrusive corner-back. In the tight he never flinched, but his positioning, timing and reading of the game enabled him to intercept many an attacking move and dispatch long, well-placed, intelligent clearances downfield. It was this capacity to intercept and cut off the danger that set him apart as a corner-back. Indeed, if a dream team from the sixties was selected it would be hard to find someone better at left full-back.

For a Cork man who spent a decade playing at a top level, his honours list is relatively bare. Yet, it seemed to me as we spoke that medals didn't mean everything to Denis: "I enjoyed playing with my club and county. Above all, I particularly loved just going to the field and practising – attempting all the skills, pulling with and against the flying ball, the drop puck from the hand, the drop puck with and against the falling ball, the sideline cut that would rise and travel seventy yards – just pucking about and enjoying the thrill of it. I always took a special pride in my hurley. It had to feel right in my hands and the balance had to be right. I was meticulous about choosing it. A hurley becomes part of you and when it gets broken you can become quite upset." He took a calm unruffled approach to the game and believed firmly in good sportsmanship. "In my career I got one broken finger and three stitches – not bad, I suppose – but then I didn't hit too many people either. Only once did I get the butterflies. It was at Limerick in the early sixties in a game against Tipperary. The sun was blazing, the crowd was huge, the gates had been broken down. The white-shirted crowd seemed to be right on top of you and the pitch seemed small. I felt the tension."

He retired in 1969 at the age of thirty and many would have felt it was a bit premature. Did he regret missing a Munster and All-Ireland medal in 1970 and another Munster medal in 1972? 'There is a time to go at the top. Missing the additional honours caused me no regrets. I felt the timing was right. You're not a machine – there comes a day when someone will get three goals off of you and then...'

Two personal achievements have meant a lot to him – Puck Fada champion in the mid-sixties on a course that follows the route of the legendary Setanta and a green jersey (number 4) in 1966, presented at a dinner in The Gresham and sponsored by *Gaelic Sport* – the equivalent then of the present All-Star awards.

Denis Murphy.

DONIE NEALON
TIPPERARY

Born: 1935
Interviewed: 1996

Donie, captain of Burgess – North Tipperary champions 1964 – receives the cup from Séamus O'Riain.

"Looking back on my hurling life I know how fortunate I was to have been born into a very Gaelic-oriented family, as my father had won junior (1924) and senior (1925) All-Ireland medals with Tipperary, had played for Ireland in the Tailteann Games of 1924, and had travelled on a never-to-be-forgotten three-month trip to the USA with Tipperary in 1926. My father spent many hours coaching my brothers Sean, Pat and myself in the basic skills of hurling and always placed great emphasis on developing both right and left sides and always striking on the ground or out of the hand when in full flight and at top speed. He ingrained a great love of hurling in me as a child that I cherish to this day.

"My first major game attended was the Munster hurling final in Thurles, Tipp. v. Limerick, in 1945 as a nine-year-old, travelling by bus with my father on the Saturday, and we were joined by my mother, who travelled by bus the next day to the game.

"I always deeply appreciated the great support and encouragement I got from my wife and family, my parents, my club players, supporters and parishioners during my hurling career, as this meant a great deal to me, and I was always conscious that I was representing them whenever I lined out for my club or county. I later tried to repay them by training and coaching school and parish teams and acting as a club official in many capacities since 1963 to the present day.

"I had the pleasure of playing in eight senior All-Irelands, fortunately winning on five occasions. It was marvellous to be a part of Tipp's greatest decade in hurling history, when seven Munster titles and four All-Irelands were won in the 1960s, along with five National Hurling Leagues and five Oireachtas titles for good measure."

Many memorable and diverse moments surfaced from Donie's illustrious career as we chatted. "My first big win was when St Flannan's defeated Thurles CBS in the Harty Cup final at Limerick in 1954. It was a tremendous game, played before a crowd of ten thousand. We beat a star-studded Thurles team by three points. I was picked to play for Munster Colleges', but we lost to Leinster.

"I enjoyed my hurling days with St Patrick's Training College in Drumcondra, whom I captained in 1956 to Kavanagh Cup (inter-faculty) and Intermediate Hurling League success.

"The college days at UCD bring back happy memories. As well as three Fitzgibbon Cup wins, we won a Dublin county title by beating St Vincent's. That was a tremendous achievement. Vincent's had five of the backs that played against Tipp. in the 1961 All-Ireland final: Des Ferguson, Noel Drumgoole, Lar Foley, Liam Ferguson, and S. Lynch. They also had the midfielder Des Foley. We had Pat Hinchy of Clare; my brother Pat; Eoin Hurley, son of Jim, from Cork; Dick Dowling; and the late Ted Carroll from Kilkenny and Eugene O'Neill from Limerick. It was a great win: UCD 3:9; St Vincent's 1:9.

"You always remember your first All-Ireland win. It is something you dream about. Even though it wasn't a great contest against Galway in 1958, the win was marvellous: 4:9 to 2:5 – my first year in senior hurling.

"I could never forget our 1962 All-Ireland win. Our start was so dramatic: two goals in about ninety seconds. We pipped Wexford in the finish by two points. I was physically and mentally drained after that match. It was so fast – very few frees in the entire hour. I remember, coming up to half-time, I ran into Nick O'Donnell; both of us fell. I don't remember much about half time; I came to myself again after ten minutes of the second half." Donie was chosen as Hurler of the Year.

In a lifetime devoted to our games, Donie, always a great ambassador, has held many offices in the GAA world, between parish, county and province: administrator, coach, trainer, selector, delegate and referee, each with its own set of memories. He recalls in particular 1984, when "we all cried after the defeat by Cork in the Munster final."

I asked Donie how he viewed the present-day game and whether he would like any changes. "I don't think the game has changed that much in the last forty or fifty years. One major change I see that is not good for hurling is the movement away from ground hurling and over-head striking. There is too much emphasis now on gaining possession and running with the ball, instead of striking it first time. I hate to see half-backs putting up the hand for the puck-out; the hand up is exposed to injury. They should use the hurley. I abhor kicked scores; all scores should be with the hurley. A change from my time that I like is the elimination of the third-man tackle: backs have to hurl now instead of holding off the man. And the protection afforded the goalie is welcome; he deserves it.

"I am concerned at the extent to which point-scoring is coming into the game to the exclusion of goals. Nothing lifts a match like goals – the green flag waving. I think it's a sign of a defect not to get a goal. When we beat Dublin in 1961 by 0:16 to 1:12, 1 felt the victory was a bit hollow. We never shook their net.

"I am privileged to have been given the talent to play hurling, a most enriching and fulfilling experience, and I thank God for the many hours of enjoyment it has brought to me and the great friends I made as a result.

"Seriously ill with rheumatic fever in 1970, having retired from County level in 1969, my hurling future looked bleak, but, thank God, I made a wonderful recovery to good health to continue playing with Burgess until the mid-eighties."

Donie Nealon

PAT NOLAN
WEXFORD

Born: 1937
Interviewed: 1993

"I have many happy memories of the great game of hurling, the game that I love. The greatest game I played in was the 1962 All-Ireland final. I think it was one of the greatest finals ever, a game we did not deserve to lose.

"I suppose I was lucky to be playing at a time when Wexford were winning titles, when I think of all the great Wexford players since 1968 who never won an All-Ireland medal. We loved to win but if we were beaten it wasn't the end of the world. My proudest moments were when we won the All-Irelands and National Leagues and captaining my club Oylegate–Glenbrien to win the Wexford Senior Championship in 1963."

Pat looks back to the days of his early youth. His father, who was a great hurling enthusiast, had gone to Enniscorthy and brought home four new hurleys. The rest of the day was spent hurling and, as dusk fell, they were sitting on a stone outside the house feeling quite exhausted. John

decided he would have one last puck before calling it a day. It was a fate-
ful decision. The ball went flying through the window. Ash was turned to
ashes. His father burned the hurleys – all four of them.

Dawn broke the following morning and, though Pat and his three
brothers didn't know it then, remorse had replaced retribution. His father
set off for Enniscorthy again and returned with four more hurleys. Hurling enthusiasm had triumphed – the game was worth more than a pane
of glass.

His father's enthusiasm found concrete expression in the fact that a
playing pitch on his farm holding was always available to the local club.
And when it was necessary to rotate the crops and till the playing pitch,
the goalposts were uplifted and removed to another field.

Pat, the second of four brothers, remembers as a twelve-year-old standing between the goalposts and the grown-ups played backs and forwards
and peppered him with shots. Thus did he learn to train the eye, sharpen
the reflexes and get down to the ground ball – the Achilles heel of many
a goalkeeper.

In a career that lasted seventeen years at top level – he was Wexford's
longest serving goalkeeper, probably their greatest, and the only Wexford
man to win three National Hurling League medals – some memories stand
out above all others.

The year 1960 conjures up moments of nostalgia – this was his first
All-Ireland win. On that first Sunday in September, Wexford defied the
odds and confounded the critics with a most convincing 2:15 to 0:11 win
over hot favourites Tipperary.

The game of greatest regret was the 1962 All-Ireland final. Again, the
opposition was Tipperary. Within two minutes, Tipperary were two goals
up. "That is one game I would love to play all over again – and win it this
time." It all ended with only two points separating the sides – 3:10 to 2:11
– and Tipperary knew they were fortunate.

The year 1968 brought another All-Ireland confrontation with Tipperary. "If we were unlucky in 1962, we had our share of good fortune in
1968 – especially in the first half. We were very fortunate to be only eight
points behind at half time – Tipp. were all over us – we were playing
badly. My full-back that day was Eddie Kelly. He hasn't always got the
credit he deserved. He was a man of great physical strength and it was

very easy play behind him. Switches made that day worked well and paved the way for victory in the second half."

Let us now look at what sports writers had to say from time to time about Pat:

In a league semi-final against Limerick in 1969, won by Wexford on the score 2:5 to 1:6, a sports writer wrote as follows: "Wexford's hero of the hour was custodian Pat Nolan. Nolan displayed wonderful courage between the posts, particularly in the second half and his saves from Éamonn Cregan were right out of the top drawer."

After victory over Limerick in the National League final of 1972–73, a report headed "Prince of Keepers" went on to say:

> Let it be said here and now [that] the one link between that game of fifteen years ago and last Sunday's, that prince of goalkeepers Pat Nolan, shone above all others in this torrid encounter. His brilliant performances for the county in the last twenty years are innumerable (indeed the Slaneysiders could not have beaten Kilkenny in the semi-final without him) but rarely has he showed such courage and split second reflexes under tremendous pressure as in this encounter.

But his *pièce de résistance* must surely have been his performance between the posts at Wembley in 1968. He admits it was his greatest ever display. Here is what the *New Ross Standard* had to say in June 1968. "Biggest individual success was that of goalkeeper Pal Nolan. The Glenbrien man's praises have been sung for many years in these columns and Wexford followers have realised for years that he is the country's outstanding custodian."

After the game in Wembley, Nicky Rackard said to Pat that it was the greatest display of goalkeeping he had seen since the days of Paddy Scanlon of Limerick. No higher praise was possible.

Pat Nolan

CHRISTY O'BRIEN
LAOIS

Born: 1933
Interviewed: 1996

"My love for the game of hurling developed by listening to tales of great deeds on the hurling fields as we sat around the open fire. Later it went a step further by attending the boys' school in Borris-in-Ossory, where my teacher was Bob O'Keeffe, president of the GAA, 1935–1938.

"My first memory of holding a hurl was when my brothers Paddy, Jimmie, Nicky – who is now Brother Basil – and neighbours Joe Whelan and his brother Pat used to play at our home in the 'Liberty'. Later our sister Mary used to join in the games. The goalposts were two chestnut trees.

"I went on to play with the school, where my first success was winning a medal by defeating Roscrea. Times have changed compared with the early years: no proper coaching, togging out under the ditches, and often hurling in the bare feet, as boots were scarce at the time. We hurled on our way to school and back again. Every chance we got we had a hurl in our hands. Hurls had to be cut by axe and saw, shaped out by hatchet, planed, spoke shaved, and finished off with a piece of broken glass."

Christy O'Brien, one of the finest exponents of our ancient game and one of Laois's greatest hurling sons, played with his native county for eighteen seasons; and in all that time it is hard to believe that he never had the thrill and honour of playing even in a Leinster final. "Sometimes you would lose heart, but the love of the game kept you going. We won division 2 National League titles in 1959 and 1965. It meant a lot to Laois. We felt we would learn from playing against the good teams. But somehow we lacked confidence when we faced them. Sometimes we would give the good teams a good game, but we seemed to lack that little bit extra. We needed someone to work on our mental approach. This was evident on a few occasions when we lost to Kilkenny and Wexford in Leinster semi-finals, days when I felt we were as good as them, everywhere except on the scoreboard."

As a youngster, Christy remembers listening to the broadcasts of Mícheál O'Hehir. At half time they would all go out and be Mick Mackeys and Christy Rings and Jimmy Langtons and Harry Grays. Those were the days of fantasy and dreams. In his playing days, he regarded Ned Wheeler, Billy Bohane, Tony Wall and "Jobber" McGrath as the best he encountered.

When Christy, who played minor for Laois for three years, closes his eyes and travels back down memory lane, three occasions stand out above all others. They relate to parish, province and an American trip. In 1956, as captain, he led his native Borris-in-Ossory to its first county senior hurling title. They beat Cullohill in the final. He was carried shoulder-high from the pitch bearing the Bob O'Keeffe trophy – bearing, too, the scars of battle. It was the club's greatest moment – a club that came into existence in the very early days of the association, a club that acquired its pitch in 1937 from the Land Commission through the efforts of the late Bob O'Keeffe, in whose honour the grounds are named.

In 1972 Christy made a comeback when "all the old comrades were gone." Christy was in his fortieth year. He lined out at full-forward and in the final against Ballyfin finished with a personal tally of 3:4 — a product of craft, guile, skill and experience. That victory brought to five Christy's county titles.

He was chosen on the Leinster team in 1956. "Injury kept me out of the final against Munster, but I did get a medal — my first of four. It was an honour to play with the great ones: Des Foley — a brilliant mid-fielder; Eddie Keher — a great forward; the Rackards — powerful men. To win against Munster was great." Those were the halcyon days of the Railway Cup competition. Christy was in the company of the élite.

In 1966 he was chosen to go to America to take part in the Cardinal Cushing Games. It was a signal honour: "Others in the company of five hurlers and twelve footballers were Pat Dunney, Austin Flynn, Christy Ring, John Doyle, and Bernie Hartigan. Ring was manager of the team. We played with Limerick (New York) against Galway (New York), the champions. Ring was playing on a big full-back called John Maher. He switched with me at centre-forward. The switch worked: we won. Ring was more competitive than any of us. We played one game in Gaelic Park, New York, and one game in Boston before a crowd of about ten thousand. The proceeds went to the missions in Peru.

"The trip lasted two weeks. I lived like a king for those weeks. We stayed at Hotel Manhattan but dined at John Kerry O'Donnell's restaurant, which was about a ten-minute walk away. I didn't know Ring until I went out there. Even then you wouldn't meet him often. He was very disciplined and retiring. There was always someone looking for him, and sometimes he had to hide to get away."

Father Sean Collier, PP of Borris-in-Ossory, a great hurling enthusiast who played with Laois in 1948, knew Christy well and said of him: "Powerfully built and with skill to match; I regard him as one of the finest players I ever saw. He had everything it takes to gain the ultimate prize. He reigned supreme for around twenty years and leaves behind a great record — the only missing link and the all-important one is an All-Ireland medal."

Christy O Brien

JIMMY O'BRIEN
WEXFORD

Born: 1938
Interviewed: 2002

"The most memorable game and the best match that I ever played in was the 1962 All-Ireland final when we were beaten by Tipp. A number of incidents occurred which had a profound impact on the result.

"I remember vividly the puck around before the game. Normally, at a time like this I would be very nervous and certainly would not notice or be interested in anything but the upcoming game. We had been pucking about for a considerable time when I noticed the late Nick O'Donnell coming out on his own. He was as white as a ghost but it was after the match I was told of what had happened. Nicko was bringing out his son to sit in the dugout with the subs when a GAA official stopped him. He refused to let the boy out whereupon Nicko made a swing at him and then went back to the dressing-room and refused to come out. Anyone who knew Nicko would know that he was a very focussed person who would not change his mind very easily. After some very considerable persuasion he relented and what I saw was a very enraged Nicko.

"However, the game started and in a flash Tipp. had scored two goals. Tipp. were awarded a sideline cut and the late Martin Lyng swore to me that it was a Wexford ball. The sideline cut was taken and we conceded a soft goal. In a rage, Nicko grabbed the ball to puck out and missed his stroke. The ball trickled to a Tipp. player who had the easiest of tasks to tap it in.

"Nicko, a Kilkenny man, was, in my opinion, the greatest player to put on the Wexford jersey. He was an absolutely brilliant ball player and to miss the ball out of his hand would have been physically impossible but for his state of mind. Two goals down against a great Tipp. team left us with a mountain to climb.

"From then on, the game exploded into life and the atmosphere was electric. Bit by bit, we edged forward and, with about ten minutes to go, we were leading by two points. Before half time Billy Rackard got a very badly broken thumb and wanted to come off. Billy was told there was nothing wrong with him and to play on. About ten minutes into the second half, the Wexford selectors decided to switch Billy with Tom Neville. Tom had an absolutely brilliant first half but, with the pattern of the play, he was redundant in the corner and Billy was in serious trouble at centre half. Unfortunately for us, the decision was never conveyed to the players involved.

"Midway through the second half, Jimmy Doyle (Tipp.) was forced to retire with a shoulder injury. Up to then the main focus of attack was through Jimmy but, when he went off, the Tipp. half-forward line started to run at us and we were immediately in trouble. Soon afterwards they scored the goal to give them the lead which they never lost. We got some chances which unfortunately for us did not come off."

Jimmy's style of play, which was always incisive, reflected spirit, tenacity, grit, urgency and verve. He was courageous and fearless, and had a grand turn of speed. He made life difficult for many a fine defender, including the stout-hearted John Doyle of Tipperary. "Going on to the field I never thought about winning. I always went out to do my best, play as well as I could – never give up."

Jimmy was captain in 1967 and led Wexford to a National League title. Throughout the sixties he was one of the game's leading right half-forwards, and was a regular on Leinster Railway Cup selections.

Jimmy played in some of hurling's most memorable contests. The opening paragraph dealt with his recollections of the 1962 All-Ireland final against Tipperary – one of the truly great hurling contests. Let's now look at the three other encounters.

He came on as a sub in the league final of 1957–1958 against Limerick – a super contest to watch; greater still to play in – that left journalists searching for superlatives to describe it. It ended 5:7 to 4:8 in Wexford's favour. "Nick O'Donnell and Billy Rackard won it for us." It was a dream beginning to Jimmy's hurling career.

He played in his first of four All-Ireland finals in 1960. Wexford's opponents were red hot favourites Tipperary. Right from the throw-in, Wexford tore into the game. There was power and majesty in their hurling – glorious stuff to behold. A stunned Tipperary team and equally stunned supporters left GAA headquarters in disbelief. Gaeldom had witnessed one of the biggest upsets in the history of the game. The scoreboard read 2:15 to 0:11. Jimmy played at right half-forward and was marking John Doyle.

Before the All-Ireland final of 1968 between Wexford and Tipperary, Jimmy had to get a painkilling injection in his knee. He lined out at right full-forward. Tipperary were firm favourites. The half-time score confirmed that rating, 1:11 to 1:3, but it didn't at all reflect their superiority. Wexford's performance could only be described as vapid and dull. Nothing in their first-half display presaged what would unfold in the second half when Wexford made switches and hurled with a fury and fluency that bewildered Tipperary. It was resurrection stuff. Entering the twenty-eighth minute of the second half, Wexford led by the incredible score of 5:8 to 1:12. In the couple of minutes remaining, Tipperary got two goals. But it mattered not. The Liam MacCarthy Cup was on the way to the Slaneyside for the fourth time. Wexford had shredded the form book.

It was Jimmy's last championship game. He was thirty years of age. The injured knee could take no more. His career had ended as it had begun – in a blaze of glory.

Jimmy O' Brien

DAN QUIGLEY
WEXFORD

Born: 1944
Interviewed: 1990

Only hurling photograph of the five Quigley brothers, taken at Croke Park, 7 May 1967. Martin, John and Jim in St Peter's College diagonal hoop jersey; Dan and Pat in the Wexford jersey.

Down the decades many illustrious and famous family names have adorned the GAA hurling calendar. The name Quigley of Rathnure holds a proud and prominent place among them. The Quigleys had a unique honour in 1970 when four brothers lined out in the All-Ireland final that was lost to Cork. The Wexford half-forward line read: Martin Quigley, Pat Quigley, John Quigley; Dan was at centre-back.

"I got on the county senior panel after the All-Ireland in 1962. I played part of the league that year, but missed out on the championship because of a broken finger. Wexford got beaten in the Leinster final. I did not play but was back for the league and played up to 1971 – but played away with

Rathnure up to 1983. During those years with the county, I won 1965, 1968 and 1970 Leinster finals, 1967 league and 1968 All-Ireland. I had the honour of being captain of the 1968 team. During your playing days those things may not look important, but when you look back it gives you great pleasure." As a result of the broken finger, Dan had the unusual experience of playing for his province before playing championship hurling with Wexford. He won a Railway Cup medal in 1964 playing at full-back for Leinster.

His "greatest moment and biggest thrill" was when he received the MacCarthy Cup as captain in 1968, "although the significance of the honour did not sink in for a long time afterwards." Later that year Dan received the Hurler of the Year award.

Despite Rathnure winning three Leinster club finals in the 1970s, the All-Ireland final was lost in 1972 and 1974 to Blackrock and in 1978 to St Finbarr's – "at club level that was my greatest regret."

Ned Power, a Kilkenny man, who taught at St Peter's College, Wexford, was a major influence on the hurling life of Dan. "He used to train the teams for the College Championship. 'Fitness through final perseverance' was his motto, except that it was not Ned Power who was suffering. During those years in college it was practise every evening and doing the skills we were least good at until we got them perfect. We won the Colleges' All-Ireland under his guidance, the first ever won by the college."

Dan departed the county scene rather early – he was only twenty-seven. It was the autumn of 1971 and Dan and three colleagues went on an approved trip to New York to play with the New York (Wexford) team in the New York Championship against Clare – "We won." The four of them agreed to stay for the next game against Kilkenny but rain caused a postponement and they returned. Meanwhile, back in Ireland, Wexford were due to play Limerick in an Oireachtas final. Efforts to contact the players, who had delayed in New York for the Kilkenny game that ended up being postponed, failed. "How could they? We were still in New York." None of them was picked for the match against Limerick.

Dan, disgusted and disillusioned at the way the matter was handled and the way they were treated, decided to retire. Efforts to entice him back failed. It was Wexford's loss. Dan Quigley – Big Dan to his hurling fans – was hard to replace.

MICK ROCHE
TIPPERARY

Born: 1943
Interviewed: 1994

"Where I came from, to play hurling was the most natural thing. It was the topic at school, work, the creamery, and, above all, after last Mass on Sunday when many a heated argument was commonplace. My father was a big influence and gave ongoing encouragement – so also was my school teacher, Clare man Tom Nealon. However, for me it was local neighbour Jimmy Henzey who did most and played a big part in any success the game gave to me. Having said that, I'll always believe the single biggest influence on the youth of this country was one Mícheál O'Hehir. It was he that turned on the Croke Park light in all our little hearts and filled us with an ambition that would sustain and remain. We all owe him a huge debt of gratitude. Long may it be the great game it is, for in my view our nation would be the poorer without it."

Mick's interest in hurling began at a very early age and was actively encouraged by his father Dan who adored the game and won a junior All-Ireland with Tipperary. "My father was the driving force. I can remember him in the winter nights – he was a carpenter by trade – knee deep in shavings in the kitchen making hurleys for us. My mother didn't want us to play at all. She wanted us to do our homework. Then my father would push back the kitchen table to throw in the ball. I don't know how we didn't drive our mother demented."

In 1961, Mick played with a Tipperary minor team that lost to Kilkenny in the final. From then on, for over a dozen years hurling followers were treated to all that was best in hurling from the stick and person of Mick Roche – natural ability, anticipation, delightful stick-work, confidence, foresight and sportsmanship.

In 1963 he won an intermediate title. In 1964, as well as winning an under-21 title, he took his place at midfield on the senior team where he was to give majestic and memorable displays in a Tipperary combination that was one of the finest the hurling world has seen – strong in defence, superb at midfield, deadly in attack. He recalled the training sessions they used have in Thurles. "We used to play ten-a-side games. The hurling was great; the sessions were treated like All-Ireland finals. You had to be dedicated because there were so many good players looking for places. I remember the clashes between Tony Wall and Larry Kiely – two army men – no mercy. And then there was Theo English at midfield. To me, Theo was a father figure. I looked up to him. Not since the days of Tom and Willie Wall of Carrick did a South Tipp. man play with Tipp. Theo, who was there since the fifties, paved the way for the likes of Babs Keating and myself. Coming to train he would say to me – 'Listen here, Mick. If you think you are going to get fit up here you are mistaken. You must train at home. Have the ground work done. Only the finishing off is done up here.'" Mick found no difficulty with this. He had spent all the spare time of his youth practising hurling skills. He even remembered getting up at six in the morning to train before going to work – and enjoying it. It was the result of a code of discipline learned from Jim Henzey – an ex-army man and neighbour with a great knowledge and passion for the game – in his juvenile and minor days: "If he had asked us to climb a mountain we would do it."

In 1967 Tony Wall retired after the All-Ireland final and Mick became a centre-back by default when Tipperary played him there in an Oireachtas game against Kilkenny. Unhappy with his display, he took a dislike to the position. "I never again got playing for Tipp. in my favourite position

of mid-field. I loved midfield. You had lots of options — it was less oner-
ous than in defence, you could go where you liked — what you needed
was stamina." Those who saw his displays at centre-back in 1968 against
Wexford in the All-Ireland final, and in 1971 against Limerick in Killarney in the Munster final, will wonder how displays of such splendour
could fail to erase from his mind his dislike of the position.

He won every honour in the game including an All-Star at centre-back
in 1971, the year of inception. He captained Tipperary in 1967 and 1968,
but both finals were lost to Kilkenny and Wexford respectively.

For the greatest moment — the most memorable game and victory, the
game he would love to play all over again — he nominated the Munster
final of 1971 against Limerick in Killarney. All the drama and tension and
controversy and splendour and swaying fortunes were packed into that
eighty minutes. Down two goals at half time, they finished the second
half with John Flanagan sending over the forty-first score of the game
from far out for a one-point victory, almost on the call of "Time!", to make
the scoreboard read: Tipperary 4:16 Limerick 3:18.

Mick retired at thirty-one. There was more left in him. "But I wasn't
enjoying training anymore. I was losing the zest for the game. In my job
I was travelling sixty thousand miles a year. Between that and playing
tournament games and championship games it wore you down. Anyway, I
didn't enjoy playing in the mud and rain of winter. I felt 'twas time to go."

JIM TREACY
KILKENNY

Born 1943
Interviewed: 1982

"My greatest memory was the 1967 All-Ireland hurling final against Tipperary. I had the honour of being captain on that occasion. It was a great honour for me to receive the MacCarthy Cup from a Tipp. win. It was the first time Kilkenny beat Tipperary in a final for over forty years.

"All the success I had in hurling I owe to my club Bennettsbridge. We had some great hurlers in our club that I looked up to; to name a few – Dan Kennedy, John McGovern, Mick Kelly and Séamus Cleere."

At about five o'clock on the first Sunday in September 1967, Jim Treacy, captain of the Kilkenny hurling team, held the MacCarthy Cup high as he stood in the Hogan Stand and listened joyfully to thousands of Kilkenny fans chant cheers of victory. It was a great moment for this left full-back from Bennettsbridge, one of the homes and strongholds of Kilkenny hurling.

When Jim was young he used to watch a car call at Johnny McGovern's home. He would see Johnny climb in with his hurley and togs and be driven off to hurl for his native Kilkenny. Jim used to dream that some day he too would be collected and taken to play for his county. That dream came true.

Being captain in 1967 was a wonderful honour. The victory had special significance: the Tipperary bogey was laid. It was forty-five years since Kilkenny had beaten Tipp. in an All-Ireland.

The statistical fact sounds worse than the reality. Since 1922 they had only met four times in finals, but each time victory went to Tipp. The losses were – 1937 (3:11 to 0:3), 1945 (5:6 to 3:6), 1950 (1:9 to 1:8), 1964 (5:13 to 2:8).

But it's a long road that has no turning; and the turning came with the final whistle in 1967. It was sweet music to Kilkenny ears, and a moment of elation for Jim Treacy. Kilkenny had played some very fine hurling in an hour of tense excitement. At the final whistle the scoreboard read Kilkenny 3:8, Tipperary 2:7. A county's pride was restored – their sixteenth title.

Jim would go on to win further honours – among them three more All-Ireland titles and two All-Stars. However, following the victory of 1967, no other of Jim's successes would be quite the same.

FRANKIE WALSH
WATERFORD

Born: 1936
Interviewed: 2000

Frankie with the MacCarthy Cup in 1959.

Frankie Walsh made his debut at county senior level in a tournament game against Kilkenny. He was young and fit and energetic.

With the game under way, Frankie headed for the corner-forward position where he would be marking Mark Marnell – now at the veteran stage. Frankie had decided to give Mark the run around. That was until he took up position beside him and "he pulled my jersey and said, 'You're not going far this evening.'"

As Frankie reflects on that occasion, he sees the humour in it and smiles. But he recalls one of his next games that could have left him maimed for life. It was his championship debut against Cork in 1956. He received a fractured skull from a swinging hurley. "I spent over a month in hospital.

I was allowed no visitors, no papers, no nothing. As I lay on my back, I wondered a lot about the future."

Thankfully, Frankie made a good recovery and was in Dungarvan the following year for a training session with his colleagues for the 1957 All-Ireland campaign. John Keane – Waterford star of yester year – was there as trainer and selector. So, too, was Pat Fanning who spoke passionately to the players and told them he believed they had what it took to win an All-Ireland title.

As Frankie, then not yet twenty-one, listened to those words, his mind went back to when he was twelve years old. "I was showing promise as a hurler. Brother Magill took me on a visit to John Keane's house. John was a distant relative of mine. We were given a cup of tea and biscuits. Then John said to me – 'Did you ever see an All-Ireland medal?' I said I hadn't. He went upstairs and brought down the medal he won in 1948 when Jim Ware was captain. When I looked at it the first thing I said was – 'I want one of those.'"

Frankie pondered Pat Farming's words and saw no reason to doubt them. "At the time Mount Sion had a strong team and were beating leading clubs outside the county." It augured well.

"I remember travelling to Dublin for the 1957 All-Ireland final against Kilkenny. Tom Cheasty, Séamus Power and myself got out at Carlow to stretch our legs. Tom went to buy orange juice – he had a pain in his head. Séamus went to a bookie's office to check on horses. I went to a hardware shop to see if there were any new tools on the market – I was a welder.

"On our way back to the car Séamus saw a weighing scales outside a chemist's shop. He got up. It registered 12st. 7lbs. He was delighted. 12st. 7lbs, and fully fit – a good weight. Then Tom got up. He weighed 13st. 5lbs. 'You get up,' said Séamus to me. 'No, no,' I insisted. 'Are you frightened to spend a penny?' said Séamus. I got up and turned the scales at 9st. 7lbs. Séamus looked at me and said, 'You should be a feckin' jockey on some of those horses I backed.' In time my weight went up to 10st. 2lbs."

The final of 1957 is one Waterford will always feel they let slip. "Carbery" had this to say: "Kikenny's recovery was reminiscent of many other finals won by a point...Waterford have never hurled a better game than this."

The 1959 All-Ireland campaign began with Frankie Walsh as captain.

117

"I realised that if we all struck form and played the kind of hurling we were capable of, that we were good enough to handle any of the teams and win a title. We beat Galway in the first round. The next match was against Tipperary. There was a wicked gale blowing. Tipperary won the toss and played against it. We ran up a huge first half score. I think it was 8:2 to nil at half time. I was the only forward to score in the second half. We won by 9:3 to 3:4. When the score was sent to Mícheál O'Hehir to announce it during his broadcast at another venue, he looked at it in disbelief and asked to have it checked. When he announced it, half the country didn't believe it. The entire team was made Sports Stars of the Week."

The Munster final against Cork was won and lost when Waterford selectors switched Phil Grimes from midfield to centre half-back to curb a rampant Paddy Barry. He outplayed both Barry and Ring who alternated from time to time with a view to unsettling the Waterford defence – but to no avail. "It was a difficult game. Ned Power in goal made great saves. We were glad when the final whistle blew – we won by 3:9 to 2:9."

The next outing would be to Croke Park for the All-Ireland final – a repeat of the 1957 final. Frankie Walsh remembers the occasion just as if it was yesterday – the honour of being captain, the thrill of leading the hurling men of the Decies around Croke Park. In particular, he remembers the closing moments when the scoreboard read Kilkenny 5:5 Waterford 0:17. "It would take a goal to save the day. We won a sideline cut. Séamus Power moved forward from midfield and raised his hand. I took the sideline cut. I shouldn't have. It only went a few yards. 'You little so and so,' Séamus shouted. He stayed forward. My memory is that Larry Guinan chased the ball and won possession. He passed it to Séamus, who scored the equalising goal with a shot that deflected off the hurley of Kilkenny full-back 'Link' Walsh and passed his namesake Ollie in goal. When the final whistle blew, Séamus thought we had won by a point – I thought we had lost by a point."

Spectators had witnessed a magnificent game of hurling between two great teams. It was one of the great All-Ireland finals: a breathtaking contest, played at remarkable speed and full of intense exchanges where courage and skill and sportsmanship abounded. We looked forward to the 4 October and more of the same. On that October Sunday, 77,285 spectators packed themselves into Croke Park, bringing the combined official attendance to 150,992.

"Our backs were tighter the second day. We got off to a bad start – a bit nervous. I failed to lift a close-in free but whipped it off the ground over the bar. I think we were six points down after ten minutes – and we were playing with a strong wind. Then it all began to happen for us. Mick Flannelly, the lightest man on the team after myself, goaled. Tom Cheasty got two more. At half time it was 3:6 to 1:8. We only gave Kilkenny two points in the second half and they with the wind. We won by 3:12 to 1:10."

"Carbery" had this to say:

As fine a hurling team as ever won an All-Ireland final…every man on the Waterford side seemed to be on the move and they moved at a sparkling rate . . . they hit ground balls from all angles…Frankie Walsh, the Decies captain, hit his most dazzling form in that winning second half. His left hand was meticulously accurate; he hit frees with rare accuracy from all ranges and angles; his play through the field was inspiring.

It was Frankie's most memorable hour and year. In the five games of the championship he scored 2:28. Six of those points came in the drawn All-Ireland final and eight in the replay. His performance in the replay won him the Sports Star of the Week award. He doesn't remember what he said in his speech. Indeed, he was so overcome with emotion and excitement that "Dr J.J. Stuart, President of the GAA, had to lift the Cup with me."

The following St Patrick's Day, Frankie captained a Munster team that included seven Waterford men to Railway Cup victory over Leinster on the score 6:6 to 2:7. It placed him among an elite that had the privilege of leading club, county and province to the ultimate prize.

Frankie Walsh

OLLIE WALSH
KILKENNY

Born: 1937
Interviewed: 1990

"Hurling has been a way of life for me as long as I can remember. Even as a little boy going for the messages for my mother, I had to have the hurley and the ball with me. I was fortunate that my mother and father loved hurling, and I was encouraged and helped in every way."

When Ollie was nine years of age he was chosen in goal for the national school team. In 1949 he was picked on the under-14 Kilkenny inter-county schools team that beat Dublin at Harold's Cross.

"In 1953 I was selected to play for the Kilkenny minor team – again against Dublin, but this time we got to play in Croke Park, which is the dream of every hurler. I can still visibly remember standing at the dressing-room door under the Cusack Stand and looking out onto the hallowed ground. Little did I think, as a boy in Thomastown listening to Mícheál O'Hehir describe the Canal End and the Railway End and the exploits of the famous men of that era, that I would get to represent my county and play in what is the mecca of gaelic games."

It was Ascension Thursday in 1956 and Ollie Walsh was enjoying the swing boats at a carnival in his native Thomastown when a Kilkenny mentor shouted up at him: "Come down – you're on the panel to play against Wexford."

Ollie lined out at Walsh Park, Waterford, against Wexford and Kilkenny and won the Dr Kinnane Tournament. It was the beginning of an illustrious and distinguished career that saw him wear the No.1 jersey for Kilkenny until 1971 – a career that won him all the major honours: All-Irelands (4), Oireachtas (5), Railway Cups (4), National League (2), Hurler of the Year 1967 and twice Poc Fada champion.

He played his first All-Ireland final in 1957 against Waterford. I saw him in action that day and never forgot his display. He was magnificent. If one man could be said to have won a game for his team, then Ollie did it that day.

Growing up, he had two model goalkeepers – Tony Reddin of Tipperary and Sean Duggan of Galway.

In retirement he guided the Kilkenny junior teams of 1984, 1986, 1988 and 1990 to All-Ireland success and managed the county senior team of 1992 and 1993 when they won All-Ireland glory.

While it is the lot of many a hurler to fade from memory as the years roll on, there are always some who live on in legend. Such a figure is Ollie Walsh. His flamboyant and swashbuckling style attracted scores of youngsters to the back of his goal in games at Nowlan Park. His brilliance between the posts, the lynx-like eye and the cat-like agility lifted his defenders above themselves, enabling them to perform *gaiscí*. It bred confidence in colleagues. It deflated opponents. His brilliance won many a game for Kilkenny.

TOM WALSH
KILKENNY

Born: 1944
Interviewed: 2007

"In the 1967 All-Ireland final, I sustained an eye injury which resulted in the loss of my left eye and the end to my hurling career at the age of twenty-three.The friendship and goodwill that has followed through my life from the GAA fraternity has been astonishing. I am extremely grateful to all those wonderful people who after forty years still acknowledge their memory of my short hurling career.

"The two most memorable games for me had to be my first and last All-Irelands, winning medals in 1961 (minor) and 1967 (senior). In both of these games Kilkenny beat Tipperary, and in each case I happened to be in the right place at the right time to score decisive goals."

Tom was known to some as the "Blonde Bombshell". He was born in 1944 to Patrick and Kathleen (née Cassin), the youngest of a family of four boys and two girls. From an early age, hurling became part and parcel

PHIL WILSON
WEXFORD

Born: 1939
Interviewed: 1996

"Hurling for me was a way of life. I grew up on a farm in Ballyhogue during the late forties and early fifties. During those years my brothers and I played hurling and football every evening in our yard, as this was the only way of entertainment during those days. So, apart from the enjoyment for ourselves, I developed a great love for hurling, which I still have today.

"I made my debut with Davidstown–Ballyhogue at club level. When I was selected to play for Wexford in 1957, one of my greatest ambitions was fulfilled, especially having the distinction to play with some of Wexford's greats, like Jim Morrissey, the Rackards, Padge Kehoe and Ned Wheeler. My determination to achieve the ultimate became a way of life. It came to fruition in 1968 when we brought home the All-Ireland cup. But, you know, hurling is not just about All-Irelands. It's about schools, clubs, counties and All-Irelands."

The biggest thrill of his youth was the 1954 hurling final between his native Wexford and Cork before an attendance that exceeded 84,000. "I'll never forget the crush going in. I watched the game from the Hill. That was something special. I was standing for hours: from before the minor game to the end of the senior game."

In 1959 Phil emigrated to London and worked in the buildings. He was now a dual player, and a formidable one at that, having played at minor level in both codes for two years for Wexford and, while still a minor, playing on the senior football team. Both county careers lasted thirteen years: the football 1957–70; the hurling 1961–74.

In his two years in London he played with Father Murphy's, a team consisting entirely of Wexford men. "Going to the field three times weekly to practise was a way of life. The field was at the back of Wormwood Scrubs prison." In 1960 he was selected for the London junior hurling and football teams. The hurlers won the All-Ireland title, beating Carlow after a replay, but the footballers lost to Dublin. "If I could hurl like you," said a colleague to Phil, "I'd go back home." And that's what he did, in 1961.

Phil, partnering Dave Bernie at midfield, won his only All-Ireland in 1968 in a sensational victory over Tipperary 5:8 to 3:12. His memories of the day? "I had written to my brother Jack, who was in England and who I hadn't seen for ten years, asking him to come home. He arrived two days before the match. On the Sunday we went to half nine Mass in the local church at Bellevue. People were saying, is that fellow going to hurl today? As it was, I was making no change in my routine. I drove right up to Croke Park with Jack, and in. I watched some of the minor match standing in the Cusack Stand. The legs began to feel awful tired. Six months' training, I thought to myself, and the legs tired even before the game starts. I went into the dressing-room and lay down on a seat.

"Before a big game I liked a period of peace and solitude: time to reflect and relax and prepare mentally for the contest ahead, away from the euphoria of supporters, away from the well-intentioned but distracting admirers."

This was Phil's third final – all against Tipp. He was on the losing side in 1962 and 1965. At half time in 1968 things looked ominous – 1:11 to 1:3, eight points in arrears, and the team playing badly. In the second half, a transformed team played inspired hurling and Wexford won their fifth senior hurling crown. Injury caused Phil to miss the 1970 final – lost to Cork.

The best Wexford team he played on was the 1962 line-out. He remembers the final against Tipp. "Martin Lyng and myself were at mid-field and facing Liam Devaney and Theo English. It was my first final. I remember I was finishing up work one evening when I said to Jim Morrissey [a star midfielder of the fifties], 'What will we do with these two on Sunday?' His reply set me back in my tracks. 'What do you care about them? If you care, don't go.' That was Jim: he always had a no-nonsense, positive mentality.

"Even though Phil and Martin Lyng won the midfield battle, it wasn't enough to win a hurling thriller that saw Tipperary two goals up after ninety seconds and Wexford two points in arrears at the final whistle. My biggest regret is losing that day and not chasing McKenna when he went on the solo that led to Tom Ryan's goal."

Phil is one of hurling's unsung heroes. He was rarely missing from the Leinster Railway Cup selection in the decade ending 1972. He was All-Star material. A man of athletic build, he was a forceful hurler, and that, combined with speed, skill, strength and stamina, made him a handful for any opponent.

Over forty years Phil has contributed much to Gaelic games as a dedicated mentor and trainer, as one of the all-time great dual players. While he agrees that it is good to win, for him, "playing the game is what counts most."

1970s

RICHIE BENNIS
LIMERICK

Born: 1945
Interviewed: 1994

"I started hurling at a very young age. With seven brothers in the family it was the thing to do. I lived in a lodge at the entrance to a big mansion. We spent a lot of time hurling a ball against the wall. Before we left for school in the mornings, lads passing would call in for a puck around.

"Playing for Patrickswell was always tops for me. Wearing the Limerick jersey was a great honour. Winning my first championship with my club in 1965 as a full-back was mighty. Winning the All-Ireland in 1973 was something special. The atmosphere in Croke Park as we ran onto the field will live with me forever."

In top-level hurling, in finely balanced contests, a team is unlikely to succeed unless it has a top quality goalkeeper and a first-class marksman. In Richie Bennis, Limerick had a marksman supreme. He proved it consistently and, more importantly, he demonstrated it under pressure. Three examples in particular illustrate this. In the National League final against Tipperary in 1971 at Cork, the scores were level, at 3:11 each, with three minutes to go when Limerick was awarded a thirty-yard free from an awkward angle. Richie sent over the winner – his eighth of the day. In Thurles in 1973 in the Munster final against Tipperary, he stood over a seventy with the teams level – the referee told him it was the last puck of the game and that he must score direct. The packed stadium held its breath. Richie steadied and looked, before sending the winner over, and all Limerick erupted with delight. His total that day was 1:5. In the All-Ireland final of the same year against Kilkenny, he showed his class when scoring ten points, seven from frees. He had the ideal temperament – cool, calm, confident, nonchalant and philosophical. He headed the county scoring charts for six successive years from 1970 to 1975. Strangely enough, and unlike many great marksmen, he didn't spend hours practising the art of taking frees. "I never really practised frees–I never dwelt on it. I began taking them in a club game when our free-taker got injured. I was always fairly steady – had great confidence – it didn't worry me what people said if I missed."

Richie was one of a family of thirteen. When Patrickswell won the county senior hurling title in 1966, six Bennis brothers shared the honours–Phil, Richie, Gerry, Pat, Peter and Thomas. A seventh brother Sean always played his hurling with Ballybrown, a half-parish of Patrickswell. Richie was hurling from an early age and as a sixteen-year-old captained Limerick City to victory over Kilkenny in 1961 in the first All-Ireland Vocational Schools' final. He subsequently played minor, under-21 and senior with Limerick.

For three great memories in his career, he chose a Munster final, a club victory and an All-Ireland final. The Munster final was that of 1973 against Tipperary when Limerick captured the title after a lapse of eighteen years. The drama of the final seconds has already been described. "It compensated for the heartbreaking one-point defeat of 1971 at the hands of Tipp. I lay down in the mud of Killarney pitch that day when the final whistle blew and cried like an elephant. I didn't go home at all that week." His club won the Munster club title in 1989 – the first Limerick club to do so. "We were ahead fourteen points at half time after playing with a stormforce wind. Gradually, in the second half Mount Sion came within striking distance. It was the hardest match I ever played – and I wasn't on the field at all. We held on to win by one goal." That recalled other club memories for Richie and he admitted to crying in the dressing-room after losing the 1991 All-Ireland club final to Glenmore of Kilkenny. "It was one we let slip. We did too much running with the ball."

The All-Ireland victory of 1973 was a special dream come true. Richie had a great game — a solo run in the second half, chased by Liam O'Brien, as he jinked and weaved his way into Kilkenny territory, ending with him being fouled and Mícheál O'Hehir uttering, "Oh, the absolute gall of the man and I mean that in the kindest possible way"; a sixty-yard point from play that had "class" written all over it and will always be remembered by those who saw it; an all-round performance of skill and endeavour, which no doubt contributed to his All-Star award of that year. He epitomised the Limerick spirit of the day.

Was it your best game? "No. I feel my greatest match was against Clare in the first round of the championship that year. We knew it wasn't going to be easy. We won a torrid encounter by just two points. Clare were very good in the seventies."

In his capacity as manager, Richie guided the Limerick senior hurling team to an All-Ireland final against Kilkenny in 2007. Though beaten by 2:19 to 1:15, they gave Kilkenny their hardest game and narrowest win of the campaign.

Richie is essentially a club man. He is very much part of Patrickswell. With a sense of pride he told me that he has been associated with all the Patrickswell successes, either in the capacity of player, trainer or mentor. Men like this are the foundation stone on which the GAA and its games flourish.

JOHN CALLINAN
CLARE

Born: 1955
Interviewed: 1994

John (left) lays siege to the Limerick goal in the Munster final of 1981.

"To have been privileged to play with and against the greatest hurlers will always be appreciated. This is what hurling has given me and I hope will give countless thousands into the future. Hurling must endure. It is, however, a delicate flower which needs a favourable environment and careful husbandry. Is it being given those things? We mustn't be sentimental about the game – but active, radical and thoughtful."

John Callinan was seven years of age when his late father look him to Croke Park on All-Ireland final day in 1962. That day, Wexford and Tipperary seniors served up a game of breathtaking hurling. There were names in action that echo on through the decades. Yet of the sixty who lined out that day it was the Kilkenny minor centre-forward Tommy Walsh with the fair hair that caught the eye of John. He can still see Tommy in action. Everything else is a blur.

John admits to having been "a terrible loser – I would brood on a defeat for a week afterwards." He admits, too, to being a bad spectator: "My elbows fly in all directions as I keep up with the ebb and flow of play. I am only learning to sit in the stand. I'm really out there playing." In his time, 1972–1987, he won two National Leagues, two All-Stars, two Oireachtas and four Railway Cups, but a Munster and All-Ireland title eluded him.

In the Munster semi-final against Cork in 1981: "I think I played my best game ever at right half-forward that day. In terms of physical power, I was at my peak. Playing well and being beaten can be a bit hollow. Beating Cork was great. It was the only time I played on a Clare team that beat Cork in the championship. Our hopes were high." There followed the greatest disappointment of his career when they lost to Limerick in the Munster final 3:12 to 2:9: "I felt deflated at the final whistle. Outfield the exchanges seemed so close. Joe McKenna destroyed us that day. He scored 3:3 and had a further 1:1 disallowed. When I look back now I feel that a very good Clare team was unfortunate to come up against the very talented Cork three-in-a-row team of 1976 to 1978 and an equally talented Limerick team of the early eighties." The Oireachtas wins of 1982 and 1983 over Limerick and Kilkenny respectively were indicators of the strength of Clare hurling but such triumphs would pale in the face of a Munster or All-Ireland crown.

The players he encountered? "I met some great ones. I had a few good battles with Pat Lawlor of Kilkenny. He was very tight and very tidy – sticky, too. Joe Hennessy of Kilkenny had the same attributes backed up by first touch mastery and long clearances. Iggy Clarke of Galway was fantastic. We played against each other in Fitzgibbon Cup matches – [he] could murder you; he'd take off and score a point. Seán Foley of Limerick was an outstanding hurler. Liam O'Donoghue of Limerick was a superb defender – kept pushing you upfield, difficult to dispossess, great positional sense. Frank Cummins of Kilkenny – well, what can I say about him? His very physical presence was frightening."

TOM CASHMAN
CORK

Born: 1957
Interviewed: 2001

Tom Cashman descended from a great sporting background. "Hurling is a joy. Best game in the world, producing great players every year, new names to take over from yesterday. Long may it continue." His father, Mick, had a brilliant career with Blackrock, Cork and Munster. He starred as a centre half-back and goalkeeper through the fifties and into the early sixties. "My father was born in 1931, the year Blackrock won the title. They didn't win again until 1956 – twenty-five years later – when my father captained them to victory over Glen Rovers.

"I saw him play in goal for Blackrock Seniors and in inter-firm matches but never with the county. He was a big influence on me. But he wouldn't say too much – only what needed to be said. And any advice was short – a one liner – but it would be important."

Tom's mother, Ann, is a sister of Jimmy Brohan, another great Cork stalwart in the era 1954–1964; Tom's aunt, Maureen, on his father's side, played camogie for Cork. So Tom had much to live up to. He faced the challenge and excelled.

The Féile na nGael competition was initiated in 1971. Blackrock won through in Cork and advanced to represent the county in the All-Ireland series. "We beat the representatives of Kilkenny, Tipperary and Dublin and were crowned champions in Thurles on Sunday, 18 July 1971."

Each of the team received a wooden plaque – a trophy Tom still cherishes. Those who saw Tom in action in the final considered his splendid goalkeeping to be on a par with the great displays of his father.

Underage success continued for Tom. A rare double came his way in 1974, when he won All-Ireland minor hurling and minor football titles with wins over Kilkenny and Mayo respectively. Two years later, he won an All-Ireland under-21 hurling medal with a decisive victory over Kilkenny.

In his early tender years, Ray Cummins and Gerald McCarthy were his heroes.

Tom first sampled senior county fare at nineteen in the National League campaign of 1976 and called it a day after defeat by Tipperary in the Munster final of 1988. "I had been playing for fifteen seasons hurling, football and a bit of soccer too. Even by the time I was twenty-one, I had played a lot of games at under-age both for club and county. At thirty-one I found the training more demanding – it was getting tougher and harder. Time to quit."

The intervening years are strewn with success. He played in six All-Ireland finals and won on four occasions. From 1977 to 1986 inclusive, the only years Cork failed in Munster were 1980 and 1981, and in those years they won the National League title. There were county titles with Blackrock in 1976, 1978 and 1979; an All-Ireland club title with Blackrock in 1979; Railway Cup wins in 1978, 1981 and 1985 with Munster; All-Star awards in 1977, 1978 and 1983. "I think my two best games were the Munster finals of 1977 and 1978 against Clare, especially 1978 when we played with a strong wind in the first half, and won in the end by thirteen points to eleven."

Being captain of the county senior team in 1986 stands out, for him, as the highlight of a wonderful career. "To captain your county to an All-Ireland title is something you never forget." Galway were firm favourites to take the All-Ireland crown. The game ended Cork 4:13, Galway 2:15. Tom Cashman had led Cork to their twenty-sixth All-Ireland crown and took the Liam MacCarthy Cup to the Leeside for the nineteenth time. His younger brother Jim, playing at midfield, shared in that success and he too was a majestic giant of the hurling scene.

Tom's favourite position was centre half-back – yet he starred wherever he played. Those who saw him play witnessed a great stick man – a player of style and quality, equally adept left and right, a master of every stroke.

One journalist summed him up as follows: "Sweetest and most stylish of hurlers. Perfect sportsman. Usually first to be called upon when an emergency arises, as against Nicholas English in the 1985 Munster final."

In *The Rockies: A Centenary Year Publication*, published by Blackrock Club, Tom is described as follows: "The true ball-player, lightning fast striker of the sliotar, left or right, on the ground or in the air. Some of his classic points from midfield shot from his hurley, as bullets from a gun and with the same accuracy. A sportsman supreme, Tom Cashman adorns the game of hurling."

IGGY CLARKE
GALWAY

Born: 1952
Interviewed: 1993

In dialogue with Mícheál O'Hehir at Áras an Uachtaráin at a
photocall with President Mary Robinson re. *Hurling Giants.*

"I am a native of Mullagh, Loughrea and it was there I gained my love for
games and, in particular, hurling. My brothers were all keen on hurling
and my brother Joe also lined out for Galway. My other brother Tony, who
died at an early age, showed great potential. My older brother Tom was a
handy corner-forward. After a day working on the farm, all of us with our
neighbours the Cahalans, Coens and Morgans gathered in our front lawn
to play hurling. It was there we grew to love the game and learned all the
skills between ourselves.

"As young players we had a fair bit of success with Mullagh, winning
a county under-21 title with two intermediate titles. One of my great

memories as a young player is being carried off the field shoulder high by a neighbour Pat Joe Garvey. It was an extremely wet evening and I was wearing short pants. Playing hurling for the parish gave us a great sense of pride and it became for the parish a uniting force. It was and is a strong force behind any country parish. It was and is a medium that makes conversation easy and the whole social fabric of the parish is enhanced. It gives the parish a focal point of which they can be proud and all, young and old, usually give their full support.

"I went to college in Garbally, Ballinasloe, better known for rugby than hurling perhaps. I played rugby as a schoolboy and represented Connaught schoolboys. There, I also played football and soccer and took part in athletic competitions. I came in contact with other players like Andy Fenton, Séan Silke and Ciaran Fitzgerald. Garbally has many happy memories for me and, as well as broadening my education, it introduced me to a wide variety of other sports.

"During this time I was called for my first minor trial. I was sowing potatoes with my father Joe when Padraic Donohue called and invited me to go. I said, 'Why me? The other lads are better than me – are they going?' Eventually I went and things took off from there. It was a Good Friday but I did not know then that religion and hurling would be so big in my life.

"After Garbally I went to Maynooth to study for the priesthood and, looking at it now, I consider myself very lucky. I was able to continue to play for Galway at under-21 and senior level and that was something that many great players before me were not able to do. I am thinking of players like Fr Paddy Gantly, Fr Jack Solon, Fr Tom Keyes and many others who had to sacrifice their best years on account of their studies. Thank God the rules were relaxed on that because I could continue what I enjoyed and loved.

"1980 was a historic year in Galway and I was thrilled to be part of it. I do not think I fully realised what hurling meant to the people of Galway until then. After winning the league in 1975, we got a taste for it and vowed to ourselves we would break the alleged curse and carry the MacCarthy Cup across the Shannon. To have achieved that is a very cherished memory. Even though I was injured for the final, it was an unbelievable thrill to be able to raise the MacCarthy Cup aloft on that historic day when the West was truly awake.

"I will always be grateful to the Maynooth authorities for their flexibility. After Ordination I was appointed to Loughrea in 1978 and I later transferred to play with Loughrea, which was a very painful decision. Playing on the field as a priest made no difference. It was open competition and profession was irrevelant. It was a great joy and a constant challenge.

"To any young person starting off I would say practise every day. I do not mean physical training. Enjoy it, for time passes quickly. I hope they will have as many happy memories as I had over the years."

The curtain came down on his inter-county career after the All-Ireland semi-final defeat by Offaly in 1984 – "not a happy memory", The final score was Offaly 4:15, Galway 1:10. It was a career that began in a game against Waterford in 1972 "when I felt lost in the midst of big men" but he made up for it in the next game against Antrim "when everything went well". As time went on, he won four All-Star awards in a career adorned with flair, skilful half-back play and sportsmanship. Did he retire a little early? "Some said I did but I felt the dynamo was dying after fourteen years hurling. I didn't feel right anymore at half-back and the thought of going into the corner-back didn't appeal to me."

But his love for the game was still very real in 1993 and found expression at corner-forward where he played for Loughrea.

BRIAN CODY
KILKENNY

Born: 1954
Interviewed: 2002

Brian with his wife Elsie (née Walsh), a great Wexford camogie star who captained Leinster in 1988 and 1991.

"I don't really remember a time when hurling wasn't a part of my life. My parents had a real interest in hurling, so from an early age I was forever pucking around. I come from a place called Sheestown, four miles from Kilkenny City, and the teacher in the local school, Joe Golden, helped to nurture the love of hurling in all the pupils. Brother Basil O'Brien of the De La Salle order played an important part in my development too, as our school played with St Patrick's De La Salle in the local schools' competitions.

"I was very lucky to belong to the James Stephens Club and I went on to win many juvenile honours with the club. My father was heavily involved with James Stephens and went on to serve as chairman for many years. St Kieran's College also played a big part in my development. I was a boarder in St Kieran's College and just about all our spare time was spent in the hurling pitch. I was a fellow student of many great players and as a result enjoyed success on the playing fields there, culminating in All-Ireland success in 1971.

"In 1972 I had the honour of captaining Kilkenny minors to All-Ireland success and went on to make my debut for the seniors in the league of that year. My first game was against Limerick in Nowlan Park. This was a golden era for Kilkenny hurling and I consider myself very lucky to have an involvement in it.

"I went on to enjoy good success over the following number of years with Kilkenny and, most importantly, with my club James Stephens. I won my first Senior County Championship in 1975 and went on to become the first team from Leinster to win the All-Ireland Club Championships. That was a real highlight of my career as we beat a brilliant Blackrock team in the final in Thurles. We were captained by the outstanding Fan Larkin who was the real driving force of that team. We went on to retain our own County Championship in 1976 also. We had to wait until 1981 to win our next county title but we also went on to win the All-Ireland Club Championship again, beating Mount Sion. That golden era for our club was all achieved under the chairmanship of my father, Bill.

"I suppose I mention my club so much because I got wonderful enjoyment from just playing at every level – be it club or county – and I suppose my biggest worry for hurling at the moment is that the club player is probably losing out because of the greater emphasis on inter-county training and preparation.

"A major highlight of my career obviously came in 1982 when I captained Kilkenny to win the senior All-Ireland. It was a great team with a great spirit and we had a great victory over Cork in the final. We were total underdogs but we prepared well under Pat Henderson and on the day turned in a great performance. It was indeed a special moment.

"I could not finish without paying tribute to Fr Tommy Maher's contribution to Kilkenny hurling. He was in charge of the team during the 1970s when I first joined the panel and was a major influence on us all.

"In conclusion, I will just say that I don't look back on my career and think in terms of what I won. I recall the great enjoyment I got from the game over a long period of time and can honestly say that playing for both James Stephens and Kilkenny was always a source of pride for me."

Brian's late father Bill was a native of Thomastown. "All his life he loved, and lived for, the game of hurling. In his time he was a county minor and senior selector. He was chairman of James Stephens club for seventeen years – it coincided with the club's great days." Brian's mother Annié (née Hoyne) was also a native of Thomastown. Growing up in that parish she spent her spare time "playing camogie and revelled in the game".

Little wonder then that their son Brian has a profound love and passion for hurling. At present, he is manager of the Kilkenny senior hurling team. He lives and breathes the game. Its presence in his daily life is oxygen to his very being. As I talked with Brian, I realised that his hurling days merge into a panorama of moments that brings to the surface his love for, and devotion to, hurling that transcends trophies and victories – although he does admit that they too are necessary and at times essential.

In 1982 Brian was honoured with the captaincy of the county senior team. A narrow two points victory over Offaly in a thrilling Leinster final, followed by a ten-point win over Galway in the All-Ireland semi-final, brought the Noresiders face to face with the men from the Lee on final day, 5 September, at Croke Park. On a day when Cork were firm favourites, Brian led Kilkenny to one of their biggest victories ever over the Rebel County. The game ended 3:18 to 1:13. Brian's late father Bill was on the Hogan Stand to relish the occasion. GAA President Paddy Buggy, himself a former Kilkenny All-Ireland hurling star, proudly handed the MacCarthy Cup to Brian. Later in the year Brian received an All-Star award.

Brian finds it difficult to single out any one success above another; instead, he picks the year 1975 as having special significance – a year when a lot of honours came his way and he just twenty-one years old. "I won my first All-Star, a second under-21 All-Ireland, a senior All-Ireland on a team that had five players from 'The Village' (James Stephens) – myself, Fan Larkin, Mick Crotty, Liam O'Brien and Tom McCormack. That was special. I also won my first county title with James Stephens – that, too, was very special. It led on to our All-Ireland club win the following March."

Under Brian's management, Kilkenny has produced the most successful hurling team in the history of the game. He took over at the helm in 1999 and by September 2011 had guided the Noresiders to five National League and eight All Ireland successes.

JOHN CONNOLLY
GALWAY

Born: 1948
Interviewed: 1991

"Apart from hurling I also played football with a city team called St Michael's and played with Galway minors and under-21s and, in 1968, with a lot of the stars of the great three-in-a-row senior football team. When I was seventeen a local boxing club was started by that great boxing man "Chick" Gillen. I joined with a few of the lads, and went on to win the Connaught Junior Light-welterweight Championship that year.

"However, I came down to earth when a fellow called Mike Berry beat the hell out of me in a local tournament.

"Anyway, I thank God for the ability to play hurling at top level. The game has helped me to be a better person in many ways; helped me to accept disappointment on and off the field and bounce back. It has given me the opportunity to make and meet friends from all around the country that I'll have until the day I die.

"I was born in Leitir Moir, Connemara, and when we moved to Bally-brit (beside the world-famous Galway Race Course), at the age of five years, hurling became as much part of my life as sleeping or eating.

"Although my father had never seen a game of hurling played before then, his interest in it had a great effect on me. I remember him carrying me on the crossbar of his bike the five miles to Pierce Stadium in Salthill to see the Galway team play. The look of admiration and expression on his face as he pointed out to me the Galway stars of the day made a huge impression on me as a young lad."

John was always wonderstruck by the way his father, who was normally a calm man, became elated and excited as he watched Joe Salmon and Paddy Egan and other Galway stars perform; and he would utter aloud their names to his young son John.

The performance of the hurling heroes appeared to mean so much to his father that, when John began his county hurling, he always hoped that he too would bring joy and entertainment into the lives of many of the spectators.

"It was a tradition of ours, even after us getting married with our own homes, we would all meet in our old home place the morning of a match, known to everybody in Galway as Mamo's, which was an old name for 'Grandmother's'. We would chat about the game, and without realising it we built up a kind of spirit that stood for us on the field. Then, as we left Mamo's, she would always shake the bottle of holy water on us, saying, 'Mind yourselves and don't be fighting, and don't come back if ye lose.' Of course we had many a fight, and we lost plenty of times, but we were always welcomed home."

John's first senior match in the championship was in 1967. His career knew many disappointments, narrow defeats and frustrations. Those frustrations peaked after the defeat by Kilkenny in the 1979 All-Ireland final. Galway were hot favourites. Kilkenny, measured by their own high standard, were perceived as "weak". On the way home, John's wife Nuala turned to him and said, "Ye'll never win an All-Ireland now." John was well aware that there was a belief in Galway that a curse hung over the hurlers, but he always laughed at the idea. Now, however, he began to think that maybe there was some substance to it.

Glorious days lay around the corner. On St Patrick's Day 1980, Connaught (all Galway), captained by his brother Joe, won the Railway Cup: Connaught 1:5, Munster 0:7. And then there was that memory that will never fade – the occasion of the All-Ireland club semi-final in 1980 against the Cork champions Blackrock. Athenry pitch was thronged. "Parish rivalry was cast aside and every Galway man became a Castlegar man that day. I never remember scores, but I'll never forget that score, 2:9 to 0:9, and we beat a Blackrock team that had nine county players, including Frank Cummins of Kilkenny. The greatest day of my sporting life was the day the seven of us – Padraic, Michael (captain), Joe, Jerry, Tom, Murt and myself – won seven All-Ireland medals when we won the All-Ireland club final, beating Ballycastle of Antrim.

Of course the other great day in our lives was Galway winning the All-Ireland in 1980. We beat Limerick and had whatever luck was going that day. You must remember that we were beaten so often for so long, by so little, to realise what it meant to Galway. On that great Galway team Michael, Joe and myself played, while Padraic was a sub. Joe played a real captain's part, and crowned it all with a famous speech "as Gaeilge afterwards." Later that year John was honoured with the Hurler of the Year Award.

John "will never understand how Galway lost to Offaly in the 1981 final", and he thinks about the goal he scored in the first half – "and the umpire waved the green flag but the referee disallowed it." The sound of the final whistle heralded a feeling of despondency that represented a nadir in John's hurling life.

As he looks back now, his biggest regret is the depth of remorse and upset he used to feel after losing a match. "I would go back over every movement and every missed stroke and all the opportunities and analyse the might-have-beens. If I could start all over again I would promise and undertake to myself, as a top priority, to set out to enjoy every match."

He singles out three hurlers as exceptional – Frank Cummins (Kilkenny), Ray Cummins (Cork), and Mick Roche (Tipperary) – and he wonders "if we will ever again see a forward unit like what Kilkenny had in the mid-seventies: Crotty, Delaney, Fitzpatrick, Brennan, Purcell and Keher".

DENIS COUGHLAN
CORK

Born: 1945
Interviewed: 2008

"I was born in Blackpool (Glen Rovers/St Nicks) and so grew up listening to the great feats of "Fox" Collins, Jack Lynch, Jim Young and many more.

"My father was a great influence on me. Being an only son, he took me to all the Glen Rovers games and especially to the great Cork v Tipperary games in Limerick in the 1950s. Mind you, I only saw glimpses from his shoulders, from time to time, but have never forgotten the excitement of it all.

"I clearly recall my first senior hurling game for "The Glen", in 1962. I was seventeen years old and we played Faughs of Dublin in Banagher, Co. Offaly. Christy Ring was the main attraction and I was marking Billy Dwyer, the well-known Kilkenny hurler.

"I played for the next twenty years for the Glen senior team, while also playing football with St. Nicks for most of that time too.

"My career with Cork hurlers and footballers ran concurrently with my club career; needless to say it was a very busy stage in my life.

"Winning County Championships was very important to the club and the two that stand out for me were hurling 1969 and football 1965. Of course, captaining the Glen team to their first All-Ireland club final was very special. Playing with Cork hurlers and footballers was a great honour and I especially looked forward to Munster final day.

"In football, Killarney against Kerry was always a special day, while strangely enough Limerick was my favourite for hurling finals. I suppose it reminded me of the days my father would take me on the train to those games.

"I enjoyed every moment of my career. I had great help and advice along the way, and met some lovely people. Some of my opponents made life difficult for me, but it was a pleasure to have been on the same field in football with Mick O'Connell, Jimmy Duggan (Galway), Pat Griffin (Kerry), while Christy Ring, Jimmy Doyle, Eddie Keher, Babs Keating and Mick Roche in hurling were wonderful sportsmen.

"Winning and losing is all part of sport and I have absolutely no regrets or disappointments. I would love to be able to do it all again."

Denis was born on 7 June 1945 to John and Margaret (née O'Flaherty). His father played club hurling with St Mary's and Brian Dillon's and won a county junior title with the latter in the early 1930s.

Denis was one of the great dual players of Gaelic games – blessed with talent and rewarded with honours. The hurling days stretched from 1965 to 1981; the football era covered the period 1964–1974. He belongs to a small elite band – probably less than a score – that won All-Ireland honours at senior level in both hurling and football.

He won his football medal in 1973. He operated at midfield. He was a key figure in a strong, talented Cork lineout, captained by their goal-keeper Billy Morgan. Denis was brilliant at centre field in a championship campaign that saw Cork romp past all opposition on their way to collect the Sam Maguire Cup.

Railway Cup honours came in 1972. On St Patrick's Day, Munster drew with Leinster in the final at Croke Park. The replay took place at Cork on 23 April. Munster won by 2:14 to 0:10. It was the first time since 1949 that the province won the competition – their seventh title in all.

"The first medal I ever won was a football one – we beat London in the All-Ireland Junior final of 1964. That day I played at left full-back."

However, it is Denis the hurler, a member of Glen Rovers founded in 1916, I remember best. I witnessed his elegant, versatile and sporting displays on the hurling pitch on many occasions.

I saw him in action in the Munster final in 1969 against Tipperary at the Gaelic grounds in Limerick. Denis stood apart in a field of much hurling talent. He gave a vintage display of classic hurling and some delightful ground striking. He made it all look so easy – a master of his craft.

Denis had a role in six All-Ireland finals. He played in midfield in 1969 and 1972 when Cork lost to Kilkenny. In 1970 he was a sub on the team that beat Wexford. Then came the three-in-a-row in 1976, 1977 and 1978. Operating at left half-back in the No. 7 jersey, Denis turned in many majestic and magical performances. And, perhaps, none more so than in the 1977 final against Wexford when his display and overall contribution were immense.

Little wonder then that Denis was chosen as Texaco Hurler of the Year in 1977 and that, for each of the three years 1976–1978, he was selected as an All-Star in the left half-back position – giving him four in all – the first in 1972.

Other hurling honours include eight Munster titles, five county titles, two All Ireland club titles and four National Leagues.

Growing up, his heroes were "Johnny Clifford, a third cousin, my first hero; the Cork three-in-a-row hurlers of 1952 to 1954; and the Glen Rovers trio of Josie Hartnett, Dave Creedon and John Lyons. The best hurler I saw in my lifetime was Mick Roche of Tipperary – out on his own at midfield."

Some moments stand out as very special for Denis. "I first wore the Cork jersey in senior hurling in an Oireachtas game against Kilkenny at Pairc Uí Caoimh in 1965. I was marking Paddy Moran. Beating Tipperary in the Munster final of 1969 was very special. Cork hadn't done it since 1954. It was a great day – one of my better ones.

"In 1971 I was sensationally dropped from the Cork football team to play Kerry in the Munster final. I came on as a sub after twenty minutes and scored ten points."

No wonder Denis remembers it. Cork went on to beat Kerry, reigning All-Ireland champions, by twenty-five points to fourteen. And, finally, there was a memory of the Maestro himself. "I played with Christy (Ring) for four years from 1964 onwards. I remember one evening in training with the Glen. Finbar O'Neill was in goal. At one stage Christy set about testing him. He began at the 40-yard line. He worked his way into the 21-yard line belting ball after ball at Finbar. We all just stood aside and watched in admiration."

Denis's last game in championship hurling was the Munster final defeat by Limerick at Thurles in 1980. He was thirty-five. Father Time was beckoning. He did play in the early stages of the 1981 National League, but before the game with Waterford "Frank Murphy beckoned, via Johnny Clifford. I was being rested, I was told" – permanently, as it transpired.

ÉAMONN CREGAN
LIMERICK

Born: 1945
Interviewed: 1993

Éamonn Cregan speaks with pride about his native city Limerick, his club Claughaun, his school Sexton St (Limerick CBS) where his hurling brilliance blossomed, and finally his lifetime in hurling.

His father Ned played in a junior All-Ireland final with Limerick against Meath in 1927 but lost. From there, he progressed to the senior team and won National League, Munster and All-Ireland honours with the great Limerick team of the thirties. He played in the All-Ireland finals of 1933, 1934 and 1935, and was a sub in 1936.

Did he ever compare the hurlers and hurling of the different decades? "No, he never made comparisons. He would never say that the fellows of his day were better. He would offer us advice – set us thinking. One day, as he watched me strike continuously with the left, he just said, 'have you got any right side?' It put me thinking."

Since retiring, Éamonn has coached Limerick and Clare and is at present (1993) with Offaly. "Of course I still play every stroke when I am sitting on the sideline and those beside me get elbowed and shouldered."

Éamonn made his inter-county debut in a National League game against Dublin in the autumn of 1964. The curtain came down on a brilliant hurling career when he came on as a sub against Cork in the 1983 Munster Championship.

Éamonn won three All-Star awards. He was a highly accomplished thinking forward worthy of a place in modern hurling beside Eddie Keher of Kilkenny, Jimmy Doyle of Tipperary, Jimmy Smyth of Clare and Jimmy Barry Murphy of Cork.

One of Éamonn's greatest displays was at centre-back for Limerick on a very wet Sunday afternoon in September 1973 against the reigning champions Kilkenny in the All-Ireland final. He had the ideal temperament – a temperament laced with steel, skill and stamina – for the task of minimising the threat of ace Kilkenny centre-forward Pat Delaney. There was confidence, discipline and class in his display, and he was flanked that day by Seén Foley who gave a superlative display and Phil Bennis who, with his uncompromising approach, didn't give an inch. "No way was I going to let Pat Delaney pass me and hop the ball on the ground and thunder through for scores as I had seen him do in other games."

His display against Tipperary in the opening round of the championship in 1966 heralded what lay ahead from Éamonn Cregan, the hurler. Tipperary had comprehensively defeated Kilkenny and Wexford in the All-Ireland finals of 1964 and 1965 respectively and looked odds on to make it three in a row in 1966. But a scintillating display from Éamonn, whose speed and skill saw him score a total of 3:5, toppled Tipperary from the hurling pedestal.

He was sent off once in a game against Clare after scoring a great goal that was immediately followed by a flare-up. When the tangle was unravelled, he was incorrectly singled out by the referee as the culprit and sidelined.

Three occasions stand out as memorable in a hurling career that was filled with memories. The first goes back to when he was eleven years of age. He won his first county juvenile medal in the under-16 category. He played in goal.

Next comes the Harty Cup success of 1964 when he captained Sexton St CBS: "We lived and died for Harty Cup success and took a tremendous pride in it. You had to be in Sexton St to understand what it meant to the school to win the Harty Cup. Our trainers were Jim Hennessy and Br Michael Burke. They knew their hurling. They insisted that we play the game at high speed and to concentrate mainly on ground hurling. We used the wings and fast ground balls to open up defences." And finally there is the success of 1973: "The highlight of my career is without doubt the All-Ireland win of 1973. I always believed that this would happen and that I would be part of it. It was an unforgettable year. Pride was back with Limerick again. We did unbelievable training for that championship. We never came off the pitch tired. We could have played for two hours."

I asked him if his dad witnessed the glory of 1973? I had touched a tender cord. It showed in his expression and in his downcast eyes. After a short silent pause, which I observed in empathy with him, he responded: "It's twenty years now but it still hurts. He died in August 1972. He stopped going to matches in 1964. He used get too excited and that was bad for him. In 1967 he got ill. After a match I would go up to the room to talk to him in bed. I would analyse for him what happened and tell him what went on. That's how he learned about the games and stayed in touch."

On the way back from Croke Park after the All-Ireland victory of 1973, there was great rejoicing. It had been a sweet victory over Kilkenny. It was a time for celebration – and mirth and laughter and song. The train stopped at Castleconnell and the team travelled from there to Limerick by road – open vehicle: "The crowd was enormous. It took two hours to travel from three miles out to Honan's Quay in the city. On the way we passed our house. Mick Herbert, Limerick full-back of the late forties said to me, 'You are very quiet.'" Éamonn's thoughts were with his father.

In retirement, Eamon has never been far removed from the game of hurling. As manager, his most memorable achievement was the success of the Offaly senior hurling team in the All-Ireland final of 1994 against his native Limerick. It was a day when the joy of success was tinged with degrees of sadness.

MARTIN CUDDY
LAOIS

Born: 1950
Interviewed: 1997

Martin (right) with his brother Jackie – both Oxford players 1972 – and their father Jack.

"As the second youngest of seven brothers, I had a lot to live up to. I went to England (1967) when I was seventeen and played with Oxford with my brother Jack. We used to bring a seven-a-side team to play in a tournament at Camross. We had some great games."

Martin played with Hertfordshire in two All-Ireland junior finals. They lost to Meath after a replay in 1970. In 1971, something unique happened in the final against Wicklow. The game ended in a draw and the referee declared that the next score would decide the winners. The "winning" point came to Hertfordshire and the score stood at 4:9 to 3:11. The referee's decision led to a dispute, and a replay was ordered. Again it ended in a draw. The second replay was won by Wicklow by one point, on the score 4:6 to 3:8.

When Martin returned from England he joined the Laois senior panel, and All-Ireland "B" titles were won in 1977 and 1979. "There were signs that Laois were moving towards competing with the best. Between 1981 and 1985 we were unlucky not to have made the breakthrough."

Four times in the early 1980s Martin was selected to play with Leinster in the Railway Cup, but defeat was Leinster's lot on each occasion. "Sometimes I used think to myself that I wasn't supposed to win."

Martin made a number of trips across the Atlantic to play hurling matches with a variety of clubs. "In 1988 in the month of June I played a match in Mountrath on a Friday evening. We got the one o'clock plane from Shannon to San Francisco, arriving at midnight. On Sunday we played the Californian final. At half time, full time and halfway into extra time it was level pegging; in the end we won by one point. Celebrations went on until ten o'clock Monday morning, when we got the plane back to Shannon via New York. We arrived in Shannon on Tuesday morning. I didn't know whether I was coming or going for a week.

"I played with the Fenians in San Francisco against the Gaels, who had in their ranks Paddy Quirke of Carlow, whom I was playing on, and Pádraig Horan, who was their coach."

Martin Cuddy ranks among the great ones, but major honours, so richly merited, have eluded him. He hails from Camross, a parish that has been to the forefront of Laois hurling for almost forty years now. He participated in their successes from the seventies and in that time won ten county titles.

His proudest moment came in 1977 at Carlow, when he captained his native Camross to a Leinster senior hurling club title with a one-point victory over the reigning All-Ireland champions, James Stephens of Kilkenny. They were beaten in the final by Glen Rovers of Cork. Seven Cuddys, from two families – distantly related – lined out with Camross: Martin and his brothers Tim, Ollie and Michael; and P.J. of Laois full-forward fame, and his brothers Ger and Seán.

He named some of the great centre-backs he encountered in a career that saw him nominated for the All-Stars: "Seán Silke, Pat Delaney, Ger Henderson, Sean Stack, Mossie Carroll and Tom Cashman – some fair men to handle."

Here is how Canon Seán Collier of Borris-in-Ossory remembers Martin:

I had the pleasure and honour during the eighties of helping Camross to restore their great tradition of success and I must say that Martin Cuddy played a major role in the success, whether at centre-back or centre-forward.

Needless to say, his ability and skills did not go unnoticed at county level and very soon he was to become one of the greatest wearers of the blue and white.

Martin Cuddy

FRANK CUMMINS
KILKENNY

Born: 1947
Interviewed: 1994

"My first outing with Kilkenny was in the Oireachtas final in November 1966 and from then on I was more or less a regular with the team. I have played with and against many players during my playing days and, to me, the most important thing above all else is the friendship. Playing the game meant more to me than victory or defeat. Hurling and the GAA played a large part in my family life. My wife Madeleine was a great enthusiast and enjoyed all the games and after-match celebrations. My family were also fortunate to see me play with Blackrock and Kilkenny and share the successes with me. I can still remember the Monday night after the 1982 All-Ireland travelling back to Kilkenny with my wife, son Alan and daughter Deirdre carrying the cup."

When Frank Cummins was growing up, the talk in Kilkenny would have been about the 1947 All-Ireland victory and, to a lesser extent, the

1939 triumph. The 1957 team is better remembered by Frank. He was ten years old and Denis Heaslip from the local club was a great favourite of his: "I remember going to the local village for a wet battery for the radio to listen to the final. Ollie Walsh was my hero. I used wear a badge of Ollie made from a paper cutting on my coat going to school. My teacher was mad about Ollie too."

Frank's career coincided with what was a great Kilkenny hurling era. He won major honours with county, province and his Cork club Blackrock. They include eight All-Ireland medals, counting his first as a sub in 1967, six Railway Cup victories and six county titles. He also won five Munster club titles with Blackrock and three of those were converted to All-Ireland club victories in 1972, 1974 and 1979. He was part of Leinster's best-ever run in the Railway Cup when winning five in a row from 1971 to 1975. His All-Irelands were won in three different decades and he became the fifth Kilkenny man to win seven All-Ireland medals on the field of play.

I decided to ask Madeleine what in her estimation were his greatest moments, because by now I had discovered she was Frank's greatest critic. She selected two: "He played a league game in Nowlan Park against Tipperary in 1971. He was at centre-back. He hit everything that came his way and cleaned up all before him. Kilkenny won and he was awarded Sportstar of the Week in the *Irish Independent*. It was richly deserved. I think it was the finest game of hurling I ever saw him play. My second choice would be the 1983 All-Ireland final against Cork. A very strong wind blew into the Railway goal and Kilkenny faced this in the second half with a six-point lead that hardly seemed adequate. Frank kept dropping back from midfield to be under the long Cork puck-outs. Himself and Ger Henderson did trojan work as they kept putting the ball down-field again. It was the toughest game I ever went through on the stand. I remember at one stage in the second half when the pressure was really on and Frank dropped his hurley to hand pass the ball – a free of course. I nearly died and said aloud, 'O Sacred Heart of Jesus, what's wrong with him?' Seconds later a Cork back did the same so I felt that there must be shocking pressure out there." Frank confirmed that it was a pressured game and reminded me that Kilkenny didn't score in the last eighteen minutes. "We played a defensive game in the second half. Those were our instructions. Our centre-field fell back hoping to pick up the breaking ball. It worked like a dream." It was a good year for Frank. He won Leinster, All-Ireland

and National League titles. He was selected as Hurler of the Year and earned his fourth All-Star award.

Frank was probably not a classical hurler in the strict sense. But he was a superb midfielder – extremely effective and always very fit. There was an attacking and defensive dimension attached to his game. He had the capacity to pace his game – an essential characteristic in a midfielder. And he could pick off long-range points – the kind of hurling skill that breaks the heart of opposing defences and, indeed, whole teams.

He was a great striker of a ball and could deliver a huge work-rate. A man of high sporting standards, he was durable and had high levels of strength, steel and stamina. It was a combination that rattled many a sturdy opponent. Tim Crowley of Cork was light years away from being a weakling, but in the All-Ireland final of 1982, when he went down from a shoulder from Frank Cummins beside the sideline on the Hogan Stand side, it shook every bone in his body. Frank was a man of bronze – immensely strong. Little wonder someone once said of him: "Frank Cummins wasn't born – he was quarried."

Frank Cummins.

RAY CUMMINS
CORK

Born: 1948
Interviewed: 1997

"There is no doubt in my mind that involvement in team sport is the best possible form of preparation for the ups and downs of life. The character formation developed as a result of the self-discipline, commitment, loyalty, self-sacrifice, dependence on others, and respect for team mates, opponents and those in authority; the ability to handle pressure, suffer defeat in a manly fashion and with resolve to do better next time, and to treat success with dignity, are not found on the curriculum of any university, college or school. I will be eternally grateful to those who sowed the seeds, and nurtured and cultivated my interest in hurling and football. They and their likes in other clubs and codes are due an enormous debt of gratitude by society – unsung heroes.

"No medal won or victory gained has given me more pleasure than the friendships made through the medium of hurling. Hurling folk are unique and nothing I have experienced binds people together quite like the love of hurling or the mutual respect of the honest hurler, whatever his skill level. I consider myself privileged and honoured to have had the opportunity to play with and against so many, many wonderful hurlers and great characters on and off the field – too many, in fact, for me to mention, as it would need a book of its own and to leave out any would be an injustice.

"There is a bond between hurling men that is born out of respect. To me, hurling has meant involvement, excitement – there is no place like Thurles on a Munster final day – and friendship. I can go to Limerick and knock on Pat Hartigan's door and feel welcome. Pat was the best full-back I ever met. He was a great hurler and sportsman – physically strong and very committed. We played hard against each other, but we always played the ball. I would be comfortable meeting an honest hurler any time. At club level in Cork, I had some great battles with Martin Doherty, a full-back for whom I had great respect too."

Ray's father, Willie, won an All-Ireland minor title with Cork in 1938 in the exalted company of Alan Lotty, Christy Ring, Éamon Young and Ted Sullivan. He won a second minor title the following year. Ray's mother Mary (née Walsh) played camogie at club level.

In 1966, Ray represented Cork at minor level in both hurling and football and in due course did likewise at under-21 level.

"In the Munster final of 1969 v. Tipperary, I was brought on as a sub in the second half of the game but I can't recall touching the ball. Cork won and laid the Tipp. bogey. In fourteen years of Senior Championship hurling, I was never on a losing team to Tipp."

Ray really got his baptism of fire in senior hurling when he lined out at full-forward in the All-Ireland final of 1969 against Kilkenny and was faced by the experienced and uncompromising Pa Dillon, and behind him Ollie Walsh in goal: "I was completely green. Such a scene was new to me."

His debut was not a winning one, but a remarkable dozen years of successes lay ahead. Ray, as a dual player, excelled at hurling and football and demonstrated during his playing career that he was one of the greatest dual players in the history of the GAA. Apart from a National League in football, he has won every honour in both codes.

Ray's eleven Munster titles in a row, from 1969 to 1979, must surely constitute a record. Three of these were in football – 1971, 1973, and 1974 – despite the fact that "they only played football seriously in Blackrock when out of the hurling championship." The pressures of playing both games began to take their toll, and in 1975 he concentrated solely on hurling, having played football since the league of 1967, "My first loyalty was to hurling."

Ray reflected for a while when I asked him to recall three events from his career that conjure up something special. "I remember going to Croke Park for the first time ever. We had won an under-16 ground hurling competition – no handling. The reward was a trip to Croke Park on All-Ireland final day in 1964. I was fascinated by Croke Park.

"Meeting Jimmy Doyle was special. It was on one of the All-Star trips to the States in the early seventies. Jimmy Doyle was like a god to me. Neither of us were drinking, so we gravitated towards each other. Here was my boyhood hero – so natural, so unassuming. In the sixties I saw him destroy Cork in Munster finals.

"To captain Cork in 1976 to the first of three in a row was a great honour. I was the first Blackrock man to do so since the days of Eudi Coughlan in 1931. Wexford were 2:2 up after seven minutes. It was a physically exhausting match; I felt drained after it."

Ray introduced a new strategy to full-forward play. He had a great sense of position; wonderful hands; anticipation and vision, especially peripheral vision. He demonstrated this to the full when he advanced outfield to grasp an incoming sliotar and laid off passes of telling importance to forward colleagues. His own abilities, coupled with his intelligent use of his forward team-mates, placed opposing defences under extreme pressure, on occasion tearing them apart and opening up gaps that led to vital scores. When the occasion was right, he took his own scores; and, as with all masters, he made it look simple. "I enjoyed the freedom of full-forward play but did not relish the traditional role of full-forwards standing in the square, wrestling with the full-back and "raising dust".'

He quit after the All-Ireland final of 1982. "I never had great speed or stamina. I felt burned out. After that I decided I had enough. Time to quit." As a full-forward, Ray's name will be remembered as one that fits comfortably into the company of Martin Kennedy of Tipperary, Paddy McMahon of Limerick and Nicky Rackard of Wexford from bygone days, together with Tony Doran of Wexford and Joe McKenna of Limerick from more recent times.

As a sportsman, Ray ranks with the élite of Gaelic games.

TONY DORAN
WEXFORD

Born: 1946
Interviewed: 1992

"I first started to play competitive hurling in the newly inaugurated Nicky Rackard Rural Schools' League in 1956. Attending national school in Boolavogue, I played with Monageer-Boolavogue. The highlight of that first year's competition in which we eventually lost at the semi-final stage to Rathnure was when we played Ballyoughter in the quarter-final and Nicky Rackard himself refereed.

"In the years since then, I have been lucky to have a number of high spots in my career with both club and county since I started with Buffers Alley in juvenile (under-16) in 1959 and Wexford minors in 1963.

"Winning the All-Ireland senior with Wexford in 1968 was a great honour and one of the highlights, while beating the all-conquering Kilkenny of the first half of the seventies by seventeen points in the Leinster final was another great moment. Losing two All-Irelands to Cork in 1976 and 1977 was very disappointing. In 1976 we played well but were still beaten by four points in a great game, and in 1977, although I think we did not do ourselves justice on the day, we were only denied a draw by a great Martin Coleman save from Christy Keogh in the dying moments.

"Winning the 1989 All-Ireland Club Championship with Buffers Alley, when we beat O'Donovan Rossa from Belfast in the final, was the real highlight of my career. Winning with a team from a small rural community and seeing the joy it brought to everyone – players, officials, supporters – was something words could not really describe. Coming, as it did, twenty-one years after winning the All-Ireland with Wexford made me appreciate it even more."

"I take it Tony that you have at last retired?" I posed the question because you never knew with Tony; he just seemed to go on forever. And then I discovered that this year (1992) he actually played junior club hurling – and he in his forty-seventh year. He won his last major title in September 1991 when Wexford defeated Kildare 2:14 to 1:8 in the over-forties All-Ireland Masters Hurling title.

He was chosen as Texaco Hurler of the Year in 1976, nine years after he had established his claims for a permanent place on the panel and won his first league medal. His vast collection of medals and trophies include every major honour in the game. I therefore wondered if there had been any one particular moment of deep disappointment.

"If there was only one it wouldn't be too bad. There were many. One of the biggest was my departure from the 1981 Leinster final against Offaly. I was stretchered off after about ten or twelve minutes – it was the only time I ever went off. The fact that I took so little part was very disappointing. I listened to the closing moments in hospital and it didn't help my morale to hear the final whistle announced with Wexford on the wrong side of a score of 3:12 to 2:13. I suppose, after that, the two-in-a-row losses to Cork in 1976 and 1977 would be high on the list."

As a hurler, I would describe Tony as inspirational rather than classical, stout-hearted rather than stylish, brave rather than opportunist. He could absorb punishment with a smile; he never drew a foul stroke. There was a Matt the Thresher air about his style – his efforts were always herculean, the stuff of legend and folklore, and he possessed the charisma to match the role. He presented all full-backs with problems and mentioned three in particular that he admired – Eugene Coughlan of Offaly, Pa Dillon of Kilkenny and Pat Hartigan of Limerick.

In 1968, Tipperary were still a formidable hurling force. So how did Wexford and Tony Doran in his first All-Ireland final hope to do in 1968 against the men of Tipperary? Well, they produced a power-packed second half that had the Munster champions reeling and Tony Doran in the forward line caused consternation in the Tipperary defence. "I was centre-forward in the first half– got a hurling lesson for twenty minutes from Mick Roche; didn't see much of the ball – and moved to full-forward before half time. We went in eight points down." Wexford came out in the second half and set about getting back into the reckoning. Tony got a goal followed by further scores, including a goal by Paul Lynch that levelled matters. I can still hear Mícheál Ó Hehir describing Tony's second goal that gave Wexford the lead. "It's a goal, it's a goal – the red-haired Tony Doran – the man from Boolavogue."

1968 was a wonderful Wexford win. The celebrations that followed awakened memories of 1955, 1956 and 1960. The defeats of 1962 and 1965 at the hands of Tipperary were avenged. The pride of the fifties stirred again. They returned bearing victory amid great rejoicing throughout Co. Wexford – in Enniscorthy, Rathnure and "at Boolavogue as the sun was setting."

Tony was still doing *gaisce* when Wexford met Kilkenny in the Leinster semi-final of 1984. His goal with a left-handed stroke in the dying moments off Dick O'Hara, after he had gained possession on the Hill 16 side of the Railway goal and moved towards the centre, put Wexford into the lead and sent their supporters delirious with excitement. Tony was no longer the nimble youth of 1968. But he was still deadly around goal and the old warrior celebrated his goal by taking a leap into the air as he came out-field. I thought the ground would shake with the thud when he came down.

In a career that spanned almost twenty years of top-class hurling, Tony has known all the joys of victory and the many disappointments of defeat. In 1992, at forty-seven, he was very philosophical about it all: "Just to have played was wonderful."

PAT DUNNEY
KILDARE

Born: 1945
Interviewed: 1996

"The under-age teams I played on enjoyed great success. The local parish priest of the time, Fr Bennett, organised an under-age hurling tournament with neighbouring counties. The pride I felt from playing with my county made me determined that I would represent Kildare at adult level, both at football and hurling."

Mention the name Pat Dunney in GAA circles and everybody calls to mind Kildare's greatest dual player of modern times – a worthy successor to his fellow county man Frank Burke, who achieved fame on Gaelic fields with his adopted Dublin, winning hurling titles in 1917 and 1920 and football titles in 1921, 1922 and 1923.

His inter-county football career stretched from 1962 to 1978, "and in that period we were beaten in five Leinster finals by Meath, Offaly and Dublin." In 1965, Pat captained the Kildare under-21 football team to All-Ireland victory over Cork. But Kildare had its hurlers too. There were no golden eras, just little pockets of success – and Pat shared in them all.

He was only seventeen in 1962 when he played in goal for the Kildare junior hurling team that beat London in the final to bring the Lily Whites their first hurling title. The Kildare success was repeated in 1966 with victory over Warwickshire at Birmingham. Pat, as captain and centre half-back, had a brilliant game. Hurling was improving in Kildare, and further honours came Pat's way in 1969 with a Division 2 National Hurling League and an All-Ireland intermediate success. "One thing I remember about the intermediate win was that we beat Cork in Thurles, and about five of the Cork team subsequently won All-Ireland senior medals."

His performances on the hurling field brought him to the notice of the Leinster Railway Cup selectors. He was picked for trial games; he impressed. It led to him being chosen at centre-back in 1971 and 1972 and at left full-back in 1974, 1975 and 1976. He won Railway Cup medals in every year except 1976. I queried the gap in 1973. It was caused by a sending off in a club game for an accidental offence – for which Pat never forgave the referee.

In the Railway Cup games he was playing with the cream of the hurling world of those days. He was at home in their presence. Among them were: Pat Nolan, Damien Martin, Noel Skehan, Jim Treacy, Dan Quigley, Pa Dillon, Frank Cummins, Pat Delaney, Eddie Keher, Tony Doran, "Fan" Larkin, Martin Coogan, Barney Moylan, Kieran Purcell, Pádraig Horan, Pat Henderson and Mick Jacob.

The seventies were rewarding times for Pat. In 1974 he won an All-Ireland senior hurling "B" medal and a Division 2 National League football medal. On St Patrick's Day he won his first and only Railway Cup football medal when he came on as a sub in the defeat of Connaught. On the following day he won his third Railway Cup hurling title when Leinster defeated Munster. That dual Railway Cup success placed him among a select band. Twice in the mid-seventies he was chosen as a dual All-Star replacement. It was a tremendous honour – a fitting reward for a great exponent of our Gaelic games.

Pat played his club hurling with Éire Óg and his football with Raheen. In 1964 they won the county double, and in 1984 he made a comeback with a view to repeating the double in the Centenary year. He had a 50 per cent success: the hurling was won.

He sees hurling as "a better game to play than football". As to which he was better at – "I would like to think I was a better hurler, but probably I was a better footballer."

GAA affairs have always been central to Pat's life and he has occupied many key positions, including coaching the youth. This affable and quietly spoken Kildare man has been a wonderful ambassador for the GAA.

BILLY FITZPATRICK
KILKENNY

Born: 1954
Interviewed: 2002

"Back in the early sixties growing up in Johnstown, hitting the ball against the gable end of our house, I dreamed of playing in Croke Park, of winning All-Irelands for Kilkenny. I was lucky enough to achieve all those things. I was lucky enough to be part of a great Kilkenny team in the early seventies – and a great Fenian team in that era. The experience I gained from that time was to stand me in great stead in following years. Hurling was a great and enjoyable part of my life. Friendships were made that have lasted a lifetime. While the 1983 All-Ireland was probably the pinnacle of my career, I get as much satisfaction from the four county titles with the Fenians as anything else in my career. I came across so many great players that it is nearly impossible to single a few out. I would like to think that I gave my family and friends some happy memories during my career and that my own kids will be proud of my achievements in the years ahead."

Billy Fitzpatrick – son of John and Bridget (née Farrell), an aunt of Pa Dillon of Kilkenny hurling renown, was only twenty-one years old when he led the men in Black and Amber around Croke Park prior to the All-Ireland final against Galway on Sunday 7 September 1975. It would be the first seventy-minute final in the history of hurling.

Though young in years, Billy had many hurling hours put up on his camán. Many victories and much success had come his way.

In 1971 he won an All-Ireland Colleges' hurling title with St Kieran's College. The following year he was captain when they lost the final to Farrenferris – one of his great disappointments. However, there was compensation. He won an All-Ireland minor medal when Kilkenny had a resounding victory over Cork. In that game he gave evidence of his scoring potency and potential with a personal tally of 3:4 from the left half-forward position.

County titles with his club Fenians were won in 1972, 1973 and 1974. All-Ireland senior and under-21 titles were won in 1974. According to Billy, "It all seemed so simple." As a consequence, the significance of the glory associated with being captain in 1975 passed Billy by: "It would have meant a lot more if it came after a lean spell."

In 1975 Billy was playing with a great Kilkenny outfit – a team with a remarkable forward unit, one of the greats of hurling – Crotty, Delaney, Fitzpatrick, Brennan, Purcell and Keher. Kilkenny were contesting their fifth All-Ireland final in a row and were about to win their third out of five appearances. GAA President Donal Keenan of Roscommon presented the MacCarthy Cup to Billy. Another triumphant hurling return to the Marble City was underway.

Billy played in six All-Ireland senior hurling finals and was successful on five occasions. It was a remarkable success rate. And yet, before each final, he experienced the "butterflies": "The worst time of the day for me was always around 12.30. You had that sinking feeling. Things improved after that, although watching the minors didn't do you any good either. You saw them sending over points from seventy yards and thought, 'I'll be expected to do that too.'"

Billy was a classical hurling forward – skilled, speedy, sporting, consistently accurate, a clinical finisher, often Kilkenny's leading marksman. He made everything about the game look simple and effortless for he played with an art that concealed art. His repertoire was vast and was displayed to the full in the All-Ireland final of 1983 against Cork.

Kilkenny won by 2:14 to 2:12. Victory was largely due to a tour-de-force performance by Billy. He finished with a personal tally of ten points (five from frees). Over the hour he caused havoc in the Cork defence. Playing with élan and abandon he gave a dream performance, with deft touches, delightful artistry, classical skills – a master craftsman. He was voted Man of the Match. He won his second successive All-Star.

His was a display to proudly recount in years to come to his grand-children – a story he can tell with lots of superlatives. And no doubt, the passage of time will add a glitter of nostalgia to his recollections.

To watch Billy Fitzpatrick in full flight, displaying all his artistry and wizardry, was a hurling delight. Kevin Cashman, sports journalist, had this to say of Billy: "Indeed it is arguable – and some Cats do so argue – that, for sheer skill and scoring potential, Billy Fitzpatrick was Keher's equal. But Fitz. had a relaxed and whimsical soul which would not drive him to the top of the inter-county heap."

Billy was one of the all-time greats. His county senior career lasted from 1973 to 1986. Carve his name with pride among the hurling immortals.

JOHNNY FLAHERTY
OFFALY

Born: 1947
Interviewed: 1996

"Hurling was always a big part of my life. I can never remember the time that I was without a hurley. I got more enjoyment out of hurling than anything in my lifetime.

"In Kinnitty, where I come from, hurling was the only game played. We had it for dinner, breakfast, and tea. After that we went to the hurling field at night to develop us as young boys and men. Little would I have thought in my early career that hurling would have been so good to me and that one day I would end up playing in an All-Ireland for the county.

"There were so many happy occasions – too numerous to mention here, because every match would have been an All-Ireland in itself. If I had one regret it would have been that when Offaly did reach its first All-Ireland in 1981 – well past my prime – that it would have been ten years sooner."

Johnny exudes animation as he talks about the game of hurling, which has played a great part in his life since his juvenile days. He had his first great day in 1957 at the age of ten when he won a juvenile title with Kinnitty. "I was on for about only ten minutes but in that time I scored 1:2." And he was still scoring thirty-seven years later when he helped Kinnitty to win a county junior final in 1994.

Johnny played minor for Offaly in 1964 and 1965 before progressing to senior ranks in 1966.

In the Leinster Championship of 1969 Offaly showed they had the potential to be a hurling force when they defeated the All-Ireland title holders, Wexford, in the semi-final. So for the first time in forty-one years an Offaly senior hurling team was in the Leinster final; their opponents, Kilkenny. They performed gallantly and lost by two points, 3:9 to 0:16; and those sixteen scores showed how much they dominated outfield. Unfortunately, it was an ageing team. The breakthrough was a decade away; only Damien Martin and Johnny Flaherty would survive from the squad of 1969, and they would both emerge with added craft, cunning, and skill.

Johnny spent from 1971 to 1977 in the US, although he did come home to play in 1973 and 1974, but without success.

Johnny had the honour in 1973 of being on a ten-day South Pacific tour. "This was arranged by John 'Kerry' O'Donnell – Mr GAA in New York. We were joined by Ollie Walsh, Mick O'Connell, Christy Ring, and Niall Sheehy. We toured Australia and New Zealand and visited Hawaii on the way back. I remember a hurling game we played in Auckland. I was centre-back and Ring was corner-back. On one occasion I wasn't clearing fast enough for Ring's liking so he lashed on the ball and in the process belted me across the knees. As I limped away I could hear him say, 'Are you all right, boy? Are you all right, boy?'"

Back in Ireland after his sojourn in North America he found himself among the substitutes when Kinnitty lined out for the county final. Then fate took a hand. Pat Delaney got injured in the pre-match puck-about. Enter Johnny Flaherty. "The Kinnitty score was 1:8. I scored the eight points and made the goal." Johnny collected his second county senior medal.

On the pitch this extrovert personality was a bundle of energy: fast, fiercely competitive, opportunist. We didn't really see him, and his vast range of hurling skills, in his heyday. Offaly were out of the limelight and

Johnny was playing most of his hurling in America. We saw him in his twilight years; he shone brightly. Let's recall those years.

It was the Leinster final of 1980 against Kilkenny. Showing grit, courage, resolve, and stamina, mingled with much quality hurling, Offaly emerged triumphant 3:17 to 5:10. Delirious pandemonium. Offaly, Leinster senior hurling champions for the first time. Johnny, one of many heroes.

Now to 1981. After a nine-month stint in America, Johnny returned in May. Offaly retained their Leinster crown with a 3:12 to 2:13 victory over Wexford. Awarding Johnny Sports Star of the Week, the *Irish Independent* wrote:

> The cheer which greeted that Johnny Flaherty point near the end of the Leinster Senior Hurling Championship final in Croke Park last Sunday was not so much a victory roar as a tribute to the veteran Offaly corner-forward. His contribution of a goal and two points in the downfall of Wexford capped an all-round quality display of class hurling which helped steer Offaly to their first All-Ireland final next September. Many believe that Flaherty's part was a vital one and it certainly earns our award Sports Star of the Week.

Now to the All-Ireland final of 1981 against Galway. Five minutes to go and Galway two points up – clinging on, yet not looking like losing. Offaly attack; Brendan Birmingham passes to Johnny Flaherty in front of goal. "I was going to palm the ball onwards as Éamonn Cregan had done the previous year against Galway to score a great goal. But instant second thoughts said don't. I grabbed it and palmed it over my left shoulder to the net." It won the game for Offaly – victory in their first All-Ireland final.

On Friday, 11 September, the *Westmeath-Offaly Independent* wrote:

> All seventeen players who participated in the game will be feted as heroes… Johnny Flaherty's contribution was probably more positive for in the years ahead nobody will forget the man who scored the winning goal. However, his reputation should not be based on that score alone for throughout the game he was easily Offaly's most dangerous forward and obviously the man whom Galway most feared.

ÉAMON GRIMES
LIMERICK

Born: 1947
Interviewed: 1997

"A moment of triumph": Éamon with the MacCarthy Cup in the Hogan Stand in 1973.

At ten years of age Éamon Grimes got his first "real" hurley, from Santa Claus; before that he used an assortment of home-made ones. His hurling brilliance quickly manifested itself. He played Harty Cup hurling for four years at Limerick CBS, and when he won his first of three Harty Cup medals in 1964 he was one of the youngest winners ever in this intensely competitive and prestigious competition. In 1966 he was proud to captain the team to its third-in-a-row success.

The triumph of 1964 led to All-Ireland success with a win over St Peter's College, Wexford. He was magnificent in that game. An article in the *Limerick Yearbook* of 1972 gave the following description: "It was in Croke Park in April 1964 and all over the field one could hear people asking – who is number 12, that blonde lad on the Limerick team? It was of course Éamon Grimes, and I doubt very much that any forward display from a college lad at Croke Park for a long time could possibly measure up to his showing, which was superb, for on top of scoring two great goals against the breeze, young Grimes never lost a tussle for possession; for his solo running was a treat, and his first-time pulling too set an example for his colleagues."

In 1965 they lost the final to St Kieran's, Kilkenny, on the score 6:9 to 6:1. But they got revenge the following year when they defeated St Kieran's in the semi-final, 8:9 to 3:9, before going on to beat St Mary's, Galway, in the final.

1966 was the year he got his call-up to the Limerick senior hurling team. "It was the first round against Tipperary, who had won the All-Ireland title in 1964 and 1965. They were favourites to win three in a row. Well, we surprised them. Éamonn Cregan had a super game, scoring 3:5 out of a winning score of 4:12 to 2:9. There were three Éamons in the half-forward line: Cregan, Carey, and Grimes. It was a great win − the first time Limerick had beaten Tipperary in the championship since 1948. It was the day before the Leaving Cert. I took an awful chance."

Éamon's county senior career stretched from that first-round game of 1966 to when he came on as a sub for Willie Fitzmaurice in the All-Ireland final of 1980. The best Limerick team he played on? "The 1966 team was by far the best. We lost the semi-final to Cork in Killarney by two points in rather controversial circumstances - a disallowed goal."

The victory Éamon got most enjoyment from was the 1973 Munster final defeat of Tipperary. He was captain. "I'd say that gave me more enjoyment than any other win. To beat Tipperary on their home ground on a terrible warm day in a final − great. Mícheál Ó Muircheartaigh says it was one of the best games he has seen." It was certainly full of drama and excitement and finished with a suspense that would do justice to any Hitchcock thriller. After about ten minutes Limerick had gone seven points up. At half time they trailed by four points − 2:9 to 3:2. A quarter of an hour into the second half Limerick had forged ahead by four points − 6:3 to 2:11. The tension was terrible. The heat was intense.

With a little over five minutes to go Tipperary go one point up. Limerick draw level and forge one point ahead. Three minutes to go; the atmosphere is electric. A point, and Tipp draw level. A little over a minute remaining; then a seventy to Limerick, and the referee, Mick Slattery of Clare, tells Richie Bennis he must score direct. Cool as a cucumber, Richie bends, lifts, and strikes, and the white flag waving sends Limerick fans delirious − the first Munster title since 1955. Seán Foley has Richie Bennis on the ground in a bear-hug of enthusiastic congratulations.

That victory paved the way to Croke Park, and Limerick faced Kilkenny in the final on the first Sunday in September. "What can you say about it? Nothing was going to beat us that day – no team in Ireland: we knew we would win the All-Ireland title when we beat Tipperary in Thurles." Éamon played a captain's part, leading by example. He received the Hurler of the Year award.

Éamon was also a first-class athlete. He represented his school in the 100 yards and 220 yards. Those were his favourite distances. He won many county events, which also included distances of 440 yards and 880 yards. He is particularly proud of the fact that the time record in Ireland for the junior relay race consisting of laps of 220, 220, 440 and 880 yards (one-mile relay) established in the late sixties by himself, Joe Laffan, Noel Spellesy and Dick Power, while representing Limerick, still stands.

Éamon won two All-Star awards, and the narrations associated with those awards tell us much about the man:

"1973. For his seemingly limitless energy; his desire to work all over the field, qualities which have made him a natural leader and a high scorer."

"1975. For his seemingly unlimited energy, his incisive running and sharpness in picking off scores."

Éamon was undoubtedly one of the outstanding hurlers of his day. So taken was J.P. McManus by the spirit of the indefatigable Éamon that he felt compelled to name one of his horses "Grimes" as a gesture to the memory of a great hurler and athlete.

PAT HARTIGAN
LIMERICK

Born: 1950
Interviewed: 1993

"Little did I think that growing up in Donoughmore, a hinterland of
Limerick City, as a young lad during the fifties that it would provide me in
the future with a culture that was to play a significant part in developing
me through boyhood, to the present day.

"The culture into which I was born blessed me by creating a platform
for me to grow, appreciate and enjoy the true values of rural Ireland. The
culture which I refer to is one where I learned to strive for success, both
in mind and body, where one's own ability to succeed was only surpassed
by one's ability to be humble.

"This culture was fashioned through school, work and play. All three
were consistently tangible to one another, where play followed work, and
work followed school. Without school and work there could be no play.
With hindsight it was a marvellous way to utilise your playtime to the
fullest.

"Playtime was dominated by the game of hurling. During the 1950s one's aim was to be a John Doyle, a Christy Ring or, indeed, an Art Foley. These were the men most often spoken of by our forefathers, and to dream of being one of these giants would almost assure you a place in eternal folklore.

"The privilege and honour to play for my club South Liberties was never surpassed by any sporting achievement that came my way through-out my playing career. Even today, every facet of my sporting life is dulled in comparison to the glorious memories I hold within myself from my playing days with South Liberties. Wouldn't it be great to be little boys again?"

A serious eye injury, in a freak accident, while training for the Munster final of 1979 against Cork, ended Pat's hurling career. He wasn't yet twenty-nine. So Pat, this warrior-like giant, in superb physical shape and health, had to abandon the game he adored and adorned at the height of his career.

Happily, he had much to look back on – All-Ireland, Railway Cup, Oireachtas, Provincial, National League and county title honours. He received five All-Star awards in a row from 1971 to 1975 in the full-back position – a remarkable record. He is especially proud of the 1973 All-Star award. He was the only nominee and therefore an automatic choice. His school days brought many honours too. With Limerick CBS he won Harty Cup honours in 1966 and 1967. The Munster title of 1966 was converted into All-Ireland honours. He played minor hurling for Limerick for four years from 1965–1968 and he played in six successive years at under-21 level from 1966 to 1971.

But it wasn't sufficient to be able to just look back. Pat now needed something to fill the vacuum. It came mainly in two forms. The first was athletics which he was always good at since his school days – especially the sixteen-pound shot putt. In that competition, he represented Ireland on four occasions, winning in Dublin in 1968 and taking second place in Spain in 1969. The second was the Puck Fada competition which he won in 1981 and 1983. "It brought me a huge element of compensation, to be able to handle a hurley again and puck the ball, to get an opportunity to compete."

Without a doubt, 1973 was the year of hurling highlights for Pat – the year of the breakthrough. In Semple Stadium in Thurles, Limerick faced Tipperary in the Munster final.

"It was a mid-July day and the humidity was overpowering. The tension was incredible. This was Tipp's home ground where they would be perceived by many as invincible. Even in the dressing-room the humidity was evident. I never saw so much water spilled in any dressing-room. It was approaching time to go out onto the pitch. Éamon Grimes spoke. Holding up his jersey he said, 'This is what it's about – today is the day. Any man who thinks this isn't worth dying for, stay here – we will go out without you.' We all shared his feelings. We didn't need motivation going out to play Tipperary.

"Running onto the pitch, the roar of the crowd was deafening. Out on the pitch I got a feeling of claustrophobia – every exit was cut off, there was a feeling of no air; it was a cauldron of noise." A tense thriller ended with the last puck of the game when Richie Bennis sent over the winner from a seventy. And then he was engulfed.

Pat recalls the dying seconds in the All-Ireland final against Kilkenny: "We were now seven points ahead. The crowd was coming in over the Canal End – massing and increasing. I asked the umpire how much time was left. He waved his hands. I wasn't sure what it meant. Then I saw the referee Mick Slattery of Clare with his hand up. I still can't remember whether I pucked out the ball or not." They followed Éamon Grimes to the Hogan Stand. The MacCarthy Cup was on the way to the Shannonside for the first time in thirty three years.

Pat was a giant of the hurling arena – 6'3" and 14 st. 10 lbs, agile and athletic, dedicated and disciplined; a modern-day Cúchulainn and a shining example to youth. His sportsmanship was impeccable. It was an unwritten precept of Pat's never to act in a manner on the hurling field that would in any way sully the image of the great game. "It would upset me to be remembered as a dirty player – or mean or dangerous. Ray Cummins was the best full-forward I played on – a friendship was forged in those clashes on the pitch. Joe McKenna was the best full-forward I never played on – nor would I have looked forward to opposing him."

PAT HENDERSON
KILKENNY

Born: 1943
Interviewed: 1994

1975 All-Ireland winners: John (minor), Pat
(senior) and Ger (under-21).

"I developed a love of hurling at a very early age when my father, who never played the game, used bring me as a small boy to games in Thurles, Kilkenny and Portlaoise. In those early days, late forties and early fifties, I remember seeing players like Ring, Langton and, indeed, Harry Gray of Laois in action. In those days I tried in the local national school to emulate the feats of those heroes of the time. In the early fifties I also watched the famous Rackard brothers of Wexford in action and when we played our own little games around the farmyard at home or in the schoolyard, we would assume the role of Rackard or Langton or Ring.

"When I left national school and went to Thurles CBS in the mid-fifties, I arrived in a real hot bed of hurling. In my second year at college I won my first medal. In 1958 Tipp. won the senior title and Tony Wall brought the MacCarthy Cup to the school. John O'Grady, one of my teachers, was in fact the goalkeeper. This occasion instilled a great desire in me to play in an All-Ireland and represent my county.

"In 1961 I first wore the black and amber at minor level and it was with this team I first came under the influence of Rev. Fr Tommy Maher.

"I have been fortunate to have lived, played and coached in a great era of Kilkenny hurling, to have won every honour in the game with my county.

"I would rate on a par with any of the great inter-county [players] the players and members of my own club 'Fenians Johnstown' who came together to form that club in the late sixties and in 1970 won the first senior title for the parish. I was honoured to have captained that team which went on to win four more senior titles between 1970 and 1977. In 1977 both John and Ger also played on the winning team and they both then went on to play inter-county with distinction.

"I have been directly involved in the game over the past twenty-five years and this has been possible because of the great interest in and love of the game by all of my family, in particular Mary, my wife, and I am delighted to see my three sons so actively involved now as players and deriving much enjoyment from it."

Pat Henderson was one of hurling's most majestic centre half-backs. A career that spanned fifteen years is dotted with numerous outstanding performances. No honour of the day eluded him. He was Hurler of the Year in 1974.

In September 1971 Pat was heading for twenty-nine years of age and was dropped. He, together with Ollie Walsh, was made to shoulder the blame for the All-Ireland defeat by Tipperary. There followed months of watching from the sideline. But Put was determined to come back. "I wasn't going to give up. It was the stubbornness in me."

Centre-back was his favourite position. In that demanding berth he gave performances that made him comparable as a hurler to the élite centre-backs of the game – John Keane (Waterford), Jim Regan (Cork), Paddy Clohessy (Limerick), Billy and Bobby Rackard (Wexford), and Pat Stake-lum and Tony Wall (Tipperary).

Watching him perform on the field, there were occasions when one got the feeling that the man was indestructible. It is therefore hard to believe that in 1990, at the young age of forty-seven, he had to undergo a quad-ruple by-pass. "I played a hurling match of sorts – Fenians Johnstown v Dicksboro – three weeks before. I played squash the week before. It all came to light when I went for a check-up.' But his physical fitness stood to him and he was back at work within six weeks. In 1993 he coached Dicksboro who ironically defeated his native Johnstown – powered by his brothers Ger and John – in the final. He finds it as energy sapping on the sidelines as it was on the pitch. "I play every ball. I should relax a bit but I can't. I got the coaching job back in 1982 (having been sacked in 1980) and was there for five years. We won All-Ireland and League doubles in 1982 and 1983."

Pat arrived on the scene at a time when a golden era in Kilkenny hurling was dawning. Between 1964 and 1978 he played in ten All-Ireland finals and was successful five times – "and the butterflies, rather than diminishing, increased as time went on." Let's recall three memorable occasions.

First of all, there was 1967. "I had lost in two All-Ireland finals to Tipp. and Cork in 1964 and 1966 respectively. I would have felt devastated to have lost a third. The fact that it was my first All-Ireland win made it very sweet. After that, the team continued to improve and go from success to success." In a Kilkenny team that had many stars that day, Pat Henderson was a stone wall at centre-back and in the course of the hour out-hurled three different opponents.

Next comes 1972. In the All-Ireland final against Cork we saw evidence of the magic and splendour of Kilkenny hurling. This was particularly so in the last quarter – when Kilkenny really took control to wipe out an eight- point deficit and win by seven points. "We were dead – but we came back. I had a reasonably good game." It was an understatement. Pat rose to great heights in what was a famous victory.

Lastly, there was 1975. This was the year he won his last All-Ireland medal – his fifth. But more especially it was a family year, a unique year for the Henderson family. As well as Pat winning a senior medal, Ger won an under-21 and John won a minor. It was a unique triple for Kilkenny and the Henderson family. It may never be repeated.

PADRAIG HORAN
OFFALY

Born: 1950
Interviewed: 1994

"The first thing I can remember of hurling was my father buying me a new hurley for my birthday. The following Sunday my brothers and some friends were playing hurling out in the field at the front of our house. I was mad to show off my new stick but nobody could find it. The following morning my mother, when making up my bed, got the hurley under my pillow. And from that day on I probably never left a hurley out of my hand, whether going for the cows or getting a bucket of water from the well.

"Hurling was always my first love in sport and being born into a hurling family always made things that bit special. Hurling would start every Sunday at about 1.00 p.m. We broke for to listen to Mícheál O'Hehir at 3.00 or 3.30 p.m.

"In about 1962, St Rynagh's was formed and from there things started to move. The years 1965 and 1966 brought the club their first Offaly senior success and the rest has now been written in history. For me, the turning point came in 1971 when I decided to opt out of football and "stick" with hurling. I believed that it would be in hurling that success would come and not as it turned out that year. But it was still great to be on the Hill in 1971 getting wet to the skin when Offaly won their first All-Ireland – even if it was football – and I probably could have been out there playing.

"I always loved Offaly and Offaly hurling and knew that some day Offaly would win an All-Ireland. So, while 1981 was a long time coming, to me it was always on the way. Looking back, I would say that winning was something I never got carried away with. But losing was something I hated. Hurling probably fits fourth into my life – after God, my family and work. When I think of the friends I have made through the game I am glad and always grateful that my father gave me that hurley for my sixth birthday."

Pádraig Horan had a long and illustrious career in hurling that stretched over a period of almost seventeen years. He was extremely versatile – reflected in the fact that he played in every position except goal for his native Offaly. Pádraig at the beginning of his career established a reputation as an outstanding and uncompromising defender. For four years from 1973 to 1976 he was full-back on the Leinster team and won three Railway Cup medals.

Centre-back was Padraig's favourite position. "I loved to play there. I found hurling easy at centre-back. I loved watching centre-backs in action – Pat Henderson, Ger Henderson, Dan Quigley, Jimmy Cullinane and Sean Stack. But my idol was Tony Wall of Tipperary. I was a better back than a forward and when playing in the centre – where I played my best hurling – I liked to play slightly behind my wing men. It's easy hurl that way."

It was as a forward that Pádraig won his two All-Ireland titles in 1981 (captain) and 1985. As a forward, he was strong and forceful. He used his defensive experience to make life difficult for his opponent. He was crafty and difficult to mark and could score even with very little room to manoeuvre. After his performance in the 1985 final, he was nominated Man of the Match. He also got his only All-Star award.

Pádraig remembers well the Centenary year final of 1984 in Thurles. "We let ourselves be made favourites and that was suicidal. It was a day I would love to have been at centre-back. I was worried from the moment we left in the bus from the hotel. It was like a carnival atmosphere and some were too confident. I knew we were in trouble. It was a game we might have won but then if we did we mightn't have won in 1985 – these things tend to balance out."

I asked him if he remembered the early moments when he gathered a ball that had "goal" written all over it and sent it over the bar? "I still dream about it. I think about it every morning. I gathered the ball behind Donal O'Grady's head and went to flick it over Ger Cunningham's head into the net – but it went over the bar. An early score would have settled us. I tend to remember the goals I missed rather than the ones I scored. I never stayed awake on a night before a match. When I did stay awake it was always the night after a match. I stayed in Cashel the night after the All-Ireland. I didn't sleep. I kept waking up thinking of the ball that went over the bar."

Reflecting in general over his long career, he had the following to say. "The 1969 team had great scoring power and was probably the best forward combination Offaly produced. In my seventeen years I played on better Offaly teams than those that won the All-Irelands. Paddy Molloy was one of the best hurlers I saw. He had ferocious speed and tremendous skill. We had a great team in 1982 – probably our best team of the eighties. We came back after an All-Star trip and beat a good Wexford team. We lost the Leinster title by two points to Kilkenny. It was the one year I felt we could have won another All- Ireland title. We were a cleverer team in 1985 than in 1981. But we missed Johnny Flaherty. We knew Galway would probably be all over us at times but that if we kept in touch we'd be OK – and that's what happened."

Padraig Horan

MICK JACOB
WEXFORD

Born: 1946
Interviewed: 1995

"I can recall waving to fans as they drove by our house on the way to the All-Ireland finals of 1955 and 1956.

"I began my adult playing career at sixteen years of age as a goalkeeper on our junior team, a position I was to occupy for four years on the county under-21 team, finishing up with them as a midfielder in 1967. During my senior inter-county career, I played first as a midfielder and then as a defender, while nowadays I usually wear the number 14 jersey for Oulart junior team. The highlight of my senior inter-county career was being picked as centre-back on the All-Star teams of 1972, 1976, and 1977; while the biggest disappointment was losing three All-Ireland finals in the seventies.

"On the club scene, the greatest day for Oulart-the-Ballagh was 16 October 1994, when we won the county senior hurling title for the first time, having been defeated in five finals in twenty-five years. I was proud to be a selector with that team. This year [1996] will be my forty-first playing hurling, as boy and man.

"I would like to see clubs and the GAA make it compulsory for players to wear helmets with face guards, in order to reduce facial injuries and to allay any fears that parents might have about their children playing the greatest game in the world."

No All-Ireland senior medal came Mick's way, although he did have the consolation of a medal as a sub in 1968 when Wexford, for the second time in a decade, surprised and shocked the favourites, Tipperary. Defeat was Wexford's lot in 1970, 1976, and 1977, each time at the hands of Cork, their bogey team. In particular, 1976 was a bitter disappointment: "We beat Kilkenny by seventeen points in the Leinster final. They were going for three in a row and had a great team. No one gave us a chance; we were written off. That's what made the win so satisfying. We hurled like tigers that day. It was probably the best team display during my time with Wexford. We then had two great games with Galway at Páirc Uí Chaoimh – won the replay by a goal. Both games were terrible fast, and the heat was intense. They were played within a week of each other and were really energy-sapping."

That brought Wexford to the final against Cork; and after the victories over teams of the quality of Kilkenny and Galway, they had every right to feel confident. And that confidence seemed well founded when, after six minutes, they led Cork by 2:2 to nil and seemed rampant. But Cork steadied and were level at half time. When the final whistle blew, Cork were ahead 2:21 to 4:11, their twenty-second title. "It was a game we could have won. We missed a number of good chances; we failed to score in the last quarter of an hour. It was my biggest disappointment in the purple and gold. The entire team were shattered – sick for months afterwards. We let it slip. Cork brought on John Horgan in defence and made switches that settled them."

Those who were at the game will remember the splendour and magnificence of Mick Jacob's hurling at centre-back, and in the course of the game he was opposed by four different Cork players: Brendan Cummins, Mick Malone, Ray Cummins and Jimmy Barry Murphy. He was equally superb three years earlier when Wexford beat Limerick in a thrilling National League final that gave Mick his only league medal. In 1975, as a replacement, All-Star he was nominated Player of the Series in the American tour.

He was a member of the Wexford team that won the All-Ireland Masters (over-forty) title in 1991. He played junior "A" hurling with his club in 1995 at corner-forward and scored 2:1 in one of those games, and he in his fiftieth year.

His style was tidy and economical. His concentration made him ever alert. Countless hours of diligent practice produced a clean striker with great positional sense. Above all, he was a ball player – yet there was no flinching in hip-to-hip and shoulder-to-shoulder exchanges, all within the canons of good sportsmanship. It all added up to a centre half-back in the classical mould. Mick's approach to hurling was one of total dedication and commitment. He was always superbly fit: "I always did plenty of running on my own – through the fields, over the ditches, up the hills. You build up stamina and then work on speed. If you want to last the pace at top level you must have strength in the legs and wind in the lungs.' His slight, sinewy figure had hidden within it strands of steel and vast quantities of energy.

He got an accidental blow of the sliotar in the eye, hit full force from four yards' range. His wife, Breda, said she used to think that if you were fit and skilful you would always avoid such an injury; but freak circumstances do arise, and that is what happened to Mick, who now maintains that "anyone who plays hurling without the facial-guarded helmet is mad."

The household is immersed in GAA affairs. Everything seems to revolve around hurling and football. Hurleys and boots are clearly visible. Breda, a native of historic Boolavogue, played camogie at junior level with Wexford and is as enthusiastic and involved as Mick in the local club and its under-age players.

The enthusiasm of Mick and Breda has proved highly infectious and has rubbed off on their family: Mick, Helena, Rory and Ursula. All four joined enthusiastically in the discussions, which went on well past bedtime, and little Ursula finished up asleep on the floor.

That was October 1995. On Sunday, 11 September 2011, Ursula captained the Wexford senior camogie team to All-Ireland glory with victory over Galway. Her sister Helena made it a family double by winning an intermediate title on the same day in a victory over Antrim.

Michael Jacob

PHIL "FAN" LARKIN
KILKENNY

Born: 1941
Interviewed: 1997

"The years 1969–1982 were very successful ones for my club, James Stephens. During that time we contested seven County Championship finals, winning four.

"One of the real highlights of my career was our championship victory over the Fenians in 1969. This was our first success since 1937, so naturally there was great excitement and celebration in the Village.

"Our next big year was 1975, when I had the honour of captaining James Stephens. We beat Galmoy in the county final and thus qualified to represent Kilkenny in the All-Ireland Club Championship for the first time. After a great Leinster campaign, we qualified to meet famed Black-rock in the All-Ireland final at Semple Stadium. After a terrific game against powerful opponents, we emerged victorious and became the first

Leinster team to win this highly valued championship. Receiving the cup that day for my club was probably the highlight of my sporting career.

"Before retiring, I had the pleasure of tasting success at local and national level again. In 1981 we beat the Fenians in the county final and Mount Sion in the All-Ireland final."

Fan's father, Paddy, small in stature and sporting a peaked cap, was an outstanding hurling stalwart of the thirties. When I mentioned this to Fan he dismissed it in mischievous tones, saying, "Sure he had nothing else to do."

Fan, christened Philip Francis, who won his first All-Ireland medal in 1963, inherited the hurling skills, the physical attributes and the grim resolve associated with his father. He had an equally outstanding hurling career, even though he had to watch the finals of 1966, 1967 and 1969 from Hill 16. "I was blamed for the 1964 defeat against Tipp. I was picked that day at left-full-back instead of right-full-back, because the selectors thought Sean McLoughlin was too tall for me to handle. So I found myself playing on Donie Nealon. He scored three goals. I was at fault for one but not the other two. I must say that Donie was the best forward I ever hurled on. He was a most complete hurler: he had everything."

Fan returned to the county scene in the 1970s. The break came for him when his club, James Stephens, won the county title in 1969. Rich harvests lay ahead.

"I grew up in a household where hurling was like religion. My mother played camogie with Kilkenny in the thirties. I remember my father often talking about Mick Mackey, Paddy Clohessy and Paddy Scanlon from Limerick. He played many times against them. He talked a lot, too, about Paddy Phelan and his lifetime friends Paddy Grace and Jimmy Langton. I think his favourite hurler was Peter Blanchfield; they were great friends.

"He took me to the All-Ireland final of 1947. I don't remember anything at all about it. I was only six. He took me again in 1956, when he had a ticket for the Cusack Stand. I had none, and an official wouldn't let us in on the one ticket. My father asked to see Pádraig Ó Caoimh – they were both very friendly. He came down and got us in." It was around this time too that Fan, in the company of his father, met Mícheál O'Hehir one Sunday in Wexford Park. He cherishes the memory.

Fan won his first Leinster title of the seventies in 1971, and from then until he retired, after the All-Ireland success of 1979, hurling honours of all descriptions flowed his way. He was one of the outstanding full-back line defenders of the decade, and due recognition for this came his way through four All-Star awards and annual selection on the Railway Cup panel from 1972 onwards. Following proudly in the footsteps of his father, he played in nine All-Ireland finals and won five. He was an extremely tight defender whose forte was first-time hurling. He was one of the few who successfully coped with the elusive Ray Cummins of Cork. "I had a good teacher: my father. He played on a big man in the 1939 final – Ted Sullivan – and he knew how to handle him. When I played on Ray Cummins in the All-Ireland club final in Thurles in 1976 I was thirty-two years of age and wiser than when I was a young player. I knew Ray Cummins loved to reach to the sky and get the ball in his hand, and I didn't let him. I saw Ray give very good full-backs a terrible roasting."

Thurles pitch and the year 1976 call to mind some of Fan's most memorable moments. "In the space of three years I came away from Thurles with three major cups. I captained Kilkenny to a National League win over Clare after a replay in 1976. I captained my club, James Stephens, when we beat Blackrock in the All-Ireland club final of 1976 at Thurles. There is something special about a win with your club. A club is like a family. We won a second All-Ireland club title in 1982 when we beat Mount Sion. On the first of April 1979 I captained Leinster to a Railway Cup title over Connacht at Thurles. Thurles was a lucky place for me."

GER LOUGHNANE
CLARE

Born: 1953
Interviewed: 1997

"I suppose listening to the commentaries of the late Mícheál O'Hehir was the first inkling I got of the excitement and passion which the game of hurling arouses – a game which is a large part of the fabric of rural life in Ireland. Watching the expressions on the faces of our neighbours as they followed every puck of the ball and commented on every score filled me with a desire to be part of such a great game. I remember when I was very young hoping that Mícheál O'Hehir would still be commentating when I was playing and that he would mention my name on the radio.

"My ambition, when I set out, was to win a County Championship with Feakle and to win an All-Ireland with Clare. It is ironic that we would win the County Championship in my last game for Feakle, in 1988, after a lapse of about forty-three years, and that finally Clare should win an All-Ireland with me as manager rather than as a player. I couldn't have asked for anything better!"

A smile of elation covers Ger's face as he recalls the day he received the postcard informing him that he was selected to play for his native Clare against Tipperary in the Munster Minor Hurling Championship.

"I remember that day well. I remember where I was standing the very moment I got the postcard. I kept it – I still have it somewhere in the house. It was a great moment for me. I couldn't wait to put on the Clare jersey."

Ger loves the game of hurling. He exudes enthusiasm as he talks about every facet of it. Every time he donned the blue and gold of Clare a deep sense of pride gripped him; he felt as honoured the last time as the first time. Wearing the county jersey meant as much to him as his Railway Cup and National League triumphs and his All-Star award. Incidentally, his All-Star award of 1974 – his first of two – was Clare's first.

Ger was a member of a quite exceptional Clare team during the seventies and eighties. Munster and All-Ireland honours eluded them. Four occasions in particular stand out. In 1977, 1978 and 1986 they failed very narrowly to Cork in the Munster final, and on each occasion Cork went on to win the All-Ireland. In 1981, they ran up against Limerick and Joe McKenna (he scored 3:3). But they did contest three successive National League finals, winning in 1977 and 1978 at the expense of talented Kilkenny teams.

"Those league victories were like All-Irelands for us. The whole county was behind the team. I can remember the home matches at Tulla. The place would be thronged – standing on the hill. You would have to park your car and walk about two miles to the pitch." Ger was an outstanding defender and formed a great half-back line with two other superb hurlers, Sean Stack and Seán Hehir. For seven years in a row, from 1975 onwards, he was a regular on the Munster Railway Cup teams.

Ger had the ideal temperament for the big occasion. He admits to loving it and never getting flustered, whether as player or manager. But he does remember one big occasion in particular when things were difficult: "It was the 1978 Munster final against Cork in Thurles. The crowd was huge – one of the biggest for a Munster final; many were locked out. There was a tension in the air that I never felt before or since. It was a very hot day: it was electric on the field – so tense." In the eyes of many, Clare were favourites. It added to their burden. The mental preparation didn't match the physical. At half time, Cork led by five points to three and faced the breeze in the second half. It looked good for Clare. But the tension continued in the second half. "A goal might have relieved it but it never came." It ended thirteen points to eleven.

In September 1994, Ger became manager of the Clare senior hurling team. He immediately set about building the team's morale. His exuberance and enthusiasm infected the players. His approach, befitting his teaching profession, was hortative. He urged and encouraged; he praised and drove. He was a generator of confidence, a moulder of spirit. A man of unshakable faith in the potential of his panel and players, he imbued in them a deep pride in the jersey they wore, in the county they represented and in the game they played. He bred a winning mentality.

"The 1995 Munster semi-final against Cork was a bit of a nightmare. I think we shot twenty-two wides – over-anxious. We were the better team on the day but lucky to win – felt it had to be our year." And so it proved.

Limerick fell in the Munster final. Clare celebrations knew no bounds. The barrier that had haunted Clare since 1932 was now no more. Galway fell next. Now an All-Ireland date with Offaly.

The atmosphere on final day was carnival-like. Glorious sunshine, a wonderful array of colour and the uniqueness of the pairing all added extra glamour to the occasion. The presence in the attendance of John Joe Doyle and Tom McInerney – both heading for the ninety mark – who played in 1932 when Clare lost to Kilkenny, brought a touch of nostalgia to the day – a day of triumph.

Clare, with Ger still at the helm, won a further All-Ireland title in 1997 with a fine win over Tipperary in a stirring final.

JOE McDONAGH
GALWAY

Born: 1953
Interviewed: 1993

"Growing up in the heartland of South Galway, still under the charismatic influence of Michael Cusack since his soujourn there as a teacher, it was obvious I would become engaged in the only past-time of the area – hurling.

"I was very lucky that my involvement in the hurling coincided with the National Coiste Iomana drive of 1965. Here in Galway the administrative challenge was taken up by a pioneering and far-sighted board. Structures, both competitive and organisational, were put in place and I began with the first under-14 bunch to compete for my club in 1965. Regular organised coaching sessions replaced the haphazard games in the Turlough and eventually we reached our first-ever county final against mighty Castlegar in 1965. Though defeated, we learned a lot and the experience assisted us in winning divisional south board under-age titles in following years.

"By 1970 I had made the county minor team. We created a big surprise in defeating Wexford in the All-Ireland semi-final. Unfortunately a powerful Cork minor side defeated us comprehensively in the final. I'll never forget the roar of the crowd as we came out from under the Cusack Stand tunnel.

"The next major stepping stone was the All-Ireland under-21 success of 1972. Having embarked on a student working visit to New York earlier that summer, I was enjoying the life in the Big Apple and playing hurling for Galway, when a sudden telegraph came through inviting me home to join the panel for the All-Ireland final against Dublin. Galway had defeated Tipperary in the semi-final. I joined my colleagues in training and an unfortunate injury in a challenge against St Rynagh's left me struggling to regain fitness for the final. Though failing to make the first fifteen as a result, I was delighted to be able to come in as a substitute in the second half at midfield, and win my first All-Ireland medal.

"Following that victory in 1972, a number of us were invited to join the senior panel. Obviously the step up to senior was a big one and it took us some time to adjust. However, the long-term building programme under-taken by M.J. Flaherty, our coach, paid off some two years later when we coasted through Division IB of the league and defeated Cork in the National League quarter-final and a lethargic Kilkenny in the semi-final, before beating much-vaunted Tipperary in an historic final in Limerick. At last the barrier was broken and we looked forward with relish to the championship.

"Having qualified for the All-Ireland semi-final against Cork in 1975, we started the game in whirlwind fashion and created yet another sensation in qualifying for Galway's first senior final since 1958. It was heady stuff, and expectations were high, but in reality we were never a match for one of Kilkenny's greatest ever teams. My opponent that day was Kilkenny's young captain Billy Fitzpatrick. We have remained life-long friends since."

Following defeat by Ardrahan in the county final of 1978, Joe was chosen to captain Galway and finished up losing four finals – Oireachtas (1978), Railway Cup (1979), National League (1979) and All-Ireland (1979): "Undoubtedly, luck was not one of my major traits as captain."

"Having suffered a long illness after the 1979 final, I was delighted to be asked to rejoin my colleagues for the 1980 campaign. Though not playing, I felt as much a part of the team as the players since we had struggled and suffered since 1975. The euphoria that attended the 1980 final had to be seen to be believed. The long wait was over and suddenly Galway's hurling passion exploded. All the curses and psychological barriers had been dispelled. I'm glad to have lived to participate in and witness such a happening."

Joe McDonagh hails from the little parish of Ballindereen in south County Galway. His first real awakening to hurling came when his father took him to the Railway Cup final of 1963. There for the first time he saw Ring – pointed out to him by his father – in action for the last time in a major engagement outside of club.

Joe's greatest regret is missing out on the 1980 campaign. It is surely ironic that, when the great breakthrough came against Limerick on the first Sunday in September, two of Galway's finest ever wing-backs – Joe McDonagh and Iggy Clarke – were absent from the lineout through illness and injury respectively. Both, however, were able to savour the ecstasy of victory. After the great victory speech in the Gaelic tongue from captain Joe Connolly, the MacCarthy Cup was handed to Iggy Clarke and then Joe broke into a rendering of "The West's Awake" and all of Croke Park was filled with emotion. There were tears, too, as the frustrations of years of near misses were buried and the psychological barrier breached. "We sung that song as we came off the pitch after UCG had beaten Maynooth in the Fitzgibbon Cup final of 1977 – it was our victory anthem."

Joe's playing days are now a thing of the past but he remains involved with the GAA. He has been an officer of the Galway County Board since 1979 and Galway representative on the Central Council since 1988.

He is justifiably proud of Galway's contribution to modern hurling and his commitment to the great game – its spread and preservation – is total.

Joe McDonagh

DAMIEN MARTIN
OFFALY

Born: 1946
Interviewed: 1991

"Hurling was always part of life in Offaly. So too was club rivalry – a rivalry so intense that parish glory took priority over county honour.

"When I came to the Offaly panel for the 1964 championship, the players did not really know each other, and a number did not even talk to each other. Neither was there even one training session or get-together. Then Brother Denis, a Presentation Brother from Bantry, joined the Birr community. He got involved in the Offaly hurling team and we were on our way.

"The first thing he did was organise collective training, with a cup of tea and a sandwich afterwards. Over the years he built up a sense of comradeship in the panel, and made the lads proud to play for Offaly.

"Throughout the seventies Rynagh's won Leinster Club Champion-ships, beating the best in Wexford and Kilkenny, exploding the 'God-given rights' myth. This attitude passed through to the county panel – that we are as good as any. In 1979 Wexford beat us narrowly in the Leinster semi-final. We got promoted to Division 1 of the National League and had a good run beating Wexford in the quarter-final.

"I went to my club St Rynagh's and proposed an outside coach for Offaly for the 1980 championship. The proposal was carried – endorsed at County Board level – and Dermot Healy was appointed. He concentrated on the skills of the game and made us believe in ourselves.

"To Brother Denis, who built the foundations, and Dermot Healy, who finished the job, Offaly's hurling world, and especially the likes of myself who played under one or both men, can only say, 'Thank You.' For without them I certainly would have no All-Ireland medal."

As Damien walked from the pitch at Ashford after his first senior game with Offaly in the National League against Wicklow in 1964, a young Wicklow enthusiast ran up to him and asked for his autograph. Damien, still a teenager, "was stunned with surprise, and wondered if the young-ster was serious."

He knew, of course, what it was to have heroes. Tony Reddin was his goalkeeping idol, and for sportsmanship and overhead striking he was completely captivated by the hurling artistry of Galway midfielder Joe Salmon.

There was no sound reason in 1964 – based on tradition, that is – for Damien to have great expectations. A look at the Offaly record showed that the cupboard was very bare.

Patience and perseverance marked his career. It spanned twenty-two years – by any standards a remarkable innings. It had many and varied highlights: an outstanding display in 1969 against Kilkenny in the Lein-ster final, when Offaly lost by two points with a team that had many top-class hurlers; the special honour of an All-Star award in 1971; the superb reflex save from Noel Lane in the 1981 All- Ireland final – a save that arguably won the title for Offaly.

Damien used to travel to New York to play with the Offaly team there, and had as a team-mate Pat Dunney of Kildare – "He was great, a fantas-tic hurler." In the Summer of 1967 Damien travelled to the US and, with-out approval from GAA Head Office, played with Offaly. He got a two year suspension, but was re-instated the following Easter by the Mercy Committee.

He travelled as an All-Star in 1971 and received the Man of the Tour award in the US. He gave credit for his success to "a superb full-back line of Tony Maher (Cork), Pat Hartigan (Limerick) and Jim Treacy (Kilkenny), that provided me with magnificent cover."

Many of Damien's successes have made him feel very humble. He thinks of great artists of the game who never became household names or won any honours because of the counties they came from – "Jobber" McGrath, Pat Jackson and Tommy Ring (Westmeath), Christy O'Brien, Mick Mahon (Laois), Gerry O'Malley (Roscommon), Paddy Quirke (Carlow) and Declan Lovett (Kerry). "One of the best goalkeepers I have seen, but has no honours or awards is Johnny Carroll of Laois."

The best man that he played hurling with or against was Padraig Horan of Offaly, while the best hurlers of his era were Jimmy Doyle (Tipperary) and Barney Moylan (Offaly).

Damien was with Offaly as they climbed slowly towards the top level, and the trip was not without its growing pains and disappointments. But when they did break through they made their presence felt and continued to rise and rise, growing in stature and competence and finesse: a Leinster title in 1980; an All-Ireland title in 1981; every Leinster final contested throughout the 1980s – concrete proof that they had arrived in the big time.

It had been a long road from Ashford in 1964 to Croke Park in 1981. "We drove in triumph in a bus through Tullamore after the 1981 All-Ireland victory. The crowd was incredible. I didn't believe there could be so many people in Offaly. Padraig Horan turned to me and said, 'Wasn't it all worthwhile?' and I replied, 'It would have been all worthwhile even if we didn't win.'"

BARNEY MOYLAN
OFFALY

Born: 1943
Interviewed: 1993

Barney proudly displays his trophies.

"My hurling days were extra special – right from the time my father got me my first hurley. I have a lot of lovely memories of playing with St Rynagh's. I enjoyed every game, whether with club, county or province. Losing two All-Ireland club finals to Roscrea (1971) and Glen Rovers (1973) were moments of disappointment, but we did our club proud. Medals didn't bother me. I played for the love of the game. I didn't like being beaten but it didn't kill my love for the game, and that's for sure.

"When I was in Canada for almost two years, I played a game every Sunday during the hurling season and practised every evening. Hurling in America was very hard and physical."

Barney Moylan was one of the finest hurlers that Offaly ever produced – a quiet, unassuming man who talked about hurling with a passion and sincerity that showed hurling was far more than just a game to him. The game was the centre of his universe. "I loved the old game – I lived for it." That sentence dominated our meeting, being repeated many times.

Those who saw Barney in action speak in glowing terms of his display in the Leinster final of 1969 against Kilkenny. He had the unenviable task of marking the legendary Eddie Keher. He performed *gaiscí*, holding Eddie, I am told, to two points from play. It was a remarkable performance – a reflection of his hurling genius.

"I played for Offaly in New York in 1968–69 and we hurled against the best teams of that time. I worked in Toronto and had to get a plane on Saturday to New York. We played our match on Sunday – I got a flight back to Toronto after the match and was back at work on Monday morning. I was often sore but I wouldn't have missed it for the world. There was a fanaticism for the game in the States.

"That same year I was picked to go on a World tour with the Offaly (USA) team but I couldn't leave the job in Toronto. It was really a great pity because I would have had the opportunity of playing against Tipperary in Birr. In my days in Toronto there were about six hurling teams."

Barney's abilities as a first-class hurler were rewarded in a variety of ways. He was on the victorious Leinster Railway Cup teams of 1972 and 1973. He was Hurler of the Year in Toronto in 1968. In 1972, he was chosen as Offaly Hurler of the Year. In 1976 – the year he retired – he was chosen as Man of the Match after the county final. With his club St Rynagh's he won nine county senior hurling titles.

Barney Moylan was All-Star material.

Barney Moylan

BRIAN MURPHY
CORK

Born: 1952
Interviewed: 1993

Being congratulated by Jack Lynch on the occasion of an All-Star.

"GAA has been very special and very good for me, ever since I started to play with my club – Nemo Rangers in Cork. I first played with them when I was fourteen years of age and I have been lucky to have had the success I had with them on the playing field." Brian's overall record on the playing field is quite remarkable – possibly unique.

"I first played with Cork senior hurlers in the 1971–72 league and that match was in the Old Athletic grounds. That day I played on Babs Keating who was one of my heroes when I was growing up. I always remember getting a lift from Ossie Bennett to Urlingford after that match. I was now stationed in Kilkenny as a member of the Garda Síochána and had yet to make the money to purchase a car. The first senior All-Ireland I played in was in 1972 against Kilkenny. Between 1972 and 1983 I played many games with Cork in hurling and football." As a dual performer, Brian was a magnificent defender in both codes.

"I mainly played in the full-back line, a position where a player cannot afford to make a mistake and where a player certainly must concentrate on marking his man. The good thing now is that you don't have to keep the man out from the keeper – that is something which was no harm to have gotten rid of. I would like to see the kicking of the sliotar to score also being done away with. Scores should be got with the hurley."

His path of glory is strewn with success and he must be one of the most wide-ranging decorated dual players of all time. It all began in his College days at Coláiste Chríost Rí – days that have very happy memories for Brian. "I was probably more interested in the games than in the books. In 1968 we travelled to Buttevant to play Limerick CBS in the Harty Cup final. We were rank outsiders. Limerick CBS had captured the previous four titles and had men of the calibre of Pat Hartigan in their ranks. We were hoping to do well. But we had a victory that leaves me with one of my most cherished memories.

"The same year we won the All-Ireland Colleges' football final by defeating Belcamp OMI of Dublin. We repeated the football success in 1970. Again the final was at Croke Park and our opponents were St Malachy's of Belfast. The one point victory 4:5 to 1:13 was very sweet. Being captain made it even sweeter."

His subsequent successes were as follows – All-Ireland minor hurling 1970; All-Ireland minor football 1969; All-Ireland under-21 hurling 1971 and 1973; All-Ireland under-21 football 1971.

At senior level he had the following successes – All-Ireland football final 1973: "When Cork won that title for the first time in twenty-eight years I was twenty-one years of age and I didn't appreciate it so much then as I do now. Cork in that period had some wonderful footballers and many fine teams but their record was terrible"; seven county senior football titles with Nemo Rangers between 1972 and 1983; and the county successes led to All-Ireland senior football club titles in 1973, 1978, 1982 and 1984. Brian clearly remembers the 1978 victory over Scotstown of Monaghan when he was captain: "I can remember the day well. Snow was falling. It was difficult to see the guys at the far end of the field." All-Stars were won in 1973 and 1976.

He won three All-Ireland hurling titles 1976, 1977 and 1978; four National Leagues 1972, 1974, 1980 and 1981. No county senior hurling title came his way but he did have the compensation of an intermediate title in 1971. All-Stars were won in 1979 and 1981.

The honours list is remarkable and yet, no matter what game or victory you talk about, his mind keeps drifting back to his school days in Coláiste Chríost Rí. "There was something special about College matches. I would have to say that the games played during my time in Coláiste Chríost Rí would go down as special and the most memorable time during my playing career." The memories and victories of those days will never leave him. They seem destined to remain indelibly imprinted on his mind. "The build up in the school – the great atmosphere – the schoolyard meetings to get support going – the songs – the flags – the speeches – all contributed to the crescendo of excitement that was reached when victory was won."

> *They flash upon that inward eye...*
> *And then my heart with pleasure fills...*
> *(William Wordsworth)*

Brian's style of play was quiet and unobtrusive. He did what every good corner-back should do – effectively marked his man, covered well, read the game, cleared intelligently and left no gaps to goal. His hallmark was dependability, consistency and sportsmanship. In the All-Ireland final of 1976, when Tony Doran was threatening to cause havoc, Brian was moved to full-back where he put the shackles on what had been a rampant Tony Doran. He had the skills and the temperament to do it.

He is very conscious that the GAA and its games have been very good to him. It brought him three trips to America: "I would never have been there otherwise." He travelled to Wembley to play tournaments. Above all, he "made many great friends." Brian Murphy was a credit to Gaelic games.

JIMMY BARRY MURPHY
CORK

Born: 1955
Interviewed: 1994

"I suppose it is inevitable that most boys born in Cork from the age of four or five years of age are going to have a hurley put in their hands at some stage. Obviously a great number of them do not partake much more. Some go on to play at various levels for either club or county. The lucky few like myself can go on to realise what was, for me, from as far back as I can remember, the only ambition I can recall and that is to play in an All-Ireland final wearing the red and white of Cork. The family's long involvement in Gaelic games also ensured that one would at least play hurling and football, and after that ability would dictate at what level. My grandfather and granduncle both won All-Ireland medals in 1919 against Dublin and my granduncle Dinny of course captained Cork to win All-Ireland honours in 1929. He also played in the famous final of 1931 against the 'old enemy' Kilkenny and often told me about the great players like Seán Óg Murphy, Eudi Coughlan, Lory Meagher and many more. My late father John won two county medals with St Finbarr's and also won a junior All-Ireland medal in 1940. With a family history like that there was never much chance of getting big headed or carried away with brief successes.

"My best memory of my own playing days is to have been part of the three-in-a-row team of 1976, 1977 and 1978. Since the forties it has always been a target to put two or three All-Irelands together and this also proves the real worth of a team. What means most to me now about the GAA is the friends I made throughout the country, and wherever I go I find somebody always wants to talk hurling and discuss prospects for future years. I am now involved in coaching, both in my own club and with Cork minor hurlers, and I hope in some small way to repay the game of hurling for all that I got from the game both on and off the field."

An rud a beirlear sa cnámh, is deacair scarúint leis sa bhfuil

Few players have been as fortunate as Jimmy Barry Murphy and it is probably true to say that he has been unsurpassed as a dual performer. He was highly gifted and richly talented in both hurling and football and played for his county in both codes at minor, under-21 and senior levels.

Victory and honours flowed in abundance right through his career. In football there was All-Ireland senior honours in 1973 at the age of nineteen. And for him it was a dream debut that produced telling scores at psychological moments – a goal within three minutes of the start to settle a team that hadn't won a football title since 1945 – a brilliant goal within eight minutes of the final whistle that clinched victory. There followed All-Star awards in 1973 and 1974; four Railway cup successes in a row from 1975 to 1978 inclusive; National League honours in 1980; and an All-Ireland club title with St Finbarr's in 1980 and 1981.

The hurling honours include ten Munster titles, five All-Ireland titles and five All-Star awards, one Oireachtas, two National Leagues, two All-Ireland club titles and six county titles. I pondered aloud on the diverse nature of all the medals. "I don't place much store on medals. At the end of the day they don't count for much. The number of honours doesn't mean anything. Don't gauge anyone by that. It's how you present yourself and play on the day that really counts."

Jimmy's most humbling experience was his failure as captain to lead Cork to victory in 1982 and 1983 against Kilkenny. "It was a good lesson – a humbling lesson."

Jimmy always enjoyed playing at full-forward. "I loved being in around the square. If you are prepard to wait and keep your patience your chance will come. You can destroy a back's day. A forward need only be lucky once. A back needs to be lucky all the time."

He always enjoyed playing against Kilkenny because "they are the ultimate in hurling." He liked the games against Tipperary because of the "fabulous atmosphere". "I played minor, under-21 and Senior Championship matches against Tipp. and never lost." And then he adds with a sense of pride – "very few Cork fellows can say that."

The name Jimmy Barry Murphy is now a household one in Cork and all hurling circles. He was an opportunist and played the percentage game. He rarely, if ever, became embroiled in intensely physical play. He was a thoughtful player with a penchant for the quick snappy score. He conserved energy. He was a visionary and had the patience to wait. When a chance – indeed a half chance – arose, he pounced. He then made it look easy. But that was because he was a master of the basic skills and the simple things. At all times he played the ball. He was the personification of good sportsmanship.

Here is how sports correspondent Kevin Cashman once described him: "The man. One of the all time greats. Matchless intelligence and composure. Predatory stalker and finisher of scores. Ability to hit the 'Killer' pass was unique until the advent of Joe Cooney. Guides and inspires all around him."

MARTIN QUIGLEY
WEXFORD

Born: 1951
Interviewed: 1997

"My first hurling memory goes back to 1960 when I was nine years old. I remember Mícheál O'Hehir broadcasting the 1960 All-Ireland final between Wexford and Tipperary. Tipperary were strong favourites in that final, but Wexford had a great win.

"When the match was over, I went out on the farm to bring in the cows, with my hurl and ball, and pretended to be both Billy Rackard and Tim Flood who had both just won their third All-Ireland medal.

"In September 1963, I entered St Peter's College and it was here under the watchful eye of Ned Power that my love of hurling flourished. As a school, we enjoyed great success in this period, winning numerous Colleges' titles at juvenile, junior and senior levels. The sixties was a great era for underage hurling in Wexford. We won All-Ireland minor titles in 1963, 1966 and 1968. I played on the minor teams of 1967, 1968 and 1969. One of my greatest memories is winning the 1968 minor final, on a historic day for Wexford hurling.

"I played my first Senior Championship match for Wexford in 1970 and my last outing was in 1989. In those twenty years of Leinster Championships, I have many sad memories and only a few very good ones. The Leinster final victory of 1976 was perhaps the most satisfactory. Kilkenny had beaten us in the previous five finals and in 1976 we beat them by seventeen points, We really should have won that All-Ireland, having been eight points up against Cork after ten minutes. We had really good teams in Wexford throughout the seventies and we were very unfortunate not to have won at least one All-Ireland title in this decade.

"As well as playing for Wexford, I also had very many happy years playing in the black and amber of Rathnure. I was part of a very strong Rathnure team and I have ten Senior Championship medals.

"For most of my club career I played as I did for Wexford, in the forwards. However, in later years, I played at full-back and enjoyed many a great tussle with the one and only Tony Doran.

"I think I retired (or was retired) in 1986. There are those, however, who would say that I had more comebacks than Lazarus. In 1988 I was a spectator at the first round of the championship against Laois. Three weeks later, I scored 2:2 in the semi-final against Kilkenny. That is the stuff that dreams are made of! Twenty years – people often ask me what made me keep going. I can honestly say that it was a privilege for me to wear the purple and gold. In truth, I might be out there still only for a dodgy knee!"

A brilliant career began in his school days at St Peter's College, Wexford with whom he won Leinster and All-Ireland Colleges' titles in 1967 against Limerick CBS and 1968 against Coláiste Chroíst Rí. Both All-Irelands went to replays.

Rathnure, of Rackard fame, was further enhanced in the hurling world by the Quigley family. In 1972, John, Jim, Martin and Dan won a Leinster club title with Rathnure but failed by one point to Blackrock of Cork in the All-Ireland final. In 1974, they were joined by Pat and, after success in

Leinster, failed again to Blackrock, after a replay, in the All-Ireland final. Martin is extremely proud of his native Rathnure.

The family created a unique record in 1970 that may stand for a long long time. In the All-Ireland final of that year against Cork, the Wexford half-forward line was an all-Quigley one – Martin, Pat and John. The centre-back position was manned by Dan – Big Dan to hurling followers. Wexford, lining out without five regulars lost by 6:21 to 5:10.

Martin is Wexford's most decorated All-Star – being honoured on four successive occasions from 1973 onwards. He was Sportstar of the Week – "I think 'twas 1977" – following a league match against Clare at Tulla. "Clare used play their home league matches there. 'Twas a graveyard for visiting teams, I think we were the first team to beat them there. They were good then – they won a couple of league titles. 'Twas a good day for us."

Martin's mother had little or no interest in the game: "I think she only went to one match ever and it wasn't an important one." His father, however – "who played a bit of football" – was a fanatical supporter. "I remember as a kid going to a lot of matches with him. That's where we got our enthusiasm from. I remember one day he invited the referee to the line to fight. I was mortified as a child. In his later years, he gave up going to matches. He used to get 100 per cent worked up and that wasn't good for him."

Martin took some hard knocks during his playing days. He was stitched several times. There are marks on the face and around the eyes. In retirement, he takes an occasional mental glance at the hurling ledger and he sees in its pages some outstanding unsettled scores. At this stage, it is most likely they will be either written off, or go statute barred.

SEÁN SILKE
GALWAY

Born: 1950
Interviewed: 1997

"It was impossible not to become involved in hurling – as I was born into a house where sport was always discussed, as hurling was played by Dad and uncles. Also, and more importantly, our house and farm was located in the parish of Meelick/Eyrecourt – who proudly remember their participation in the first All-Ireland final v. Thurles of Tipperary in 1887. Memories of great games, and great hurlers, were shared, as neighbours, uncles or visitors paid a visit. Men like Joe Salmon, Billy Duffy, Fintan Spillane (all locals) were mentioned with reverence and put up as stars to emulate. Thus, we were given targets to aim at. However, success didn't arrive easily. In fact, my first memory of representing my club was as a sub for the under-14s – who received a great dressing down without calling on my services.

"Highlights of my career were our successes in making the break-through in 1974–1975 league – recording victories over Cork, Kilkenny and Tipperary on the way. That was an especially joyous occasion and was followed three months later by the All-Ireland semi-final victory over a well- fancied Cork side. We met the 'Cats' in the All-Ireland final. Unfortunately we played well below our best. They were the team of the early 1970s. It would have taken a good performance to deny them, which we were unable to give.

"The following year in Cork, Wexford denied us after a replay in the All-Ireland semi-final. I always believe our drawn game was the best hurling game I played in and a point from Frank Burke – at least 100 metres out – is still vivid in that very hot, humid day.

"After our failure, again to Kilkenny in 1979, victory twelve months later against Limerick was both well overdue and well deserved. It was like being released from a prison. Many supporters had lost faith through our continuous defeats. More than anything else, the victory provided great encouragement to mentors of club teams within the county and was also a fitting reward for longer-serving stars who experienced so many bad days – especially players like John Connolly, who was a colossus on weak Galway teams a dozen years before. Essentially, victory was attained from great displays from about twelve players, with another three neutralising their opponents.

"The following year provides the low point of any player's career – losing a final as captain. Unfortunately, the 1981 final was played between two non-traditional counties – minnows of hurling, as someone said, and Offaly gradually, gradually, stole away the Liam MacCarthy as we missed many good scoring chances, while Pat Delaney and especially Johnny Flaherty ended our dream for two in a row. Their uncanny ability to stay in touch, while defending against our superior forwards in the first half contributed immensely to their victory."

While at college, Seán worked in the US in the summertime and hurled with Harry Bolands in Chicago. There, his right arm, first broken in a Minor Championship game with Cork, was again broken. The setting was defective so the arm had to be rebroken and reset. A glance at the arm confirms the damage.

Seán was in the US in 1973 when London surprisingly defeated Galway in the All-Ireland quarter-final, but the following year he was flown home for the semi-final against Kilkenny: "I arrived on a Friday evening – didn't cope well with jetlag–and played rubbish."

The Fitzgibbon Cup titles won with St Patrick's College, Maynooth in 1973 and 1974 were very special, breaking the stranglehold the other universities had on the title, especially UCC and UCD. "It was during those days I had the privilege to win county junior and intermediate medals with Meelick/Eyrecourt. What an occasion – and how our small parish celebrated and enjoyed our success. It was during this time I received the call for Galway seniors – and played, commencing initially in 1971, continuously in 1972, and for the next twelve years, finishing after the Centenary year in 1984."

His championship displays of 1975 and 1980 earned him two well-deserved All-Star awards at centre-back. The following narration accompanied his 1975 selection: "For being the essence of shrewdness in his county's defence where he dominated so impressively throughout the year."

In the championship of 1980, Galway defeated Offaly in the semi-final 4:9 to 3:10, and had three points to spare over Limerick in the final. The breakthrough after countless frustrating failures since 1923 heralded an unleashing of jubililation, celebration and emotion, rarely seen in Croke Park.

It was probably Seán Silke's greatest day in the maroon of Galway. He was majestic at centre-back and in the course of the game faced three different opponents in John Flanagan, Joe McKenna and Willie Fitzmaurice. His contribution to Galway's win was incalculable. One small banner in the crowd proclaimed "Silke is not a soft touch." The surname – hurling-wise – was never more apt, for Seán's display was a silken one.

Peadar O'Brien in his report in the *Irish Press* on Monday, 8 September 1980 voted him "the outstanding player on the field – the immaculate Seán Silke" – immense praise indeed on a day when there were several brilliant individual performances.

NOEL SKEHAN
KILKENNY

Born: 1944
Interviewed: 1993

"I started playing with Bennettsbridge on the under-16 team when I was thirteen years old and played minor club at fourteen. I played on all club teams from there on. I played senior at sixteen and won my first Senior County Championship in 1962. In 1962 I played minor for Kilkenny and won the All-Ireland that same year. In 1963 I was a sub to goalkeeper Ollie Walsh on the Kilkenny team that won the senior All-Ireland.

"I played in and captained the 1972 Kilkenny winning team. It was my first senior All-Ireland to play in and to captain it was a bonus. After that I played with the county until April 1985 when I retired.

"In those years I won nine All-Ireland senior titles, eleven Leinster titles, four Oireachtas, three leagues and one minor – also six county titles, seven All Stars, four B&I awards, one Texaco award, two Man of the

Match awards in the 1972 and 1982 All-Irelands, several Sport Star of the Week awards and many others. During my playing days I made friends in all the counties we played and on trips to USA and Railway Cup matches."

Noel was reared in the parish of Bennettsbridge in an atmosphere that lived and breathed hurling. It was much easier to be absorbed into the game than to escape from it. There were lots of heroes to look up to and to emulate. Among them was his uncle Dan Kennedy, who gave many sterling displays for Kilkenny in the forties.

He belongs to the top bracket of goal-keepers and ranks with the great ones since the foundation of the GAA. When he stood on the goal line and looked out at the opposing team he never feared any forward or forward line. He had supreme confidence in his own ability to deal with anything that came his way.

Noel has very special memories of the 1972 All-Ireland final: "I was captain that day. It was the first All-Ireland final I took part in. About mid-way through the second half, Con Roche sent in a ball from about ninety yards. I looked up and watched it as it sailed over my goal at the canal end. I think it left us trailing by eight points. I felt that was it. I felt very downhearted. I just grabbed the ball and pucked it out with a feeling of complete indifference as to where it was going or how far it was going. Around that time Keher was brought out from the corner to the wing and Martin Coogan came on at right full-back. In less than fifteen minutes we were in the lead and the next thing is I am going up on the Hogan Stand to collect the cup having won by seven points." Honour for Noel; glory for Kilkenny – their eighteenth All-Ireland crown.

SEAN STACK
CLARE

Born: 1953
Interviewed: 2002

Sean (left) with two hurling superstars, John Joe Doyle, Clare captain 1932, and Noel Drumgoole, Dublin captain 1961.

"If this great game holds bad memories for me, it is that the disappointing days keep haunting. The pains that we felt after our Munster final defeats are still tangible. Those Mondays will never leave my memory and still, to this day, hurt greatly. There were days when any kind of company was avoided – especially those keen on talking about the 'game'. 1978 keeps on coming back – excuses that Cork had a marvellous team, their great forwards were held goalless, etc. etc. are just not erasing the pain. This was to be the pinnacle of all our careers. Croke Park beckoned, but damn it, we did everything in our power. Two miserable points separated us from glory. Five years of growing up together, working up and down that field of Tulla. This was to be our dream. The fact that Cork subsequently 'sailed' away with the All-Ireland made it even worse.

"But this great game of ours is not easily left aside. I love everything about the game of hurling. Watch any player on the pitch over an hour and then you know what kind of character he is. Now, I had my great days too. The Clare Championships won with Sixmilebridge are special; 1983 in a replay was one of those 'moments in time'. Coming back to the village in late December 1984 with the provincial trophy was memorable. We sang everything that night from 'Singing in the Rain' to 'Jingle Bells'. I took as much joy in winning the County Championship in 1993 [at the age of forty] as any of the others."

Sean Stack was born in 1953 in Listowel, Co. Kerry, where he spent the first year of his life, followed by a three-year spell in Glin, Co. Limerick. His father, Stephen, "a great friend of Gus Cremin's of Kerry football fame in the forties", was a Kerry man, while his mother Bridget (née McNamara) – affectionately known as Pydge – was a native of Glin. In 1957, Stephen purchased a farm of ninety-seven acres in East Clare, together with twenty-five cows and a range of machinery for £7500. And so fate ordained that Sean would star in the colours of Clare, rather than those of either Kerry or Limerick.

His hurling days were many; the glory days were relatively few. However, in a most illustrious career, which ended following a National League game against Wexford in 1987, he did have his moments of success, interspersed with quite a few near misses, particularly in Munster finals. The late Raymond Smith referred to Sean as "a hurler of cultured grace". A most apt description, indeed, for Sean was a sportsman to his fingertips. And he was versatile too – a forward in his juvenile days, a midfielder in his college days, a corner-back in his first Munster final in 1974; he was later moved to wing-back and finally to centre-back, where he played many magnificent matches.

Sean first gripped the camán with the juveniles of Sixmilebridge. And from that moment, a hurling fervour gripped him. In 1993, at the age of forty, he won his seventh Co. Clare senior hurling title and played in the Munster club final against Toomevara (a team he was then coaching). He lost to the team he had coached.

Sean captained the Clare minor hurling team in 1971, but suffered a heavy defeat at the hands of Cork in the Munster final at Killarney. In 1972 and 1974, Sean came tantalisingly close to Munster titles at under-21 level. Again, the Fates frowned on The Banner. Victory went to Tipperary and Waterford by three points and five points respectively.

In 1981, Sean received a well-deserved personal honour when he was named at centre-back on the All-Star team. He was centre-back on the victorious Munster Railway Cup teams of 1984 and 1985. He played in three successive league finals, all against Kilkenny, in 1976, 1977 and 1978, winning in 1977 and again in 1978 when he was captain. Around this time, Clare hurling was reaching new heights. An All-Ireland title seemed a possibility. Sadly, a dream it remained as hopes were dashed in stories of so near and yet so far.

Let's look at them. Sean played in five Munster finals without success:

1974 v. Limerick (6:14 to 3:9)
1977 v. Cork (4:15 to 4:10)
1978 v. Cork (0:1 3 to 0:11)
1981 v. Limerick (3:12 to 2:9)
1986 v. Cork (2:18 to 3:12)

Apart from 1974, when everything went wrong for Clare early on, the other four finals all carried the label of might-have-been. I asked Sean which final, on reflection now, left him with the greatest sense of loss. Was it 1977, when Clare saw their fine full-back Jim Power sidelined in the first half, or 1978, when Clare were firm favourites playing before a huge crowd of 55,000 – one of the largest ever for a Munster final – and facing the second half only a point behind and the wind in their favour; or was it 1981 as they watched Joe McKenna at full-forward for Limerick find the net three times and match it with points – "John Flanagan, the farmer from Feohanagh, gave me a terrible time that day" – or 1986 when Sean trained like a Trojan in the US, flew home for the defeats of Limerick and Tipperary and flew home again to face Cork?

His answer: "It was 1986. I knew that day it was going to be my last chance to win a Munster medal. In the other defeats I knew there would be other days. We gave away two soft goals that day. My chance was gone – that made it sad for me."

Disappointments there may have been but Sean's hurling fervour lives on, active and healthy, as reflected in his successful coaching of Toomevara and his deep concern for the future of our ancient game.

Sean Stack

1980s

JOE CONNOLLY
GALWAY

Born: 1956
Interviewed: 2001

"Due to a bad knee injury, my career finished when I was just twenty-eight. However, I can honestly say that I had a wonderful hurling career and finished up winning nearly everything there was to be won.

"Today a great deal of the contentment that I have in my life comes from my past experiences as a hurler. I consider myself to be so unbelievably lucky that I finished my career with All-Ireland medals with both my club and my county. I am married to a Limerick woman, Cathy, and my five sons, Paul, Brian, James, Barry and Joseph, all wield the camán at underage level for Castlegar. *Tá súil agam go mbainfidh siad an sult agus an aoibhneas as a gcuid saol iománaíochta is a bhain mise.*

"The two greatest hurlers of the modern era I consider to be D.J. Carey and Brian Lohan. The greatest hurler I ever saw was Eddie Keher and I would love to have seen Christy Ring. He must have been something really special. I love the company of people who really love their sport, whatever it may be."

As a youngster, Joe remembers directing a car into a parking space at his home during race week. It was worth a half a crown to him. "Well, who stepped out only Jim Treacy of Kilkenny, an All-Ireland medal holder. I was in awe. I ran in and told Michael and Ger to come out. Mother invited Jim and his wife in and gave them tea. We looked at the mug he drank from afterwards and held it. Imagine, we thought, an All-Ireland medal holder drinking tea in our house and parking on our grass. It shows you where we were coming from as regards winning All-Ireland medals." For Joe the winning of an All-Ireland medal became an ambition and a daily dream.

Hurling was central to the Connolly household. All the boys played. Joe's father was a great enthusiast. Their mother was a great supporter. But she never saw them play. Instead she stayed at home and prayed. "She went once to watch John at underage in a club game. She left at half time. She spent the half hour with the rosary beads, head down – *Sé do bheatha, a Mhuire...A Naomh Mhuire, a Mháthair Dé...*" – an occasional quick glance up – "*Guigh orainne peacaithe...*"

Not since the championship of 1923, when Galway won their first All-Ireland title with a victory over Limerick, had the men of the West been victorious on All-Ireland final day. The disappointments, disillusionments and frustrations of decades would be buried on the first Sunday in September 1980 when Joe Connolly, potent and prolific in the art of score-getting, would lead a great Galway team to a thrilling victory over Limerick.

"The intensity of the effort put into the preparation for the final was fantastic. In the dressing-room on final day there was no screaming or roaring before the game. I was six months injury free. I worked hard at training. On the day I felt totally in control. I knew I was right. There was a feeling of confidence – a feeling it could be our day. We looked on Limerick as equals. Mentally, Galway were free of the baggage associated with the hurling tradition and successes of the 'Big Three' – Cork, Tipperary and Kilkenny. Not until the last ten seconds could we say we were going to win."

At the call of time the scoreboard read Galway 2:15, Limerick 3:9. Joe Connolly (All-Star 1980), at centre-forward, played a valiant captain's part and contributed four points. His brother John at full-forward (Hurler of the Year 1980), Michael at midfield and Padraic on the substitute bench made it a very special day and year for the Connolly family.

Winning an All-Ireland medal in 1980 made Joe feel very proud – proud because it represented reaching the Everest of the hurling world. And as each year passes nostalgia adds a deeper glow and lustre to that cherished medal. The success also made Joe feel humble – humble because he often thinks of the many great players who aspired to hurling's Everest, only to be denied by fate and circumstance.

Joe delivered one of the finest post-match victory speeches that Croke Park had ever heard. The Irish language part of his speech opened as follows:

> *A mhuintir na Gaillimhe, tar éis seacht mbliana is caoga tá Craobh na hÉireann ar ais i nGaillimh. Is mór an onóir domsa, mar chaptaen, an corn seo a ghlacadh ar son an fhoireann uilig.*

Joe's mother didn't go to the game, nor did she watch it on TV. Instead, she walked the nearby Ballybrit Racecourse – and prayed, rosary beads in hand, *"Sé do bheatha, a Mhuire . . . a Naomh Mhuire . . anois agus ag uair…"*. Sara, her daughter, hailed her at full time. It was time to conclude with *Fíor na Croise* and hurry in to celebrate.

Joe Connolly

JOE COONEY
GALWAY

Born: 1965
Interviewed: 1997

"I first went to an All-Ireland final in 1980. My brother Jimmy was playing for Galway in that match. I was sitting in the stand and thinking would
I ever get a chance to play in Croke Park. Galway won that match and I
played three years after that for Galway, in a minor final which we won
also. Mick Jacob, Seán Silke, Iggy Clarke, Jimmy Barry Murphy, Tony
Doran and Sylvie Linnane were some of my idols in those years."

Joe is one of a family of fourteen children – six boys and eight girls.
When Sarsfield's – a rural club located a few miles from Loughrea
town – won the All-Ireland senior club hurling final in 1993, all
six boys participated in the great victory. Jimmy, who won an All-
Ireland medal with Galway in 1980, with a brilliant display at corner-
back, was among the subs. The full-back line was an all-Cooney one,
Packie (capt), Brendan and Michael. Joe was at midfield and Peter was

a corner-forward. That victory over Kilmallock by 1:17 to 2:7 ranks as Joe's greatest hurling moment and rivals the All-Ireland triumphs with Galway in 1987 and 1988. The following year, the club repeated the success with a two-point win over Toomevara and, in so doing, created a number of records that may never again be repeated. The exact same fifteen lined out in the exact same positions. They were led by the same captain. It was the only time up to then that the same club won the title in successive years. "After being beaten by Ballyhale Shamrocks (they had seven Fennellys in the team) in the semi-final of the 1990 championship, I thought we'd never win a club title." The successes generated immense parish pride in a club that "depends on six or seven families for its playing members."

Joe's journey into hurling greatness began when he played in goal for Galway under-16s in 1980. Minor and under-21 All-Ireland titles were won in 1983 and 1986 with victories over Dublin and Wexford respectively. He entered county senior ranks for the league campaign of 1984–1985. Soon, this richly talented player, holding his hurley right-hand under, caught the eyes of the All-Star selectors. He won his first of three in a row and five in all to date, in 1985. Hurling followers were witnessing one of the all-time greats of the game – a player of vision with a penchant for despatching "killer" precision passes.

In many respects, Joe had his greatest year in 1987. It began with a league title win over Clare. This was followed by an All-Ireland title in a tense struggle with Kilkenny. Leinster were defeated in the Railway Cup final in October. He received his third successive All-Star award. And, finally, to crown everything, he had the wonderful personal honour of being chosen as Texaco Hurler of the Year. "Yes, it was a fantastic year. It isn't too often things happen that way for you – it was probably my best year."

In Galway, the year 1989 will always conjure up memories of a lost opportunity – memories of a three-in-a-row that might have been. Galway faced Tipperary in the All-Ireland semi-final – minus outstanding half-back Tony Keady who was suspended in controversial circumstances for having played in the US. Reduced to thirteen men in the second half, Joe moved to midfield where he played inspired hurling that almost turned the tide. It wasn't his fault that Galway lost a game that was within their capacity to win.

The most painful year of Joe's hurling career was 1990. They faced Cork in the final and were firm favourites. Joe was captain. He gave a scintillating first-half performance, scoring 1:6 – all but one point from play. Galway dominated much of the game and at times looked rampant. "We scored 2:21 – it would have won most finals." But they had costly lapses – the first before the game was one minute old. They conceded five goals – most of them due to lapses of concentration and lack of attention to key basics. But when your luck is out even the gods can frown on you. Less than ten minutes from half time, Joe sent one of his "killer" passes to Éanna Ryan, whose shot bulged the net, but the referee blew for a foul on Joe – no goal. Then in the second half Martin Naughton bore down on the Cork goal and his rasping shot, with "goal" written all over it, glanced off the forehead of the advancing Ger Cunningham, and the umpire, instead of giving a seventy, signalled a wide. Joe's recollection is that, from the puck-out, Cork scored a point. He knows that a game that was lost by three points could have been won and won well. "Yes it is my most painful memory."

He sees hurling as "going through a great era, great games – with Offaly, Wexford, Galway, Clare and Limerick all contributing and challenging seriously for major honours – has to be good for the game."

Now in retirement, this genial and exemplary sportsman can look back on a career to be proud of – a career that is dotted with great performances – a career in which he has won every honour in the modern-day game and stood shoulder to shoulder with "great defenders like Ger Henderson, Joe Hennessy and Tom Cashman".

EUGENE COUGHLAN
OFFALY

Born: 1956
Interviewed: 2009

"Living in Clareen, I knew from an early age I was going to be hooked on hurling as there was a great hurling tradition, both in my family and my club Seir Kieran. My grandfather, Edward, was on the first team that won a Junior Hurling Championship in 1912. My father, John, was a great hurler for the club; he won junior and captained the side to intermediate success and also wore the Offaly jersey. He was looked up to in the club. He played at centre-back and centre half-forward. My uncles, Eamonn and Jim, also played and won medals with the club. On my mother's side there was also a strong hurling tradition; her brothers Seamus and Johnny Guinan won Senior Hurling Championship medals with Coolderry. So, hurling was in my blood.

"Growing up at home on the farm in Bellhill in the sixties was different than it is today. At that time there was a lot of physical work like milking the cows, saving the hay, thinning turnips and harvesting the corn. There were no televisions, computers, playstations or mobile phones, so it had to be the hurley. We played a lot of hurling between ourselves. We always went for the cows on time, but the hurleys and sliotar were also brought along, and as a result the cows were often late being milked. Saving the hay was a great time of the year, as we used the trams of hay as goal-posts. The weather seemed to be great that time and there was also lots of time for the hurling. My father often dropped the fork for the hurley and played with us.

"I have five brothers, Brendan, Sean, Michael, Noel, Liam, and two sisters, Bernadette and Carmel. Five of us played in county senior finals and my oldest brother Brendan played in an under-21 county final. Carmel was a very good camogie player and won a championship medal with Birr, and also played for Offaly. Michael was on the Offaly panel that won the All-Ireland in 1985. He played centre-back in 1988 when we beat Wexford in the Leinster final. Liam was on the Offaly panel in 1995. He played in goal in the 1996 championship.

"I went to Seir Kierans National School. Everyday during lunch break we used to play hurling. I won a Leinster schools medal with the Presentation Brothers College, Birr. I played for the Offaly minors and went on to play for two years with Offaly under-21s.

"I joined the Offaly panel in 1976. I played my first game at senior level in the Offaly jersey against near-neighbours Laois at Birr in a league game in 1976. And, by a strange coincidence, my last game for Offaly was against the same opposition at the same venue in the National League of 1990–91.

"In 1980 Diarmuid Healy joined the Offaly back-room team. His main focus was on the skills of the game, and he gave us the belief that we could be successful. Diarmuid was a brilliant coach and played a major part in Offaly's breakthrough. This was a great decade for Offaly hurling. Between 1980 and 1990 I played in eleven Leinster finals, winning seven; I played in three All-Irelands, winning two. The highlight was winning my first All-Ireland in 1981. The homecoming was very special, and when the cup came to Seir Kieran, Padraig Horan, our captain, handed me the cup on the outskirts of the parish and said to me 'this is your night.' It was a great feeling to bring the Liam MacCarthy Cup into club for the first time.

"In 1988 my club made the big breakthrough, as we won our first Offaly Senior Hurling Championship. It was a great honour for me to captain the side to victory, bringing back the biggest prize in Offaly hurling – 'the Sean Robbins Cup' – to our club.

"There is something extra special about the club and club success. When you know all the people, approximately 400 in the parish, it makes it a very special occasion. This is the great thing about the GAA: it can be so big in such a small place."

According to John Harrington, *Evening Herald*, 3 Aug 2000:

Couglan was an unusually skilled hurler for a back man. He seemed to have double jointed wrists and extendable arms as he flicked, battled and drove balls away from danger. Even when it looked like a full forward had gotten the better of him and was about to score a certain goal, Coughlan would somehow manage to flick the ball off his hurl and stifle the attacker with a hook or block

Offaly didn't win a Leinster title until 1980. They defeated Kilkenny against the odds and expectations. The attendance at the game confirmed this – just 9,613 spectators. Injury kept Eugene off the starting fifteen on the memorable and historic day, but he did come on as a sub at corner-back to share in the glory.

Eugene was born on 18 November 1956, and in his playing days he stood 6'2" and turned the scales at around 13 st. He was a first class full-back. He had a commanding presence in front of goal. Imperturbable in temperament and calm under pressure, he produced many sterling performances. He hurled on many of the leading full-forwards of his time: "Jimmy Barry Murphy, Joe McKenna, John Connolly, P.J. Cuddy and Christy Heffernan with whom I had many clashes, and, of course, Tony Doran."

Eugene's hurling displays in the mid 1980s earned him the Texaco Hurler of the Year award in 1985 and All-Star awards at full-back in 1984 and 1985. However, he was still capable of vintage performances in the autumn days of his playing career. I am thinking in particular of the Leinster semi-final of 1990 against newly crowned National League champions Kilkenny. Offaly entered the fray as underdogs. They emerged victorious. Kilkenny suffered one of their heaviest defeats: 4:15 to 1:8. Eugene Coughlan was Man of the Match.

In his own mind Eugene had planned to hurl until he was fifty. The knee, however, was a problem. In 1995, following keyhole surgery, his surgeon suggested to him that he should take up "a more relaxing game – like golf". Not yet forty, Eugene wasn't too impressed. He worked on the weights. He played club hurling until 2002, having been selected in 2000 at full-back on the Offaly millenium team. In 2003 the knee was bothering him again. He wouldn't be forty-seven until November that year. He knew the knee was on its last legs. He had to quit.

Ní bhíonn tréan buan.

Eugene Coughlan

GER CUNNINGHAM
CORK

Born: 1961
Interviewed: 1997

"My memories of my early hurling days are of the bell ringing to signify the end of the ten o'clock Sunday Mass at the Lough Church. At the base of the hill leading up to the church, the Lough Leagues run by the 'Barrs Under Age were taking place. It was here that I first played in goal for 'Earlwood'. It was here at the Lough that many players who were later to play for the 'Barrs first played.

"The Lough area, with its vast green space, was the ideal place to practise and it was here that I played hurling with my dad Jim, whose interest and love for hurling was passed on to me, and my brother Brian at an early age. Jim, together with Mum's family, the Finn's from Lough Road, were deeply involved with the 'Barrs. Indeed, the Finn connection goes back to the early 1900s when Tim 'Gas' Finn played for the 'Barrs.

"A graduation to Coláiste Iognaid Rís continued my hurling education and it was here that the influence of the great Billy Morgan helped me to think seriously about playing in goal. Up to this I was playing in the forwards.

"Winning the under-16 county with the 'Barrs in 1977 for the first time in the club's history led to my call for the Cork minors in 1978. This began my connection with Canon Michael O'Brien who was to have a major influence on my hurling career over the next fifteen years.

"My senior career with the 'Barrs and Cork followed on from winning minor All-Irelands in 1978 and 1979, and under-21 in 1982. In 1979 I took over in goal from Jim Power, who had played for the 'Barrs since 1959.

"My début for Cork seniors came in 1980 in Carrickshock against Kilkenny, in a challenge game, with my first league game to follow against Wexford in New Ross in October 1980. There have been many highlights in the intervening years – All-Ireland victories in 1984 (Centenary year), 1986 and 1990 versus Galway – together with some disappointments – losing in 1982, 1983 and 1992 to Kilkenny. Captaining my club to county-final victory in 1988 will always be remembered. My brother Brian, who was eighteen, was playing. That gave so much pleasure to my dad – it was very special for him.

"Through the years I have had the pleasure to play with and against some great players within and outside Cork. The All-Star and Cork trips to places like San Francisco, New York and Toronto gave the opportunity to get to know well players from other counties. I regret their passing, as it gave the opportunity to meet players other than on the playing pitch.

"Over the years, it has been my privilege to play for a great club like the 'Barrs and to play for Cork. The games have taken me to many parts of Ireland and abroad and I have enjoyed every minute of it. It would not be possible to thank everybody who helped me in my career personally, but being involved in the GAA has given many opportunities that I may never have had."

The name Ger Cunningham – Cork's longest serving goalkeeper – ranks proudly with the great goalkeepers hurling has known. His height, agility and athleticism, combined with sharp reflexes and a hawk-like eye, have made him one of the most consistent and outstanding goalkeepers of his era – indeed, of any era.

His puck-out from goal has always been of prodigious length. Little wonder that he won the Poc Fada competition for seven successive years. He dethroned Pat Hartigan – twice winner– and retired undefeated in 1991.

A goalkeeper has a rather unique view of a game as he observes proceedings from his goal line. I asked Ger to recall some of the players who had made a really lasting impression on him over the years. Understandably, he went mainly for forwards. "A goalkeeper tends to keep his eye on corner-forwards and full-forwards. There was my boyhood hero Charlie McCarthy – brilliant corner-forward – I carried his bag for many years. Ray Cummins was one fabulous player – played against him in club games with Blackrock." Did he send many goals past? "No, no he didn't," Ger affirmed with a smile of satisfaction. "Eddie Keher was a big hero of mine. I have always had great admiration for George O'Connor. We toured the States together and I liked his honesty and toughness. Éamonn Cregan had a great hurling brain and was very sharp. Nicholas English was a forward of superb skills probably at his best in the years before 1987. Pat Fox was as good in a different way – an under-rated corner-forward. D.J. [Carey] is tremendous and of course there was big-hearted Tony Doran and the very dangerous Joe McKenna."

Glancing through his achievements, I was particularly taken by the range of honours that came his way in 1986. It began with a Munster title win over Clare in July, followed by an All-Ireland medal in September when Galway were defeated. His performance that year brought him his third All-Star award and he was chosen as Texaco Hurler of the Year. Add these to the Poc Fada success and 1986 was surely a year for Ger to remember and be proud of.

PAT DELANEY
OFFALY

Born: 1955
Interviewed: 1994

"Where I lived in the Sliabh Bloom mountains the only pastime we had when we were young was the game of hurling. We listened to the broadcasts of Mícheál O'Hehir and played stormers after it. We became the John Doyles, Jimmy Doyle, Mackey McKenna, Liam Devaneys until dark. Tipp. were the hurling power of that era 1964–65. Then, at about the age of twelve, my job in Kinnity hurling field was to puck the ball back from behind the goal to the senior players who won a championship in 1967 against Coolderry after thirty-seven years – ironically, it was Coolderry they beat in 1930. It was the late Tom Mitchell from that team who brought me to my first All-Ireland in 1969.

"Offaly's Paddy Molloy, a hurling genius, was my idol at that time. Little did I think myself that I would be playing in Croke Park in a Leinster Minor Championship semi-final in 1973 at centre-back. We lost by two points to a very good Wexford team who subsequently lost to Kilkenny and who won the All-Ireland easily. There were a lot of disappointments between my first day hurling in Croke Park and 1980."

Offaly were outsiders in 1981 against Galway in the All-Ireland final. Throughout most of the first half there was a fluency about Galway's hurling that threatened to turn into a torrent and engulf Offaly. And yet, despite playing what at times looked like exhibition stuff, they weren't reflecting their superiority on the scoreboard.

Each Offaly man was sticking grimly to his task – no frills or fancy stuff, just total concentration on the basics. On every countenance there was resolve and determination – especially on Pat Delaney's. At centreback, he was cool, steadfast and inspiring. Within a minute of the start, he pointed a seventy-yard free and throughout the game demonstrated his accuracy from long distances. He finished the game as Offaly's top scorer with five points. Throughout the entire game, Pat dominated at centreback – a key position on the hurling field. He deserved to be Hurler of the Year in 1981.

Pat had his own views on training. "I would puck a ball all day and love it but I detested physical training. I cycled three miles to national school and back. I cycled three miles to hurl. I thinned turnips and beet and saved hay. I never had hamstring trouble or broken bones. I didn't need physical training." He recalled that in 1985, for the first round of the Leinster Championship with Kilkenny, he had done no physical training. "I was down in Cork where I did the kind of training I loved – pucking the ball around. In the game against Kilkenny, which ended in a draw, I had my finest hour. I felt super fit. No matter where I went that day in Croke Park, the ball followed me." The year 1985 was a testing one for Offaly as they attempted to erase the memory of the Centenary year defeat by Cork. This they did with a victory over Galway that brought Offaly a second All-Ireland crown. For Pat, 1985 was the year of his first All-Star.

In decades to come, two memories that will remain vivid in Pat's mind relate to occasions of defeat. His first day in Croke Park was for the Leinster final of 1969 between Kilkenny and Offaly. He was one of fourteen that a neighbour carried in a van to the match. He cried that day in Croke Park when the match was over. His heroes had come so near – 3:9 to 0:16. "Paddy Molloy was my idol. He scored the best point I ever saw that day. My namesake on the Kilkenny team Pat Delaney of Johnstown got the three goals."

In the All-Ireland semi-final of 1989 against Antrim, Pat wished in the last quarter that the ground would open up and swallow them. His legs were giving up. "When you were young you could cover off for colleagues. Now at thirty-four I couldn't do it. And when Antrim put on the pressure and got vital scores in the final stages, we hadn't the reserves to respond and come back." For Pat it was a defeat of deep disappointment. With a Leinster title at the expense of Kilkenny under their belt, backed up by the vast experience gained in contesting ten successive Leinster finals – victorious in six – it was felt that the team had the necessary ingredients to take another All-Ireland title. *Ní mar a shíltear a bhítear.*

Pat was a thoughtful player and he planned ahead. Every Christmas he purchased six Randall hurleys. Special attention was paid to the balance and the weight was paired down to one-and-a-half pounds. He always took three of those hurleys to Croke Park. As a defender, he was rock-like rather than stylish, composed rather than classy, calculating rather than flamboyant. In a distinguished career, opponents learned that Pat was an extremely difficult player on which to excel.

LEONARD ENRIGHT
LIMERICK

Born: 1952
Interviewed: 1994

"I first hurled for Patrickswell under-16 — managed by Richard Bennis. Richard Bennis would be my favourite club man. Both for underage and senior Richard is prepared to do any kind of work for the club.

"Seán Foley, in my mind, would be the greatest half-back I ever saw playing the game. The greatest example of his play was lift and strike in the same movement and send a fast ball to his forwards — the ideal ball for forwards.

"Great full-forwards I played against — Ray Cummins, Tony Doran, P.J, Cuddy and Noel Casey.

"My hurling days with Patrickswell and Limerick were great days. I wish I could live them all over again. If I got my chance again I would try to improve my game. The friendships I made will last forever. If hurling was for making enemies I would never have played the game."

Leonard was a talented all-round athlete and sportsman. Success came early in life. At the age of twelve he joined Redgate Athletic Club and won trophies for jumping, running, discus and javelin. In 1966 he won the County Limerick decathlon — a fiercely demanding ten event contest. He set a record for the Munster discus. He tried his hand at soccer too for a while — the club suspended him; the county warned him. He also played football for his club at all grades.

However, it is as a hurler that Leonard is best known. He played minor, under-21 and senior hurling with his native Limerick. One of his first games at senior level was in 1971 when he played in goal in a vital league match against Wexford at Enniscorthy. He shared in the Limerick league and Oireachtas victories of that year.

For most of the seventies he played intermittently with the county senior team. Then, in 1979, Limerick suffered a severe blow when shortly before the Munster final Pat Hartigan, their outstanding full-back, received a serious eye injury and had to withdraw. Limerick had to search for a successor to Pat. They found it in the person of Leonard Enright. He was an outstanding full-back — one of the best of his era and comparable to any of the all-time greats. He had a safe pair of hands, had first-touch mastery, could read a game well and was quick to size up a situation; he was mobile, tight and utterly dependable. He won three All-Star awards at full-back, bringing the Limerick total in that position to eight.

He has always admired the Cork style of hurling where they make the ball do the work. And he often noted that, when their half-forward line send the ball goal wards, they tend to follow up and add to the pressure on the opposing defence. He feels Limerick have always been at their best playing ground hurling.

His "nightmare game" was the 1984 championship clash with Cork. It was the day Limerick gave away three gift goals and Leonard was one of the donors. "I was clearing the ball close to goal. As I struck it, my leg slipped — the ball hit off my leg and dribbled over the line. It was a bad day — it turned out a very bad day." And what about John Fenton's goal from a sideline cut fifty yards out that went all the way to the net through Tommy Quaid's fingers? "I remember that too. John had a great pair of wrists."

His most memorable win was the Munster title of 1980 when Cork were defeated. "It was the biggest we got in my time. It was the one that gave me greatest satisfaction." He puts it ahead of the league victories of 1984 and 1985. Cork were heading for a record six in a row in Munster. On paper the team looked invincible – hurling talent and experience in abundance. They had beaten Limerick earlier in the year in two great games – a league final that went to a replay. "We were quietly confident that day – we went out to win. We knew if we got the breaks we would win."

For once, Limerick did get the breaks. Victory hinged on a number of things – an early first-half goal by Éamonn Cregan; a great opportunist second-half goal by Ollie O'Connor; Cregan's deadly accuracy from frees; the switch of Liam O'Donoghue to right-half-back, where he proceeded to give one of his many superb displays for Limerick; the hurling aggression of John Flanagan at centre-forward; and finally superb defensive play by Leonard Enright at full-back.

The one that got away – the game he would want to play all over again – was the first-round Munster Championship game against Waterford in 1982. "We had won the Munster title in 1980 and 1981 and were confident of making it three in a row. It was something Limerick hadn't done since the thirties. We felt we could go on to win the All-Ireland. A lapse in concentration lost it for us." It was Leonard's greatest disappointment, a one-point defeat.

What changes does he see in the game? "County hurling is now like your work. The demands are immense – on fitness, on time, on family. With so much emphasis on physical fitness, the basic skills of hurling have suffered."

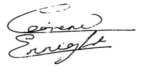

GER FENNELLY
KILKENNY

Born: 1954
Interviewed: 2002

"[I was] Born in Piltown. My earliest memories are of my father, Kevin,
bringing home four or five new hurleys from Henry Giles, who was a
working colleague of my father's – a rent collector – and taking great
pride in that hurley; after playing a game with the brothers, hiding the
hurley and cleaning it. Moved to Ballyhale at seven years of age where my
father bought a farm.

"My mother was big into the hurling – worrying about us a lot of
the time in case of injury. But she had many great days. It was hurling for breakfast, dinner and supper when we were young. It was hurling
every evening of the week. My father was a great inspiration to me. Work
finished on the farm at six o'clock and then off to the training field with

the whistle in his pocket as referee. Them were the days that made us so successful.

"My memory of great players I came up against would have been many – men like Mick Jacob of Wexford, John Fenton of Cork, Pat Delaney of Offaly, Seán Foley of Limerick, the Connollys of Galway and, of course, Tony Doran."

Ger Fennelly, son of Kevin and Teresa (née Hoyne), comes from a great hurling family. Seven brothers – listed from eldest to youngest: Michael, Ger, Kevin, Brendan, Liam, Sean and Dermot – all played the game and all wore the black and amber jersey of Kilkenny at some grade at county level. And, of course, their first cousin Mary won All-Ireland camogie titles in 1974, 1976 and 1977. Hurling was Ger's passion. A cool, calm exterior camouflaged the internal nervousness that preceded every game. A man of quiet disposition, he always gently encouraged those around him.

An inspirational figure in the household was their late father Kevin, whose whole life revolved around the game of hurling and its promotion. He played a key role in 1972 in getting the two teams in the parish of Ballyhale to unite under the new name of Shamrocks.

Ger Fennelly first tasted All-Ireland success in 1972 when he played at centre-field on the Kilkenny minor team that overwhelmed Cork in the final. Further honours came to Ger in 1974 and 1975 when Kilkenny defeated Waterford and Cork respectively, in the under-21 finals of those years. Ger was captain in 1974. "Two weeks earlier I won an All-Ireland senior medal as a sub on the panel. Two weeks later I was off on a trip to America – all in the space of four weeks."

As the years sped onwards, the success rate gathered momentum. Honours and bouquets came from every quarter. Ger won National League titles in 1982, 1983 and 1986.

Sunday, 2 September 1979 was a proud day for Kilkenny and a special day for Ger. "It was a great honour to be captain; first full year in championship hurling; coming from a small club; playing in a game that was being covered all over the world. Playing on All-Ireland day was big in itself."

Following the final whistle against Galway, Ger held aloft the MacCarthy Cup in the Hogan Stand – a proud captain signalling Kilkenny's twenty-first All-Ireland senior hurling title. Two more senior titles came

Ger's way in 1982 and 1983. His performance in 1983 brought him an All-Star award. He called it a day at county level in 1989.

Let us now look at the three All-Ireland club titles won by Ger's club Shamrocks.

1981 – beat St Finbarr's (Cork), 1:15 to 1:11 at Thurles
1984 – beat Gort (Galway), 1:10 to 0:7 at Thurles, following a 1:10 apiece draw at Birr.
1990 – beat Ballybrown (Limerick) 1:16 to 0:16 at Croke Park

It was Ger who scored the all-important goal against Ballybrown in the 1990 final. "I got a shoulder and got a free – about fifty yards out. I was probably going for a point but it ended up in the net – badly needed at the time. I played that game with five stitches in my finger – injured it the week before the game, kept it quiet; thought I wouldn't make it, but I did."

These club victories represented for Ballyhale parish and the Fennelly family a *coup de grâce*, a *piéce de résistance*. It brought the parish on level terms with Blackrock of Cork – three titles each. It brought the Fennelly family a unique honour that we can safely bet will never be equalled, not to mind surpassed. All seven brothers played in each final. The family collected twenty-one All-Ireland senior hurling club medals – a wonderful achievement.

Ger Fennelly

LIAM FENNELLY
KILKENNY

Born: 1958
Interviewed: 1994

"My basic skills were built into my game at a very early age at home in Castlebanny, playing hurling up against the wall, in the paddock, and hunting cattle around the family farm. I suppose the greatest influence on my career was my father and older brother Michael, who insisted on teaching us all the skills. Hurling was part of growing up and probably was the most important part of our school days. It was in school that we started getting used to playing fifteen aside under the close eyes of Peadar O'Neill and Joe Dunphy.

"I suppose every child's dream in Kilkenny is to wear the black and amber and I was delighted to get that chance, and it was a bonus to play alongside great names such Frank Cummins and the rest of the 1982–83 teams. Really, the game of hurling was born for small parish teams and I had that great luck to win championships with the Shamrocks and knock a great fifteen years of unbelievable satisfaction for our local area.

"If I had to condense my life in hurling into one sentence and to say what I most achieved from the game I would have to say the friends I made and also the fact that it is the greatest way of all to start a conversation. To conclude, I suppose, I will never forget the 1992 final – the sense of satisfaction and achievement I felt when the final whistle sounded and knowing that this was to be my last day to wear the black and amber jersey. I hope for the future that the GAA will remain close to the grass-roots of rural Ireland and long may it continue to create enjoyment and surprises for all."

Not surprisingly, Liam's greatest moment – "the biggest moment in my lifetime; the biggest moment in the club" – was when Ballyhale Shamrocks won the All-Ireland club hurling title in 1981 by defeating St Finbarr's of Cork with the score 1:15 to 1:11. Finbarr's were powered by men like Ger Cunningham, Donal O'Grady and Jimmy Barry Murphy. "It was our greatest performance ever. In the dressing-room before the game there was silent determination on every face. There was no shouting or speeches – just silent, grim resolve. The game itself was a great one – probably the best ever club final. We were the first rural parish to win the title and the homecoming was indescribable." But parish glory did not end there. In 1984 they captured the title for the second time when defeating Gort after a replay by 1:10 to 0:7: "two very tough games. I came on in the drawn game in the closing stages when we were four points down. I had broken a bone in my leg in a league game and removed the plaster myself the Wednesday before the match. In the replay I played for the full hour but the damage I did to my ankle lasted for a good while afterwards." The club won the title for the third time when they defeated Ballybrown of Limerick in 1990 – 1:16 to 0:16. In the 1984 line-out, five Fennellys played in the forwards – each knowing what the other was thinking – and the full-forward line read Dermot, Kevin and Liam. Happily, their father was alive to celebrate all three victories and share in a great family triumph.

Liam captained Kilkenny to their twenty-third and twenty-fourth All-Ireland successes and a further glow was added to the glory of each occasion by an All-Star award. There was a uniqueness about those captaincies that may never be repeated. In 1983 Liam brought home to Kilkenny the original MacCarthy Cup, presented for the last time to Declan Carr of

Tipperary in 1991. In 1992 a new MacCarthy Cup arrived on the scene and Kilkenny and Liam Fennelly were back after a lapse of nine years to take it to the Noreside.

He remembers both occasions very well. "In 1983 I couldn't help feeling to myself: who am I to lead out these great ones – men like Noel Skehan, Joe Hennessy, Ger Henderson, Frank Cummins and Billy Fitzpatrick, all more experienced than me? The occasion was emotional. I felt tears come down from my eyes running onto Croke Park that day. It was a horrible day for hurling – a very strong wind – an awful hard day to win a match." Kilkenny played with the wind in the first half. A typical Liam Fennelly goal – the opportunist variety at which he was so adept – less than ten minutes to half time stretched Kilkenny's lead at the interval to six points. At the final whistle, the scoreboard read Kilkenny 2:14, Cork 2:12.

By 1992 Liam had become the elder statesman – the only survivor on the first fifteen from the 1983 winning side. "As I held the cup aloft to jubilant Kilkenny followers, I took a good look around Croke Park. I was savouring the moment. I knew it would never come again for my mind was firmly fixed on retirement. When I was young it never dawned on me that I would play for Kilkenny and now here I was leading them to victory for the second time – a great honour."

Liam was a potent forward who operated mainly in the left corner and switched regularly to full-forward during games. He was a worker and a forager who challenged for every ball. This, together with a combination of skill, vision and positional sense, enabled him to seize rare opportunities and steal snap scores.

The family has garnered a large collection of trophies and awards that includes seven All-Ireland medals, five All-Star awards, eleven National League titles, twenty-one All-Ireland club medals, several Leinster senior titles, a number of underage titles and in excess of fifty county medals. "As the years pass, it is not the medals but the memories that will mean most to me."

Liam Fennelly

JOHN FENTON
CORK

Born: 1955
Interviewed: 1994

Homecoming celebrations for John Fenton (captain) following victory
in the Centenary Final of 1984.

"My father, Dan, played with Carrigtwohill and the Cork junior team and
he encouraged and helped me in every way. One of my great friends and
mentors in later years, Willie John Daly, played with my father on those
teams and this was an inspiration to me to follow in their footsteps.

"When we (Midleton) finally succeeded on 9 October 1983 in beating St
Finbarr's in the final, it was the culmination of all my hurling dreams. It
was a fairytale ending to a story that nobody thought would ever be written. It was without doubt my greatest moment in sport and one which will
always give me my fondest memory. The following twelve months were

all go, with Midleton, Cork and Munster all being successful in what was a great year for the GAA – it being the Centenary year.

"Looking back on my career I find that it helped me in a great way in developing my personality and character. The greatest memory I have is the friendship and comradeship I had with the players I played with and the players I played against. There will always be disappointments in playing games, but, if you approach the game in a proper manner and play the game fairly, it will always bring enjoyment and great memories to look back on when that final puck of the sliotar is struck."

John Fenton began playing with Cork in 1975 but there was so much hurling talent in the county during the three-in-a-row years of 1976–1978 that it took John until the early eighties to firmly establish himself on the first fifteen. "I was raw in those early days," he said of his attempt to bridge the considerable gap between intermediate club (which Midleton was at the time) hurling and county senior hurling. "I had to learn fast and I needed space. I found that at midfield, which was my favourite position." The most disappointing moment in his career was when he was taken off in the second half of the All-Ireland final of 1983 against Kilkenny. "The temptation to quit the game altogether was very great." Fortunately, he didn't. The good days lay ahead in the Centenary year of 1984 and thereafter. The spur to keep going came when his club Midleton won the 1983 County Cork Senior title. After that, John captained Munster to Railway Cup honours in 1984. Under his captaincy, Cork reached the Centenary final of 1984 and faced Offaly in Semple Stadium, Thurles on a glorious first Sunday in September. They emerged victorious. Further honours included an All-Star award and Hurler of the Year in 1984.

John was one of the finest midfielders of his time and won five All-Star awards in a row in that position from 1983 to 1987. He was excellent at the art of ground striking and a master of the sideline cut. He was a reliable long- distance free taker and was deadly with frees in front of goal. All his attributes stemmed from perseverance and painstaking practice.

There was a precision about John's hurling and his shots at goal were radar-guided. Let's look at a few examples:

* In the 1980 National League final replay against Limerick, he blazed a penalty to the net and scored a point from a sideline cut

- In the Munster Championship of 1984 against Limerick, he took a sideline cut from about fifty yards out. It floated into the hands of Tommy Quaid in the Limerick goal and through his fingers to the net

- In the 1986 All-Ireland final against the favourites Galway, Cork won a twenty-one yard free eight minutes after the throw-in. Up stepped John. The net shook. Galway's confidence sank

- In the 1987 Munster Championship against Limerick at Thurles, about forty-five yards out and dead centre with the Limerick goal, John sized up the approaching ground ball – total concentration – then the swing and the stroke, beautifully measured timed and executed, goalward soared the sliotar and, before Tommy Quaid could react, the ball was in the top corner of the net. It was undoubtedly one of the great goals of hurling. So dramatic was it that it subsequently became the background action for a farming advertisement. It was rated the "Goal of the Year" by RTÉ and won for John a magnificent Waterford Crystal trophy appropriately inscribed

Following retirement, John put in a lot of work with underage players. He tried to instil into them a policy of ground hurling and a philosophy of letting the ball do the work – "something which Fr Bertie Troy bred into us." He discouraged solo runs. At training sessions he picked out the fastest player and gave him a thirty-yard start on a solo run. From where he took off, another player struck a ball, which travelled about sixty yards. "No contest," said John as he looked at his students and hoped he had driven the message home.

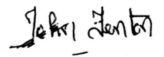

PETE FINNERTY
GALWAY

Born: 1964
Interviewed: 1996

Pete Finnerty (right) with Peter Quinn, Uachtarán CLG. Railway Cup presentation 1991.

"During my years in the maroon and white I have had many great days and nights. The first day I played senior in 1985 against Cork in the downpour at headquarters, the two All-Ireland victories in 1987 and 1988, the All-Star awards, the trips to the States and the general convivial atmosphere that surrounded those ten years were brilliant. The one occasion that stands out above all the rest was in 1986, the All-Ireland semi-final against the Cats. With fifteen minutes remaining in the game I looked at the scoreboard, and we were leading by nine points. We had out-hurled the Cats in all areas and we had also outfoxed them.

"The reason that this victory was so sweet was, when I was a young lad I played hurling in the field behind our home from evening till dusk. I imagined myself as Brian Cody, Fan Larkin, Eddie Keher, or Billy Fitz – these were the great heroes, and they were all Cats. On that day in August 1986 we gave the youth of Galway their own home-grown heroes: Cooney, Ryan, Keady, Lane. Could this be true? Was it a once-off? No, we confirmed the result in 1987 by beating them again in the All-Ireland final."

Having greeted Pete, I reminded him that he had retired at thirty and that now, at thirty-two, he could still be playing. He went early. Why?

He paused, smiled, and reflected for a moment. "When I was in my early twenties I often heard of the great three-in-a-row Galway football team of the sixties. Nearly all of those retired on or before the thirty mark. I couldn't understand it – that is, not until I reached that age myself. Then I understood. It was easier to get injured; took longer to recuperate; the demands on energy seemed greater. In my young days, training was effortless; as you headed for thirty it became more demanding. It was five nights a week. As well as that there was the job and the family. I'd love to have continued, but I knew the speed wasn't there any more. All considered, it was time to go."

When Pete was six, his mother died. There were three other boys: John, Paddy, and Tom, aged ten, eight, and four, respectively. His father, also Pete, a farmer and psychiatric nurse, reared them all. "He would pack nine or ten of us into his estate car and drive us to play the national school competition games."

Pete's father loved going to matches. "It gave him a new lease of life" after the shattering blow of losing his wife. Knowing he was on the sideline made Pete want to play better and to excel. Performance assessment from his father was always positive and supportive. A lovely relationship developed between father and son and has continued to this day. They go for a pint together, reminisce, and discuss the matches.

Pete Finnerty was an outstanding right-half-back, a position where he gave many a superb display of classic defensive hurling. He was always very fit. Concentration, tenacity, timing, positional sense and well-honed skills were his hallmarks. His display against Cork in the All-Ireland semi-final of 1985, when he reached great heights, was arguably his greatest. It earned him the RTÉ Man of the Match award and also a B&I award.

He won his first of five All-Star awards that year. Indeed, it might well have been a record-breaking six in a row if the Tony Keady controversy of 1989 had been avoided. All the awards were in the right-half-back position, and five in the space of six years reflected a series of consistently high performances – a sure mark of greatness. He won Railway Cup medals in 1986, 1989, and 1991. He was absent for the victories of 1987 and 1988, when he was in America in a temporary capacity with his colleague Gerry McInerney.

Pete packed a lot of hurling into an inter-county career that began in minor ranks in 1980 and continued for fifteen years until the All-Ireland semi-final defeat by Offaly in 1994, after which he called it a day. As the years pass and great wing-backs of modem hurling are recalled and discussed, the name Pete Finnerty will certainly be among them.

PAT FLEURY
OFFALY

Born: 1956
Interviewed: 2001

Pat (right) with Michael Connolly, the Galway captain, and referee George Ryan (Tipperary), before the 1985 All-Ireland final.

"It would have been inconceivable, when my senior inter-county career began in the 1975 championship, that by the time I would decide to retire after the Leinster final of 1986, Offaly hurling would have reached levels which were beyond our wildest dreams.

"One sentiment which remains constant is of being fortunate enough to be part of a great team which made the breakthrough in Leinster in 1980, won our first ever All-Ireland senior hurling title in 1981 and was equally fortunate to captain that team in two successive All-Ireland finals 1984, when we lost the Centenary final to Cork, and 1985, when we overcame an emerging Galway side to win our second title.

"While there were many great occasions and great memories, pride of place must go to the Leinster final of 1980. On the basis that something can only be won for the first time once, it will always be special.

"The Centenary final must rank as the greatest disappointment but, happily, we compensated our supporters in 1985.

"My club, Drumcullen, supplied me with my childhood hero in the shape of the incomparable Paddy Molloy, and wonderful encouragement and support throughout my playing career and during my term as Offaly senior hurling manger. My single greatest regret is that we failed to win an Offaly Senior Championship during my time with them."

Pat Fleury was born in 1956 and grew up in the parish of Drumcullen. In his hurling days he was 6ft tall and weighed 12st. 7lbs, "but there were days when I was sorry I wasn't a stone or more heavier." The local hurling hero was Paddy Molloy of Offaly and Leinster fame. "He was our Cú Chulainn and when you saw him walking or cycling down the road you felt like genuflecting. I was fortunate to get on the local team, where it all starts and ends, at an early age and had the privilege of playing with Paddy. He played all over the field for the club. Then there was Tom Dooley who came from a great hurling family. He used to organise young teams and bring us to matches."

An All-Ireland senior "B" Colleges' title with Presentation Birr in 1973 paved the way for Pat to progress to county minor and under-21. He made his senior debut in 1975 and won the Fitzgibbon Cup in 1977 with University College Galway – a famous victory over Maynooth 1:14 to 1:12.

Hurling was always strong in Offaly but it was weakened at county level by fierce parish rivalry. "In the Autumn of 1979 the county board brought in Dermot Healy to train the Offaly players. He made a big impact. His contribution was enormous. Success came earlier than people anticipated. Dermot placed emphasis on doing the basics well – tight marking, blocking, hooking and direct hurling. These became the trademark of Offaly hurling."

In 1980 an open draw was introduced in Leinster. It led to a provincial final meeting of Offaly and Kilkenny. In almost all eyes Offaly were perceived as sacrificial lambs. Only 9,613 turned up to witness the slaughter. But Dermot Healy had prepared them well. He covered much detail. He dealt with the mental as well as the physical aspects. It was, after all, only Offaly's sixth Leinster final with no success to date.

Dermot's words rang in every Offaly ear. "At no stage look into the stand at the crowd. In the parade just keep your eyes on the man in front of you. Either get the ball or stop your man scoring if you're a back; stop him clearing effectively if you're a forward. Eradicate frees. Close-in frees should all be scored."

"For over twenty minutes of the first half we had played a good game and made Kilkenny come from behind. But at times in that half we saw all the hallmarks of the same old story. We were behind at the break, 3:6 to 1:10, yet we knew we should be ahead. Dermot didn't come into the dressing room until a little while after us. There was a big smile on his face. He said he was delighted with the way things were going. He was using psychology. He pointed out we had been ahead in the first half so why couldn't we do it again. We could now accept what used to be inevitable defeat in the past or go out and do something about it.

The second half was enthralling. It was fast and furious as the ball moved to and fro about the pitch. With ten minutes to go the pressure was unreal."

The final whistle presented the incredible score line of Offaly 3:17, Kilkenny 5:10. A new hurling force was on the march.

Unfortunately, the famous victory became overshadowed by sadness. A cloud descended on the occasion when it was learned that Tommy Horan, father of Pádraig, one of Offaly's heroes of the day, had died in a car while listening to the match.

Offaly lost the All-Ireland semi-final to Galway by two points but a year later they defeated the Tribesmen in the All-Ireland final by three points. Glory days had begun. The victory qualified Offaly for an All-Stars trip to America. "It was very beneficial to the team. It was our first time away as a group. We were relaxed. There was a togetherness."

Pat's hour of captaincy glory came in 1985 when he displayed great leadership qualities in leading Offaly to a two-point victory over Galway in the All-Ireland final.

Pat felt that they owed that All-Ireland victory to their supporters after the homecoming reception they received the previous year, despite falling to Cork at Thurles in the Centenary final of 1984. "The journey home from Thurles was difficult in 1984. We were very disappointed. We didn't play well. I didn't feel the gap between us was as great as the final score of 3:16 to 1:12 might suggest. The reception that awaited us in Tullamore was unbelievable. The crowd was as big as when we won in 1981. We were blown away by the reception. We were so moved and so shocked by it all. As captain, I had to make various speeches. I found it hard to compose myself – the emotion of it all. I had a lump in my throat. All that was missing was the cup. It made a huge impact on the players. They resolved to deliver in 1985."

Pat was a stalwart defender – staunch and uncompromising. At corner-back he was like a sentry on duty. He cleared his lines with speed and without ceremony.

His hurling career brought lots of honours – the major ones being two All-Ireland titles, two All-Star awards and four Leinster successes.

Pat quit the county scene in 1986 after losing the Leinster final to Kilkenny "'Twas a big decision. It was hard to leave. You leave a big part of your life behind."

AIDAN FOGARTY
OFFALY

Born: 1958
Interviewed: 1996

"The most important and significant influence on me was that of my family. All our family were involved in the game, with my late father [Tom] the mainstay. The interest shown by my father, who regularly took half-days off work to attend college matches – my mother always travelled to keep him company – motivated one to work harder to fulfil ambitions.

"All my brothers – Gerard, Declan, Frank, and Andrew – played hurling for the club and county at various levels, with Declan featuring with the Offaly seniors in the eighties, including the All-Ireland years of 1984 and 1985. My wife, Theresa, was always a keen follower and travelled to all the games."

In the years that lie ahead, irrespective of what direction Offaly hurling takes, Aidan will be able to look back and say that he was there at the dawning of a great spring – a spring that bore much fruit and yielded rich harvests all through his career.

He first donned the Offaly jersey in a challenge game against Tipperary at Birr in 1976, having had as the hero of his youth, Martin Coogan, stalwart Kilkenny half-back.

The last inter-county game played by this forceful and competitive hurler was against Dublin in the Leinster semi-final of 1991. "I only played because one of the lads was injured. At thirty-three I was finding it hard to stay there. In training you found yourself marking younger fellows; you go for the break of the ball; he passes you out; you know you are gone. Time to go."

Aidan excelled as a defender, operating mainly at right full-back and right-half-back, although in 1988 he captained Leinster to his only Railway Cup success, playing at full-back. Aidan's style was tight and first-time, his covering highly effective.

After the Centenary Cup senior hurling quarter-final, in which Offaly defeated Kilkenny 1:17 to 2:11, Sean Kilfeather wrote: "...it is fair to say that their inspiration came mostly from Aidan Fogarty, who had a superb second half. He continually broke up Kilkenny attacks with timely inter-ceptions, and his clearances, whether short or long, from the hurley or from the hand, invariably found a strategically placed colleague and lifted siege after siege...".

The many honours that came his way were spread evenly throughout his career: seven Leinster titles between 1980 and 1990; two All-Ireland titles, 1981 and 1985: two All-Star awards, 1982 and 1989; Railway Cup, 1988; National League, 1991; eight county titles between 1975 and 1993; Leinster club titles in 1982 and 1993.

Let's now look at the great breakthrough by Offaly. It came in 1980 and it caught hurling followers and journalists by surprise. They faced Kilkenny in the Leinster final. The magazine *Sports World* carried a front-page heading, "Easy for Kilkenny". Hurling followers seemed to agree; only 9,613 turned up for the game, the smallest attendance of modern times. The final score was Offaly 3:17, Kilkenny 5:10. Those who came witnessed a piece of hurling history: Offaly's first Leinster senior hurl-ing title, achieved against the odds. It was a triumph for courage – a great moment for hurling.

Surprisingly, it doesn't rank with Aidan's great moments. "Matt Ruth was causing problems for our full-back line, and I was switched from the half-back line to corner-back to mark him. A minor flare-up between the two of us led to my name being taken. Following this Dermot Healy took me off. I was disappointed. I think he thought I was going to lose the head."

A year later Offaly defeated Galway in the All-Ireland final – their first victory in their first appearance. For Aidan, the 1981 success was his greatest sporting moment and most abiding memory. I wondered what his thoughts were before that game. "The lead-up was all unknown to us. Dermot Healy, who guided us through the pressure of interviews and publicity, kept emphasising that we should try to imagine it as just another game – a game against our neighbours. I reminded myself I went to school for a year with Galway's centre-back, Seán Silke – anything to play down the hype factor.

"In the dressing-room before the game everyone was nervous – didn't know what to expect; trying to concentrate on the game. Then the speech before you go out. I always found it hard to take in what was being said. I would be concentrating on my own game; the person I would be playing on – saying to myself it was just another game, telling myself not to let the occasion get to me."

They returned to the dressing-room at half time six points in arrears. "We were extremely nervous. It was a first half in which no player could feel he had done himself justice. We had given away thirteen points but no goal. We had scored the only goal. We were hanging in."

And hang in they did too in the second half, and with five minutes to go they were within two points of wasteful Galway, 1:10 to 0:15. Two minutes later came the winning move involving Joachim Kelly, Pat Delaney, and Brendan Bermingham, who parted to Johnny Flaherty, who expertly engineered a palmed goal. It finished 2:12 to 0:15. The journey home, like all victorious journeys, would seem very short; the celebrations to follow would be protracted.

In 1984, the Centenary year of the GAA, Offaly faced Cork at Semple Stadium, Thurles. It was Offaly's second final, Cork's fortieth – a unique hurling occasion. Aidan's memories? "I don't like to talk too much about it. It sticks in the craw. It was one of those days when little went right. We were confident – had beaten Galway by fourteen points; had played in the 1981 final; knew what it was like to be in a final. There are always nerves on the big day, but the awe barrier had been broken down.

"I felt we had a reasonable first half. Cork got a run in the second half and we couldn't cope. We had first-half chances for goals that didn't come off. I don't like talking about 1984."

PAT FOX
TIPPERARY

Born: 1961
Interviewed: 1997

Pat (centre) with stars of other sporting fields,
Ken Doherty (left) and Michael Carruth (right).

"As far back as I can remember I had a love for hurling. With six boys in my family there were always hurleys behind the kitchen door. At the age of eight I went to every training session with my club, Éire Óg, Annacarty. I would stand behind the goal and puck the ball in to them, hoping my day would come.

"Bill O'Donnell, who played for Tipp. in the early forties, taught me in national school, and he was a man I admired. Thanks to my brother Séamus for starting me off. I went to Cappawhite Vocational School at secondary level; I played county vocational schools with Tipperary. I started playing with Éire Óg senior team at the age of fifteen, and intend to play for another fifteen!

"My first big thrill was getting called to play minor county in 1978 and 1979 and then winning three under-21 All-Ireland medals, 1979, 1980, and 1981. Everything looked rosy until late 1982. When I tore my knee ligament it looked all over. With a lot of hard work I built my knee up again, and in 1985 I got back on the county senior team. The big breakthrough came in 1987 – was one of my greatest memories. Winning the All-Ireland in 1989 was great, but I knew that we must win another one to be remembered, as people considered beating Antrim was no big deal! 1991 was the icing on the cake, beating Kilkenny in the All-Ireland final. For me that night, receiving the Man of the Match live on television, was one of my proudest moments. I knew I couldn't achieve anything higher."

Pat was a spirited, quick-thinking and whole-hearted performer, a tenacious forager who could turn on a sixpence and when in possession had the skill to produce scores, even when his options were limited and he had little room to manoeuvre.

He was corner-forward when Tipperary faced Cork in the Munster final replay at Killarney in 1987. The game went into extra time. Tipperary only took the lead for the first time four minutes into the second half of extra time. They kept coming from behind in a game that Cork seemed capable of winning and in which they seemed in general the more composed. The final score of 4:22 to 1:22 belies the closeness of a bruising, epic contest, full of drama, changing fortune, fierce excitement.

Pat Fox was outstanding – a constant worry to the Cork defence. He scored eleven points, seven from frees. "In some ways it was a frustrating game for me. I drove the first three frees I took wide. I was pulled down in the square and the ref blew the whistle when all I had to do was tip the ball into the net. In the second half a shot I sent in rebounded off the stanchion at the back of the goal. It was a goal which we didn't get. There were times in the first half when it looked as if Cork would destroy us. We never gave up, and our hunger wore Cork down at the finish."

If ever hunger won a game it was this Munster final replay. Hurlingwise Tipp were ravenous. They hadn't won a Munster title since the 1971 epic contest with Limerick at Killarney.

Pat's wife, Marita, was in Fitzgerald Stadium to share in the jubilation. "What a win! They were back in the big time after so long. The excitement was unbearable. The jumping for joy could never be the same again after 1987. I thought Pat was something else that day." He won his first of three All-Stars in 1987. On display in his bar in Cashel is a clock superimposed on a lovely night picture of Boston, presented to him by the Tipperary Association in Boston "in appreciation of his dedication to hurling and in honour of being selected an All-Star."

1991 brought a repeat of 1987, except that the replay – a battle royal, intense and uncompromising, full of fury and played in intense heat – didn't go into extra time. Cork again, on both days, looked the more composed and complete unit, and when they went nine points up fifteen minutes into the second half it seemed to be all over. But when the final whistle blew it was Tipperary 4:19, Cork 4:15. Pat had given a regal display in the blue-and-gold jersey, and Tipperary had won a contest that for long periods seemed beyond their grasp. They went on to defeat Kilkenny in the All-Ireland final.

Without a doubt it was Pat's greatest hurling year. He gave brilliant displays all through. "I probably had one of my best hours in the replay in Thurles. I got 1:5 from play marking Denis Walsh. It was one of the best games Tipp were ever involved in for excitement. The All-Ireland final of that year against Kilkenny was the game that gave me the greatest pleasure. It mightn't have been the greatest hurling, but when you win an All-Ireland – that's the ultimate."

All kinds of awards and honours flowed Pat's way in 1991. He received his third All-Star at right-full-forward; he was nominated Texaco Hurler of the Year; he was awarded RTÉ Man of the Match after his display against Kilkenny – for Marita, "my proudest moment"; he was voted most consistent player of the year; he was chosen by the Tipperary Association in Dublin as Tipperary Person of the Year, 1991. And then came a signal accolade: Supreme Sportsman of the Year, 1991, at the Texaco awards – the first GAA man so honoured.

Pat made his last appearance in the blue-and-gold jersey when he came on as a sub in the closing stages of the Munster final replay of 1996 against Limerick, but even his presence failed to swing the game in favour of the Premier County.

CONOR HAYES
GALWAY

Born: 1958
Interviewed: 1994

"Hurling has always been in my life. Fr Jack Solan (RIP) claimed that I was so young and small that he had to get a special short hurley made for me for the school's team. That would have been in the late sixties when Galway hurling at juvenile level was undergoing a revival that would have a major knock-on effect in later years.

"Club hurling was played with Kiltormer who, along with Laurencetown and Clantusbert, won several minor and under-21 titles in the seventies along with making the breakthough to senior level in 1976 and winning the Senior Championship in 1976 and 1977.

"Galway minor hurlers were well beaten in 1975 and 1976 but success was to follow at the under-21 final of 1978 when we beat Tipperary in a replay at Limerick. All-Ireland senior success was more difficult to achieve but finally came in 1980, after fifty-seven years waiting and having been beaten by Kilkenny the previous year. Offaly were to make the big breakthrough the following year at Galway's expense – a final for which I was injured. A few barren years followed up to the Farrell era of 1985–90, when Galway contested a total of five All-Ireland finals, winning two, in 1987 and 1988, when I was fortunate enough to be captain. Should have won more but that's the way it goes.

"The team of 1987 and 1988 was by far the best that I have been involved with, and won all that was to be won in hurling, producing some of the most dedicated and skilful hurlers that I have ever played with. It also signified a major breakthrough for Galway, defeating Kilkenny and Tipperary in All-Ireland finals which would have been unheard of twenty years before that.

"A hurling career always seems short because of the enjoyment one gets from it and so 1990 saw me finished with the county scene to revert to the club and finish on an absolutely unbelievable note of two County Championships and an All-Ireland Club Championship before I called it a day."

When he was a child in the sixties, when Galway had poor hurling teams, Conor remembers hearing his father, who was a Clare man, talking in awesome tones about Munster finals and in his youthful mind he used to wonder what it was that was famous about them. And his father would come back from those finals and tell great stories about Christy Ring and Pat Stakelum and Vin Toomey and a host of others – stories of deeds and daring and gallantry; *misneach is teasbach is gaiscíocht*. It seemed that there wasn't anyone in Galway like them and hopes of Galway winning an All-Ireland title were a mere dream in that barren decade. But the dream became a reality in the days of Conor Hayes and his generation of Galway hurlers. "There was a lot of confidence coming through at underage level during the seventies and most fellows believed an All-Ireland would be won at some stage."

He played in six All-Ireland finals – 1979 and 1980 and four in a row from 1985 to 1988. He can look back with satisfaction on the three victories against traditional strongholds. They were all won in close contests – Limerick in 1980 with three points to spare; Kilkenny in 1987 with six points to spare; Tipperary in 1988 with four points to spare. Offaly proved to be a bogey team, beating them in 1981 and 1985 and "we struck our lowest point in 1984 when they hammered us in Thurles in the All-Ireland semi-final, and I was captain." I suggested that Galway might well have won two sets of three in a row during his time. "1979 to 1981 was possible. It's strange that in those three finals we beat what was easily the best of the three teams – in the only one we won – when we beat Limerick in 1980." The semi-final defeat at the hands of Tipperary in 1989 was his biggest disappointment – "more so than the final defeat by Cork in 1986. We were fairly naive in 1986; we should have known better in 1989 – we had a lot under our belt; we had the luxury of a lot of good players coming through – three in a row was on."

Great moments that will live in his memory and that time will not dim are the historic victory over Limerick in 1980, when the alleged "curse" was expunged, and the defeat of Kilkenny under his captaincy in 1987 in a hard tough game – "it was a test of Galway mettle" – when he had perhaps his most satisfying hour and there followed the second of his three successive All-Star awards. 1987 was also the year when Galway won every league game they played and Conor captained them to league honours.

The winning of the All-Ireland club title by Kiltormer in 1992 was another unforgettable moment. "The club victory parallels anything I won during my career. It means so much to a rural club. Hurling is deep rooted in Kiltormer. Even in the sixties when Galway were winning three in a row in football, it was hurling rather than football that was played in Kiltormer. We had three fantastic games in a saga with Cashel – the third at Croke Park. All three games could have gone either way. It was a sin that either team had to go out. Those games gave us great confidence and the experience gained stood to us in our victory in the final against Birr at Thurles." This was Conor's farewell to hurling.

JOE HENNESSY
KILKENNY

Born: 1956
Interviewed: 1993

"I was born in the old Dean Street in 1956. There is none of the old street, houses or children left. It has all been replaced by modern buildings. I spent my early life there and, for as far back as I can remember, I had a hurl in my hand just like most of the other children. We hurled and played in the Water Barracks. It passed many hours of fun for us.

"Why did I hurl? I owe it all to my dad, the late Paddy Hennessy. He had a love for the game that I never saw in anyone else. He organised street leagues that took in parishes adjoining the city and that included all grades from juvenile to senior. He refereed many of the matches and he brought truck loads of children to the matches on Sundays. I often went to two matches with him on Sunday afternoon and to another one in the evening. To him, hurling was the greatest game in the world and his enthusiasm and spirit rubbed off on me. My dad was my greatest hero.

"In 1976, our club James Stephens won the County Senior Hurling Championship, and from there we reached the All-Ireland club final. This one will always be special to me. Blackrock, Cork were our opponents. Their record was great – and they were loaded with county players. I remember Dermot McCurtain, Pat Moylan, Ray Cummins, Eamon O'Donoghue, John Horgan – all of Cork – and the great Frank Cummins of Kilkenny. They were five points up at the break but in a superb second half we won by 2:10 to 2:4. We were the first club outside of Munster to win the All-Ireland Club Championship and we had beaten the Kings – Blackrock. It was like a dream to me but it all happened in Thurles. There was a surprise follow-up. We had a great meal in Hayes's Hotel and later Paddy Grace, county board secretary for years, stopped me going up the street: 'Hey boy, there'll be a car to collect you next Sunday.'

"He said no more. I was walking on air. I was a sub on a great Kilkenny team. It meant the world to me. I was among the greats of that time – Pat Henderson, Fan Larkin and Mick Crotty, to name but a few. I came on a sub at corner-back against Wexford in 1976. We were skinned by seventeen points. In 1979 I played at midfield and we went on to win the All-Ireland against Galway. 1982 and 1983 meant an awful lot to me as we defeated Cork in both All-Irelands. I hurled up to 1989. I felt I had a great long run.

"The game and the GAA meant everything to me. It was as important as going to Mass on a Sunday. The game also provided me with hurling friends all over Ireland. This is a story about one friend:

"In a Railway Cup match, Leinster v. Connaught, Sylvie Linnane and myself had one hell of a tussle for possession. Both of us eyed one another. We threw down the hurls and boxed. The referee sent both of us to the line. We walked off together, sat down on the sideline together, and talked during the rest of the match. We are still the best of friends."

Joe's calibre and consistency as a hurler is reflected in his All-Star achievements. In a county senior playing life that spanned a dozen years, he was honoured with five All-Star awards – the first in 1978; the last in 1987.

One of his great fortes was his "first touch" brilliance. He had an exceptional positional sense, got to the ball quickly and despatched it immediately, without fuss, even when under pressure.

Joe has many successes to look back on, including the personal awards of Man of the Match when he played on Joe Cooney in Thurles in the All-Ireland semi-final of 1986, and Kilkenny Hurler of the Year in 1987 – "as hard to win as any All-Star award because of the competition in Kilkenny."

Three events stand out as special in Joe's hurling life. We will deal with them in reverse order of importance. The third was Kilkenny's double-double of 1982 and 1983 when they captured All-Ireland and National League titles – a rare achievement.

Next came the All-Ireland victory of 1979 against a talented Galway fifteen. "It was my first All-Ireland win – it's always a dream to win one. You look at the great hurlers winning – and then to win one yourself...".

Now we come to his most cherished hour and victory: the minor All-Ireland success of 1973 against Galway. It was won the hard way. A side-line cut to Galway from their own 21-yard line in the closing stages when they held a slender lead suggested they would lift the siege and hold out. But the cut was poorly hit and driven out over the sideline within yards of where it was taken. The resultant sideline cut to Kilkenny brought a goal and victory by one point – the score Kilkenny 4:5, Galway 3:7. What made it so special for Joe was the fact that his father and mother were present. There could be no repeat. A year later his father was dead. He was Joe's hero. "I'm glad you were there, Dad."

NOEL LANE
GALWAY

Born: 1954
Interviewed: 2001

Noel (second from right) awaits developments.

"My first hurley was made by Pat Monaghan (RIP) and I was very proud of it and treated it like a precious jewel – linseed oil, hanging up each night and running repairs by my late father. Playing with my three brothers and some neighbours we used 'stones' for goalposts and generally a sponge ball.

"My brothers were the first to influence me locally and my father, but it was probably Mícheál O'Hehir on radio that developed my passion and spirit for the game. Of course, my club Ballinderreen – playing with Joe McDonagh, Michael Coen and many others – was also a huge influence. My wife Carmel was probably my greatest supporter and biggest influence of all.

"I had many special moments, good and bad:

- Captain of Ballyglass NS and winning a South final v. Labane NS was special. We met a delivery truck while cycling home from the game – they stopped and filled our cup with orange – it was fantastic; we felt so proud. Tom Doherty brought us on a tour around the area and the parents had a big bonfire and all the goodies to celebrate

- Seeing my name in the *Irish Press* – in my bedroom in digs in Aughrim, Wicklow – as being selected for the Galway team to play Clare in Tulla in the 1977 NHL. That's how I found out – no mobile phones in those days

- Winning the 1980 All-Ireland final, the homecoming and having the MacCarthy Cup in my home, local pub and club – very special

- Scoring a 'Goal of the Year' in the 1979 final v Kilkenny

- All my goals, but particularly the goal v Tipp. in the 1988 All-Ireland final

- Finding out about my All-Star selections in 1983 and 1984

- On Galway 'Team of the Century'

- Watching my kids play for Ballindereen

"The year 1986 was very mixed. I was captain. The thought of leading my county on All-Ireland final day was the stuff of dreams. Playing two inside forwards in the final – a repeat of the semi-final against Kilkenny – backfired badly and Cork beat us.

"The subsequent days and weeks were the worst ever in my life – such a disappointment for myself and my family, but also for Galway. However, we were a young team and went on to win the next two finals.

"I played in eight All-Ireland finals, winning three, and I'm happy enough with my lot as a player. I would love to have won a county senior final with my club.

"I love hurling and did since I was four or five. I still puck around with my kids – it's my favourite way to unwind after a day's work."

Noel hails from the rural parish of Ballindereen in South Galway. So rich in hurling talent was Galway in the 1980s that there were occasions when Noel found himself in the role of "super-sub". So let's recall two in particular.

In the All-Ireland final of 1987 against Kilkenny, Galway, having played with a strong wind in the first half, led by only five points to four at the break in a game of tense, tough, torrid exchanges. Five minutes into the second half, Noel Lane emerged from the subs bench to replace Michael Naughton. It was to prove to be a vital move. With eight minutes to go, it was still anyone's game. Two points separated the sides. It was then that goal-poacher Noel Lane pounced. He finished a build-up, involving Steve Mahon, Éanna Ryan and Joe Cooney, to the Kilkenny net with a hard, angled shot. With that goal – the only goal of the game – the match was won and lost. A further point followed from Tony Keady. The game ended Galway 1:12, Kilkenny 0:9.

The following year, 1988, Noel was again to the fore in a similar role. This time their opponents were Tipperary. Galway played with a strong wind in the opening half and led by ten points to six at half time. Noel, who had played in the earlier games of the championship, replaced Anthony Cunningham in the second half. In the closing stages of the game, with Galway under fierce pressure and clinging to a two-point lead, Noel went into action. He rounded Tipperary full-back Conor O'Donovan and his well-placed ground shot found the net. It clinched victory for the Tribesmen. As in the previous year, it was the only goal of the game. Noel had demonstrated once again that he possessed the flair, temperament and opportunism to produce a winning score in tight, pressured situations. The final of 1988 ended with the score Galway 1:15, Tipperary 0:14.

Throughout the eighties, Noel won major honours on a regular basis. The list is impressive: All-Ireland titles 1980, 1987 and 1988; Railway Cups 1980, 1982, 1983, 1986 and 1987; National Leagues 1987 and 1989; and All-Star awards 1983 and 1984.

In 1990, Galway met Cork (underdogs) in the All-Ireland final and lost a magnificent game by three points. (5:15 to 2:21). Noel was thirty-six. Retirement beckoned. He called it a day.

His fame, however, will live on in hurling circles and his scoring deeds will always be remembered in the folklore of Galway hurling.

JOE McKENNA
LIMERICK

Born: 1951
Interviewed: 1994

"I was educated at St Flannan's College and played Dean Ryan and Harty Cup, winning a Dean Ryan medal. I played minor and under-21 with Offaly for four years and played senior for two years before transferring to Limerick."

The big Shinrone man – 6'2" and 14 st. – blended beautifully into the Limerick team of the period 1973 to 1985. He played in several positions but eventually settled into full-forward where his hurling talents blossomed and captured the imagination of the hurling world. It was the position to which he was best suited. "I didn't have the stamina to last a full hour in the half-forward line. I also found that if I pushed my training beyond a certain point my performance deteriorated. If I trained too hard in the summer my energy suffered."

He was a superb full-forward – one of the all-time greats – ranking in the modern game with Ray Cummins of Cork and Tony Doran of

TERENCE "SAMBO" McNAUGHTON
ANTRIM

Born: 1964
Interviewed: 1997

"My earliest memory is a Sunday afternoon in July 1977, when my manager, Alex Emerson, handed me the sliotar and told me to lead the under-12s onto the field for the championship final. As I won my first medal that day, I had no way of knowing the unforgettable joys and sorrows, the memories and the passions, but above all the wealth of friends that I would encounter from my love affair with hurling.

"Like every other young hurler in Ireland, I dreamt of playing in an All-Ireland, and in 1989 that dream came true when Antrim faced Tipperary. The pride throughout the county was palpable, yet out of the desolation of defeat came a special sporting memory. We were astounded at the welcome we received from fans all over Ulster on our return. We went on a tour of the county to thank the fans for their support. At two o'clock one morning we arrived in the footballing village of Glenavy, where the fans had waited for us over four hours in the pouring rain. The incongruous sight of Ulster's beaten All-Ireland hurlers being cheered to the skies by hundreds of football supporters, while Union Jacks fluttered over our heads, will stay with me forever."

Sambo's every expression radiates his feelings as he talks about Antrim and Cushendall and hurling. Pride and passion are words often tossed about, but in the case of Sambo he personifies them, both on and off the field. Seventeen years and plenty of defeats at top level haven't quenched his ardour for the game he deeply loves. Where that love came from is difficult to trace. "There is no Antrim blood in me: my father came from Co. Cavan, my mother from Co. Derry." Perhaps the hurling spirit of the Glens inspired him; or perhaps his natural aptitude urged him on; or perhaps it was his realisation that progress and prowess on the hurling field were matched step by step with the elimination of a speech impediment that had afflicted him from childhood. Hurling bred confidence in Sambo.

When it came to playing a game of hurling, no sacrifice was too great, no distance too far. In 1982, he played a club match against Ballycran of Co. Down and was marking Hugh Gilmore: "The following Sunday, I was in Melbourne, Australia, to play with Sinn Féin against Young Irelands in the Australian States Championship. Well, you won't believe who I saw running down to mark me when we lined out, but none other than Hugh Gilmore of Ballycran. We won that Australian medal. Billy Fitzpatrick from Kilkenny also played in some of the games for Sinn Féin."

In 1985, Sambo played with Harry Bolands of Chicago to win an All-American Championship medal in Philadelphia. Add to the above his successes in Ireland and you have a player who won hurling honours on three continents.

He was so upset after the semi-final of 1991 against Kilkenny that he left the pitch crying. Victory had come so close, and Antrim had played so well: "We were leading by a point with time running out when Kilkenny got a winning goal to make it 2:18 to 1:19. Experience on the sideline would have won it that day. I felt devastated. To beat Kilkenny would have been a great coup."

But it wasn't all sadness in 1991; it was the year Sambo won an All-Star: "It was a great honour, something you dream about. It will mean more to me as time goes on." He was voted Player of the Year in Ulster and also Ulster Hurler of the Year. After his All-Star award, a "This is Your Life" presentation was made to him by his club. From many lovely tributes, I have chosen the following: "The powerful rounded shoulders, the Henderson-like playing of the sliotar, the powerful determined striking, the courageous blocking, never pulling out of a tackle, combined to create his trademark. 'No frills and direct' has been his maxim..." (Peter Quinn).

During his career, Sambo has given many brilliant displays in a variety of positions. "I have programmes at home showing me playing in every position, from full-back to full-forward." His most recent outstanding performance was in the All-Ireland semi-final of 1996, when he played at centre-back and was opposed by the ace Limerick forward Gary Kirby, whom he described as "one of the gentlemen of hurling". As a youngster, the player he admired most was Ger Henderson of Kilkenny: "I'd love to have modelled myself on him. And then when I got to play against him – just fantastic. He was a great centre-back. John Fenton of Cork was another hurler I admired – different from Henderson. He was a most graceful performer – showed hurling to be the art form it is."

Sambo has a soft spot for Cork and its people: "Whenever we went down there they couldn't do enough for us. In my first All-Ireland, I saw the great Cork three-in-a-row team of 1976–1978. John Horgan sticks out from that game, also Ray Cummins and Jimmy Barry Murphy. Hurlers over the border have always seemed like gods: bigger, stronger, faster. This belief is still a problem in Antrim: some Antrim hurlers freeze when they see Jones's Road. But I honestly believe an Antrim hurling title is not far away. Look at the way Clare were devastated in the Munster final of 1993 – beaten by Tipperary by eighteen points – and yet they came back and won the All-Ireland title in 1995. Heart and passion: to me hurling is all about heart and passion. I was there that day. I love watching a game nearly as much as playing. To be sitting in Croke Park when Clare won – unbelievable. What an atmosphere! Whenever I watch a game I always play the role of manager – for both sides – plotting what I would do if I were in charge. As I watched Limerick against Offaly in the final, there were things I would have done that would have won the title for Limerick."

Sambo was the youngest of eleven children, six boys and five girls. In his family, five of the boys played hurling, three of them assisting Antrim and Ulster. His mother never saw him play. "She never saw me hit a ball in real life – she would watch the telly; but she always lit a candle for me when I went off to play."

No finer exponent of the noble game has come out of Antrim since the days of the great Kevin Armstrong.

Lawrence McNaughton
(SAMBO)

TOMÁS MULCAHY
CORK

Born: 1963
Interviewed: 2001

"Coming from a family background of 'hurling madness' − my late father was a staunch member of Glen Rovers Hurling and Football club − I suppose it was inevitable that at an early age I would be the recipient of a new camán and sliotar to follow in his footsteps.

"The tradition and folklore of Glen Rovers is now household in GAA circles, and to meet and get advice and encouragement from stalwarts such as Jack Lynch, Christy Ring and Jim Young will long stand in my memory.

"To represent your county and achieve the success I had was a great privilege. I remember travelling to Thurles for Munster finals and to Croke Park and the pride in wearing the famous red jersey will be with me forever.

"My wish for hurling in the future is that we go back to basics and concentrate more on the skill levels than the physical side of things and promote the game even further in the so called 'weaker counties'. I would like to see a situation arrived at where players only practise two nights a week and played one match at the weekend. As regards lying on the ball – a habit creeping into the game – very dangerous; should be penalised immediately."

Tomás played minor for Cork for two years without success. He was rewarded, however, in 1982 at the age of nineteen when he came on as a sub in the under-21 All-Ireland final against Galway. In his senior county debut at Jack Barrett Park in Kinsale in a tournament game against Waterford in 1983, the full-forward line read: Seanie O'Leary, Jimmy Barry Murphy and Tomás Mulcahy.

Three great men, I suggested. "Two great men and a little greenhorn," he replied. From then until 1995, when he retired, Tomás gave many outstanding performances for club, county and province. Nowadays, he gives a very erudite analysis of hurling games as a panellist on TV.

He won all the major honours the game had to offer: a county title with Glen Rovers in 1989; a National League title in 1993 after a three-game marathon with Wexford; All-Star awards in 1984 and 1986; Railway Cup medals in 1984 and 1985; six Munster titles that led to five All-Ireland finals (Galway beat them in the All-Ireland semi-final of 1985); and All-Ireland victories of 1984, 1986 and 1990.

Football success eluded him. He played minor at county level and "was sent on as a sub in the 1985 Munster senior football final against Kerry in Killarney to mark Páidí Ó Sé and try to get a goal."

Ray Cummins was his hero. "I watched him a lot – a dual player, a good leader, a great presence of mind and a great distributor of the ball – a star man."

What were his most memorable moments? "North Mon. was a haven of hurling. There was a half day on Wednesday – not to go home – when everyone went to the Old Mon field to play hurling and football. It was part of the curriculum. 1980 was a great year for the school. We won the Dean Ryan Cup and the Frewen Cup – the junior competitions in hurling and football. The senior team won the Harty Cup – we beat St Colman's, Fermoy, in the final and then went on to beat St Kieran's, Kilkenny, in the All-Ireland Colleges' final." Tomás felt very honoured to have participated in all those successes.

In 1989 Tomás was captain of Glen Rovers when his club won the county title after a lapse of thirteen years. "We were the first team to bring the Cup across the Christy Ring Bridge. The first man to meet us at the Bridge was Jack Lynch. He was a hero for me off the field as well."

Tomás will always remember victory in the Centenary hurling final in Thurles in 1984 under the captaincy of John Fenton. "It was special. It halted a Cork losing sequence of 1982 and 1983. It was victory in the Centenary year. It was my first All-Ireland senior medal. It was a success that gave you the ambition to do more."

The year 1990, when Tomás captained Cork, probably holds pride of place in his hurling heart. "Cork City witnessed great celebrations that year. After 100 years, Cork again won the football and hurling double. When the footballers returned on the Monday after the final, we were there on the platform. Larry Tompkins and myself exchanged the Sam Maguire and Liam MacCarthy Cups."

Tomás's father, Gerald, now gone to God, was at the hurling final – and an exciting and hectic one it turned out to be. "He had a heart complaint and was advised not to go to the match." However, go he did.

Gerald was treated to a thrilling spectacle. At half time, Galway led by five points and, within five minutes of the restart, had stretched their lead to seven points and appeared to be in the ascendancy.

But the Cork mentors had made a second-half switch that was to prove vital. Tomás was switched to centre-forward. In the seventh minute he scored a goal that cut the Galway lead to four points. That, coupled with a fine overall performance from Tomás – supplemented by attention to the games basics and the use of ground strokes by the Cork team in general – paved the way to a surprise victory in which Lady Luck and the gods also played a role.

The game produced forty-three scores – Cork 5:15, Galway 2:21. And really, from the moment the ball was thrown in – Kevin Hennessy netted for Cork after forty seconds – to John Moore's final whistle, this thrill-a-minute contest was no place for weak hearts, be they neutral or partisan. Great, therefore, must have been the strain and pressure on the heart of Gerald Mulcahy as he watched his son Tomás captain Cork, in glorious weather conditions, to the county's twenty-seventh title.

"When the game was over I said to myself, 'I hope he is alright.' After the presentation of the cup, I was in the dressing-room in a corner after interviews. There were fellows beating down the door trying to get in but there was high security keeping them out. Again, I was thinking of my father and hoping he was all right. The next thing I saw was my father coming through the door. There were tears in his eyes. He came over and put his arms around me and hugged me." A special moment; an enduring memory.

NIALL PATTERSON
ANTRIM

Born: 1962
Interviewed: 2002

Niall, the second eldest of a family of four boys and three girls, was born on 2 January 1962. He played hurling from an early age – full-back at nine years of age and goalkeeper for the under-12s, a position in which he made his senior debut for Antrim in a National League game against Kilkenny in 1979.

In a career that spanned thirteen years, Niall played for club, county and province with distinction. He captained Ulster in the Railway Cup in 1983. He has many and varied memories of his hurling days.

"One of my mates, and now a life-long friend, Ger Rogan was playing with me in a Leinster minor final against Kilkenny in 1979. The night before the match we got our new jerseys. Rogie, as he was affectionately known, was so proud of his jersey that he slept with it on all night. That was the first Antrim jersey we got to keep.

"Noel Skehan was probably the best goalkeeper I have seen. John Commins of Galway was a fine goalkeeper too. Then there was Joe Cooney, midfielder, half- forward, full-forward – play him nearly anywhere. Brian Whelehan has to be one of the most complete hurlers of this modern era. Also, D.J. Carey, Nicky English, Eugene Cloonan – where do you stop?

"I have never come across anything like what Offaly did, lining up a Guard of Honour for us after us beating them in the All-Ireland semi-final of 1989. To be knocked out of a game like that and still have the presence of mind to realise what the occasion meant to the people from Antrim is something I will never forget, and I have, and will have until the day I die, the greatest respect for Offaly hurling."

Among the many honours that came Niall's way are:

- B&I "GAA Personality of the Month" for April 1983 – regarded then as being second to an All-Star award

- Two All-Ireland "B" medals in 1981 and 1982

- O'Neill Sports Star award for Antrim in 1983

- Two All-Star nominations 1983 and 1991

- Ulster GAA Writers' Award 1990

- RTÉ Save of the Year 1990

On the Silver Jubilee of the All-Ireland Club Championship, twenty-five years after the inception in 1971, a team was chosen from all the players of that era. Niall was selected as goalkeeper and found himself in the company of hurling giants – each a master of the craft.

The greatest day in Niall's hurling life was when Loughgiel, under his captaincy, won the All-Ireland club title in 1983. It was really fairytale stuff. With nine under-21s on the team, Loughgiel beat reigning Antrim title holders Cushendall in the county semi-final by two points. Favourites Ballycastle fell in the county final. Clontibret of Monaghan were defeated next in a bruising encounter and Ballygalget of Down were overcome in the Ulster final. In the All-Ireland semi-final Loughgiel found themselves facing Moycarkey-Borris of Tipperary – favourites for the title. The Munster men were most gracious in a 2:7 to 1:6 defeat on Loughgiel's home ground. The final against St Rynagh's of Offaly at Croke Park was a draw. The replay at Casement Park, Belfast a week later on 24 April was

won by 2:12 to 1:12. A proud, proud day it was – glory for Niall, Loughgiel, Antrim and Ulster.

Niall's father Neil played for many years for Antrim. His claim to fame
was holding Christy Ring scoreless from play in a game at Corrigan Park,
Belfast around the mid-fifties. He was involved in hurling all his life. He
held a very special place in Niall's heart. "Hurling was his life. He died on
22 February 1993. I buried my stick in his coffin and never played again.
He was a great man and was my main motivator. I played just to please
him and when he died a big part of me died with him."

PADDY QUIRKE
CARLOW

Born: 1956
Interviewed: 1996

Paddy (left) receiving a presentation from
Club Chairman Andy Jordan.

Where Gaelic games are concerned, Paddy Quirke is arguably Carlow's greatest dual player – a player who has excelled at hurling and football for club, county, province and replacement All-Stars.

Paddy played hurling for Carlow from 1974 to 1990 and football from 1974 to 1987. He is one of a family of seven – five boys and two girls – all of whom played our Gaelic pastimes.

Paddy's skills at games came from a natural athleticism rather than from an inheritance in the genes. He does, however, say that he had two aunts, Minnie and Lill, "who were good camogie players" and that his Uncle Packie was "a fine athlete".

Growing up, Paddy had no special hurling heroes "but there was great talk about Mick Mackey, Christy Ring and John Doyle; they were talked about regularly, even though their careers were back decades."

He had clear memories of his first senior game with his club Naomh Eoin. "I was about sixteen at the time and playing in goal. I was afraid of my life, but all was well because I had the three strongest men in Carlow in front of me – Pat Keogh, Brian Fox and Ted Butler." It was the beginning of a senior club career that between 1974 and 1995 brought Paddy fifteen county titles.

He has never forgotten the 1978 county title against St Mullin's. It was a hurling saga. After four games and four hours' play, the teams were still level. Extra time in the fourth game heralded victory.

Paddy's performances for Carlow in both hurling and football caught the attention of the Railway Cup selectors and he was chosen to represent his province. He was a dual player in 1979 and 1981. No football medal came his way. He won a Railway Cup hurling medal as a sub in 1977 and in 1979 he became the first Carlow man to line out with a winning Railway Cup hurling team. The final against Connaught at Thurles on 1 April was a very special day for Paddy. He was playing at midfield with one of Kilkenny's greats, Ger Henderson, and he was marking another outstanding player, John Connolly of Galway.

In 1980 he was chosen as a dual replacement All-Star for a US trip. That represented the pinnacle of his personal achievements. In one of the football games Paddy found himself marking Eoin Liston of Kerry at midfield. He did well. At a subsequent banquet – out of the blue – he was honoured with the Man of the Match award.

Paddy used to go to San Francisco to play some games. Those games were hard and tough. On one of those occasions he got a nasty injury. Friends took him to a doctor's surgery. It was obviously not the first such case the doctor had seen. He looked at Paddy and said, "Were you playing that crazy Irish game?"

Patrick Quirke.

BOBBY RYAN
TIPPERARY

Born: 1961
Interviewed: 2001

"Having been born into a family that was steeped in hurling, I always felt that I would someday play with Tipperary. When that day finally arrived it was one of the proudest days of my life.

"As a young boy growing up in Borrisoleigh, hurling was almost like religion. Everything revolved around the game. Our family were very involved in the game locally. All my brothers would have played for our club, my sisters would wash the togs and my mother used to pray! My mother in particular played a huge role in my development as a player and a person. She taught us how to accept defeat as well as victory.

"My greatest disappointment has got to be the Munster final of 1984 against Cork. I was captain of the team and it was also Centenary year.

Cork stole the game on Tipperary in the final minutes and I ended up with a broken leg.

"Winning the All-Ireland in 1989 and captaining the team was for me the biggest thrill in my sporting career. To captain your county to All-Ireland success is the greatest honour any player can get.

"I have many great memories from my years of hurling with Tipperary and Borrisoleigh and, indeed, Templemore CBS. But what I treasure most is the friendships that I have made both inside and outside the county.

"I have many reasons to be grateful. I played a game I loved at the highest level. I hope in years to come I will be remembered as a great sportsman rather than a great player."

The thought of not playing county senior hurling for his native Tipperary never entered Bobby Ryan's head. "It was always a case of when will I play for Tipperary – never would I play for Tipperary? It was the same with my brother Aidan." After all, his late father Tim, Uncles Ned Ryan and Pat Stakelum had all excelled in the blue and gold of Tipperary.

Bobby's major honours include the following titles: Harty Cup and All-Ireland Colleges' with Templemore CBS in 1978, All-Ireland (2) Munster (5), National League (1), County (3), All-Ireland under-21 (2) All-Ireland Club (1) and All-Star awards (3).

Bobby's mother, Bridget, never went to watch her sons play. But she did instil in them a great sporting philosophy, a great attitude to both victory and defeat. "It takes a great man to accept victory but an even greater one to accept defeat," she said to Bobby after the heartbreaking Munster final defeat of 1984 at the hands of Cork.

"With my mother the important thing was that we didn't get a belt and that we didn't hurt anybody – well and good if we won. Before a game we used have to kneel down in front of the Sacred Heart picture and say a decade of the rosary – three Hail Marys if time was against us. Mother gave us great values."

Bobby will never forget that 1984 Munster final. "Nothing prepares you for a Munster final. It was about half way through the second half. I contested a high ball with Tim Crowley about forty yards out near the Old Stand. I don't know who won the pull but I fell and Tim fell on top of me. Tim got up. When I went to get up, I couldn't. I must have cramp, I thought, I'll be able to run it off. I got up but fell again. I had broken the fibula bone. Even then I didn't want to go off. For me it was a terrible tragedy, a terrible disappointment. I wanted to hurl on but I couldn't.

With about six minutes to go, Noel O'Dwyer struck over a point to put us four points up. He danced a jig. There I was on the sideline lying down, injured. I couldn't imagine a worse nightmare – only twenty-two, Centenary year, captaining Tipp., playing Cork in Semple Stadium. I won't be able to accept the cup – not with this leg, I thought to myself. The honourable thing would be to ask Noel to accept it. After all, he won an All-Ireland away back in 1971. Why I was chosen over Noel I don't know. Those were my thoughts. Then, bang, bang. If I live to be a thousand I won't forget that day – my worst day, my greatest disappointment."

By nature, Bobby was gentlemanly and sporting on the field of play. His style was brave, dashing and spirited. Largely due to the influence of his mother's sporting philosophy, he was equally gracious in victory and defeat.

Bobby was sitting in the stand with his wife Elaine as the Tipperary and Clare teams paraded around Croke Park prior to the All-Ireland final of 1997. He watched them go by. For him, it was an emotional moment. He saw the No. 7 jersey, the jersey of his favourite position, left half-back. He said to himself, "I should be out there." He was now within two months of his thirty-sixth birthday on 23 October. But the legs were gone. He would never again wear the blue and gold of Tipperary. Tears filled his eyes and a few flowed down his cheeks. "Elaine said, 'I understand'; I said, 'You don't, you couldn't.'"

Ní bhíonn in aon rud ach seal.

1990s

CIARÁN CAREY
LIMERICK

Born: 1970
Interviewed: 1997

The winning point against Clare in 1996, described by journalist Kevin Cashman as "the greatest winner ever scored".

Ciarán was from his infancy surrounded by a hurling atmosphere – in his home, in his parish, in school at Limerick CBS and at Croom Vocational School.

"My uncle Eamon, my father Pa, and my brother Pa all played at county senior level for Limerick. It is an honour for me to follow in their footsteps. I must pay tribute to John Enright who guided me faultlessly through the under-age ranks and Phil Bennis, a man who has influenced my career immensely, for his unerring guidance and advice.

"On the inter-county front I represented my county for two years at minor level and had the unenviable record of losing four consecutive under-21 Munster hurling finals to Cork and Tipp. I got that dream call-up to represent my county at senior level against Dublin in 1988 in the National League quarter-final. My real blooding was to come at Páirc Uí Chaoimh when I was selected to play at corner-forward against a Tipperary team at the pinnacle of its power, which boasted such luminaries as Nicholas English, Pat Fox and Bobby Ryan, to mention but a few. That same Tipperary team was to continually frustrate us as they defeated us for four consecutive years (1988 to 1991) in the Munster Championship. While I would never be a defeatist or a person to drop the head, even I began to have nagging doubts as to when we would ever make that break-through. That came when we triumphed over Tipperary in the National League final in 1992 after overturning an eight-point deficit at half time. Words cannot describe the emotion I experienced that day."

On our visit to Ciarán, we met his wife, Miriam, daughter of Phil Bennis, who played minor camogie for Limerick. We also met Sara, their four-year-old daughter who didn't hesitate to say, "Daddy is the best on the Limerick team – he won two cups."

Miriam is an avid hurling fan. But she suffers the tortures of tension at many of the games. She gave us an example. It was Sunday, 16 June 1996. Clare, All-Ireland champions were playing against Limerick at Páirc na nGael, Limerick, in the Munster semi-final before a capacity attendance of 43,534. With five minutes to go, Limerick trailed by three points and looked like losing. Three points from play brought them level. The game was in injury time when the Clare goalie, David Fitzgerald, pucked out the ball. Miriam saw Ciarán soar into the air for the ball. She couldn't look; she buried her head in her lap. She heard the rising cheers of the Limerick fans; still she kept her head buried. Then Damien Quigley's wife, who was beside her, shouted, "He's scored!" She looked up. Someone had thrown Sara up in the air. The place was a mass of green and white. Soon the agony was over.

Let's recount that last score. As the puck-out from David Fitzgerald descended, Ciarán rose lynx-eyed into the air. Cleanly he caught the sliotar. He set off on a solo run like a greyhound from the traps. He was on a mission. A point or a free, he thought to himself. He veered slightly left. Fergal Hegarty, in hot pursuit, fell. Clare backs retreated to cover their men. Ciarán had now run all of sixty yards and handled the ball twice. Now, about thirty yards from goal, he turned to his right – his weak side

– clipped the sliotar off the hurley, and struck the winner with control and composure. The Guinness advertisement summed up the feelings of all Clare supporters: "This man can break hearts from seventy yards."

Kevin Cashman, writing in the *Sunday Independent*, described it as "the greatest winner ever scored," and continued:

> a truly unique occasion; made so by excitement and tension and passion and sportsmanship (not whiter than white, but still terrific) and a pre-match atmosphere, in the grounds and its *environs*, such as many of us had thought had gone with the days of the fifties.

The Clare captain, Anthony Daly, described the solo run as the four most agonising seconds of his life. And Ciarán's recollection of the day? "It was the hottest day I ever hurled – unbelievable heat. I don't know where 1 got the energy to run."

There was more agony for Miriam at the Munster final against Tipperary at Páirc na nGael on 7 July. Down ten points at half time, Limerick had a huge task on their hands. Miriam prayed to her grandmother. In the dying seconds Frankie Carroll scored the equaliser. Miriam's prayers were answered – and on the eve of the replay she said a few more.

Tom Humphries in the *Irish Times*, the day after the drawn game, had this to say:

> Extraordinary. A game which jangled the nerves and brought the memory of great days vaulting out from the recesses of the mind. Unbelievable. An afternoon of jack-knifing fortunes and twisting, lurching narrative. Incredible. A game with jagged edges and a deservedly even finish…The greatest Munster hurling final of recent times…

The might-have-beens of the finals of 1994 and 1996 were in Ciaran's mind as I talked to him about Bobby Rackard and his two All-Ireland medals of 1955 and 1956. "One of those would do me," he said. "I think 1994 would have to be my biggest disappointment. That day we hurled well as a team – not so in 1996. 1994 looked good for us." Miriam interjected to say: "I never want to experience another loss."

What did he feel was his best display? He paused; it was a difficult one. "Miriam, give me a hand," He said. And she did: "I felt he had a brilliant game against Cork in 1994." Well, he certainly had, for he hunted all over the field: fielding, passing, linking; and in the closing moments he sent in the ball that Pat Heffernan flicked to the net for a great overhead goal. "Yes, I played well that day," Ciarán said. Miriam was wearing the watch he won as RTÉ Man of the Match.

In 1996 he captained Limerick and led them through as testing and demanding a Munster campaign as any team ever encountered. First it was Cork at Páirc Uí Chaoimh, where they hadn't suffered a champion-ship defeat since 1922. The final score made everyone blink, for Limerick had beaten their bogey team 3:18 to 1:8. Next it was Clare, reigning All-Ireland champions, at Páirc na nGael – a game with which the name of Ciarán Carey will be for ever linked. Then it was Tipperary in the Munster final at Páirc na nGael. Ciarán proved his calibre as captain that day when he spoke to his team colleagues at half time and lifted their spirits. It was a memorable moment for him when he lifted the cup after the replay defeat of Tipperary, and Limerick were crowned Munster champions.

It had been a superb Munster Championship, demonstrating to the full the peerless spectacle that is hurling. The ancient game – in craft and skill and heroics, thrills and excitement and drama – was never seen to better advantage. And at all times Ciarán was an inspirational captain, a utility man, one of the great hurlers of the present-day game, who has displayed his repertoire of skills in the backs, at centre-field, and among the forwards. Before a game he likes a few quiet moments to himself: to focus his thoughts, to concentrate, but in particular "to have a little chat with Himself." At times on the pitch he seems like a hurling magician as he bobs and floats and wafts and glides through the field. A man of pace, artistry and courage, he can execute deeds of skill while moving at great pace.

A delight to watch is Ciarán.

D.J. CAREY
KILKENNY

Born: 1970
Interviewed: 1997

Growing up in Gowran, D.J. Carey – nicknamed the "Dodger" – was introduced at an early age to the game of hurling, and before he went to St
Kieran's College he had tasted success at under-age level. Hurling brilliance was, of course, in the genes. His grand-uncle Paddy Phelan, who
featured in *Hurling Giants,* gave many dazzling displays at left half-back
for great Kilkenny teams in the thirties and played into the early forties.
His aunt Peggy Muldowney (née Carey) played camogie for many years
with Kilkenny and won four All-Ireland titles.

At St Kieran's, D.J. further developed his hurling skills and won two
senior All-Ireland college titles in 1988 and 1989 with victories over
Midleton CBS and St Flannan's, respectively. In 1988, he won an All-
Ireland minor title with Kilkenny, and in 1990 – the year after he made his
debut in goal for Kilkenny seniors in a game against Offaly – he won an

All-Ireland under-21 title. So, at a young age, the medals were beginning to accumulate.

At the same time, he was having a successful run in the handball court. As with hurling, he blossomed into a master. His list of twenty major successes is highly impressive and includes All-Ireland titles at under-12, under-14, under-16, college, club, minor, junior and senior level, and two under-23 world titles. The handball activity was, of course, tremendous for building up stamina. It also created a keen eye, sharp reflexes and strong wrists.

But back to hurling. A technically brilliant player, he is a classical performer and an outstanding artist of the modern game. Modest and genial, he is blessed with a placid temperament – a factor, no doubt, that contributes immensely to his powers of concentration. He has flair, perception, pace and creativity, In his solo runs you are treated to grace of movement, tremendous acceleration once he rounds his man, the side-step, the dummy, magical control and a deadly clinical finish. It all adds up to a superbly fit hurling master – a teetotaller and non-smoker – who is the ultimate in sportsmanship and a most worthy holder of five All-Stars in a row, from 1991 to 1995. He rarely fails to find the net, can engineer goals from any quarter on the field, and can, on occasion, cause havoc. He did it with a display of genius and wizardry in a league game against Galway at Ballinasloe in March 1997, scoring 2:9 out of a total of 3:11 and, to quote from Clíona Foley's report on the game, giving "a new meaning to the phrase 'playing a captain's part'...that had even Galway's most loyal supporters in the 6000 crowd singing his praises." And Seán Kilfeather in the *Irish Times* wrote: "What can be said of Kilkenny's captain D.J. Carey? What more can he do to join those great players like Ring, Mackey, Power and his fellow Kilkennyman Keher?" Well, he advanced his cause still further with a virtuoso performance against the same opposition in the All-Ireland quarter-final at Thurles on 25 July 1997. He scored 2:8 of Kilkenny's 4:15 in their two-point win and in the process teased, tortured and tormented the hurling men of Galway, who will have some nightmares about a game in which they held a nine-point lead at half-time.

Sunday, 20 October 1996 will always live in his memory. It was the day he captained Young Irelands of his native Gowran to their first county senior hurling title, in a replay with James Stephens – a success that had its roots in an under-12 team of the early eighties. That day, out of a total score of 3:9, he scored 2:4. His goals were a study in psychology. Twice, his marker Philip Larkin remonstrated with the referee and twice the referee moved the ball forward. So a 40-yard free became a 21-yard free. D.J. placed the ball. Then he stepped back a few yards. He stood and gazed at the James Stephens players who lined the goal. Then he advanced. His intentions were clear. He was moving at pace as he tossed the sliotar goalwards. With a swing and perfect co-ordination – well inside the 21-yard line – he struck the ball with force. The green flag waved. Within three minutes, Young Irelands were awarded a penalty. This time only three players could line the goal. D.J. went through the same drill and ritual – mesmeric stuff. The attendance of 15,000 watched in anticipation. The net shook again.

Sharing that county success with D.J. were his brothers Martin, who kept a fine goal, and Jack, who, as the game was heading towards the final whistle and another draw seemed likely, took a pass on the run to score the winning goal. Earlier in the championship, another brother, Kieran, was on the panel.

Every competition, irrespective of level, has its own Everest. Those who participate want to reach the highest point. To conquer the top leaves its own trail of special memories. D.J. has many of them and finds it hard to pick one above the other. "I still remember the under-12 handball success; the All-Ireland win of 1992 – my first; I remember the defeat of 1991. You know you're better off losing in the first round than in the final. When you get to the final you're there to win. The club win of 1996 was great. I would say to people that there is nothing greater than a win with your club, because it's the parish you grew up in. You step onto a higher level when you play with your county, and of course the biggest honour is to win the All-Ireland title."

ANTHONY DALY
CLARE

Born: 1970
Interviewed: 2001

Clare lost the Munster final of 1993 to Tipperary 3:27 to 2:12. Anthony Daly played in the position of corner-back that day.

"I walked from the pitch after the final whistle feeling numb and dismayed. The team had lost badly and played badly, and after twenty minutes the game was a lost cause. I was very disappointed with my own display – felt stuck to the ground, couldn't get going. I felt ashamed too, ashamed for my brother who had come home to see the game and for all the family who were there as well – and of course for our supporters."

Anthony felt even worse after the defeat by Limerick the following year. At the time he saw little future for the county team.

"My club was doing well, however, and I began to think in terms of winning county and provincial and maybe All-Ireland titles with Clarecastle."

Yes indeed, after the defeats of 1993 and 1994 Clare's hurling future did look grim. The county felt shattered. A dense, dark cloud descended on Clare hurling. But, phoenix-like, they were destined in 1995 to rise from the ashes of defeat. Anthony Daly was captain.

He was born in 1970, played his club hurling with Clarecastle, which won county honours; he captained the team for one of those successes. He won a Harty Cup and All-Ireland Colleges' title with St Flannan's in 1987. And in 1989 he donned the Clare senior jersey for the first time in a National League game against Waterford.

He became part of a great Clare half-back line – Liam Doyle, Sean McMahon, Anthony Daly – that represented the county from 1995 to 2000.

Anthony's own performances earned him All-Star awards in 1994, 1995 and 1998. He captained the men of Dál gCais from 1992 to 1998 and led them to two memorable All-Ireland triumphs in 1995 and 1997.

Clare defeated Cork and Limerick to win the Munster title of 1995. The celebrations that followed buried all the frustrations of a sixty-three-year gap of unrewarded endeavour. Next to fall were Galway. Clare then faced Offaly, reigning All-Ireland champions, in the All-Ireland final. They won in a heart-stopping encounter by two points.

The final was watched by two surviving Clare veterans, Tom McInerney and John Joe Doyle, from the 1932 final – a game Clare lost to Kilkenny by 3:3 to 2:3. Their presence added a touch of nostalgia to a day of sunshine and glamour when a unique pairing contested an absorbing final.

Anthony Daly delivered a wonderful winning speech from the Hogan Stand – one of the finest ever heard on a final day. It was comprehensive, dignified and thoughtful – a credit to him and the team he represented. "This was as close as All-Ireland-winning captains come to a Gettysburg Address," wrote Enda McEvoy in the *Sunday Tribune* on 24 February 2002. In mentioning team manager Ger Loughnane, Anthony said "his obsession has become a reality." Writing in the *Sunday Tribune*, Kevin Cashman beautifully described a key point scored by Anthony in the second half and added: "The year of 1995 was exclusively The Banner's."

The Irish Times ran an editorial:

> The All-Ireland hurling final was a victory for the brave: for Clare, a county long accustomed to defeat, which showed more resilience than most observers thought possible…
>
> The circumstances conspired to make the occasion memorable. Here was a county whose last appearance in a Hurling Championship final was in the 1930s, whose last success coincided with the outbreak of the First World War. Yet its teams had never lacked enthusiasm or courage and their followers invariably travelled in hope, even when the odds against them seemed overwhelming…
>
> It was the celebration of neutrals on the journey home which delayed a long procession of Clare cars at towns and villages in the Midlands even before the team's plane landed at Shannon Airport and the county's own celebrations, at Newmarket-on-Fergus, Clarecastle and Ennis, began in earnest.

In 1996 in the Munster semi-final, Clare, with Anthony Daly still at the helm, fell to Limerick in the sweltering heat of a June afternoon. However, in 1997 Clare were back with a bang and intent. They indulged in practice shooting in their opening game with Kerry. Then one by one the three superpowers of hurling, Cork, Tipperary and Kilkenny, fell before the awesome might of Clare hurling – full of power, passion and precision.

Victory over Cork confirmed Clare's 1995 superiority over the Rebel County. By defeating Tipperary for the first time in a Munster final, Anthony Daly and the men he captained dismantled a huge psychological barrier. They captured the scalp of the third hurling superpower when they triumphed over the men from the Noreside.

The All-Ireland final brought Clare face to face with Tipperary for the second time in the 1997 championship. Tipperary, as defeated Munster finalists, re-entered the championship and worked their way to the final. It was a clash of neighbours, a clash of clans, and a clash of Titans. Victory for Anthony Daly and the men of Clare would carry with it a seal of greatness. Defeat would leave question marks.

The game was a stirring contest. It built up into a gripping climax. Tipperary led by four points at half time. Playing with precision and purpose, Clare led by 17 points to 12 with fifteen minutes left.

Everything that makes a contest memorable was packed into the closing stages. Tipperary got a goal. It left them one point behind, with nine minutes to go. Then another goal. Tipperary one point up; five minutes to go. Pandemonium. Tipperary followers went wild. All Clare hearts missed a beat. In a flash, Ollie Baker equalised for Clare and Jamsie O'Connor, with a truly smashing point, gave Clare a one-point lead. There were maybe three minutes to go. Even neutrals can feel the tension of an electric atmosphere. Suddenly it was a contest between John Leahy – menacingly alone inside the Clare defence and less than twenty yards from goal – and facing him with concentration written across his face was Clare custodian Davy Fitzgerald. The Clare man won glory with a fine save. The Banner triumphed by one point. The seal of greatness was theirs.

In 1996 Anthony Daly captained Munster to Railway Cup honours with a convincing 3:20 to 0:10 win over Leinster. In so doing, he joined the select company of a few players who had the privilege of captaining club, county and province to ultimate honours. The 1990s finished up a wonderful decade for Anthony. The dust of the early years of the decade turned to gold as the decade advanced – county titles, Munster titles (3), All-Ireland medals (2), Railway Cups (2), All-Stars (3) and a Munster club title.

After the Munster defeats of 1993 and 1994, to have aspired to such awards would have been tantamount to dreaming about the impossible.

Anthony has had undreamed-of success with the Dublin senior hurling team. In 2011, he guided them to victory in the National League final against Kilkenny – the county's first such success since 1938–39, and followed up later that year with a superb performance against red-hot favourites Tipperary in the All-Ireland semi-final. At times in the course of the game, they seemed set to create a major surprise but in the end lost an epic battle by 1:19 to 0:18. He instilled in the team self-belief, controlled aggression, tenacity and verve.

TOM DEMPSEY
WEXFORD

Born: 1965
Interviewed: 2002

"Much of my youth was spent banging a sliotar against the wall at the front of my house in Kilmuckridge village. Every so often, a badly directed shot made short work of my mother's roses and, no matter how hard I tried, I couldn't get across to her that the shot just taken was the winning goal for Wexford in an All-Ireland final.

"I was lucky enough to realise the aforementioned dream and score that vital goal in 1996. The deaths of my mother's roses were not in vain.

"It was a great privilege to serve with thirty wonderful men in 1996 and also, of course, to have hurled with many wonderful Wexford men over fifteen years in the purple and gold jersey.

"It saddens me to think of the unlucky players who served Wexford so well but did not win a 'Celtic Cross', as they were all as entitled to the honour as the 1996 players.

"So, as I look back now, I feel lucky and honoured to have achieved the two main goals in my GAA life – All-Ireland titles at club and county level. I appreciate the fact that I played with and against many great men (better than me) that weren't so lucky.

"Finally, thanks to my family and to Sinéad for the patience."

Tom hails from the same territory as Mick Butler and the great Tony Doran. He was three years old when Tony was doing *gaiscí* for Wexford in the All-Ireland final of 1968. In due course, Tom would play beside his childhood hero in the Buffers Alley colours and win an All-Ireland club title. Tom's potential as an athlete was in evidence from an early age. For three years in a row he played minor hurling and minor football with his native Wexford. At St Peter's College, Tom captained the senior hurling team that won the Leinster Colleges' title in 1982.

The year 1993 was one of bitter disappointment for Tom when he captained the men in purple and gold. Lost opportunities saw Wexford lose – after three games – a league title that was there to be won, especially in the first game that ended 2:11 each and also in the second game that ended level – Wexford 3:9, Cork 0:18 – after extra time.

But even greater heartbreak lay in store for Wexford and Tom Dempsey in the championship of 1993. They met Kilkenny in the Leinster final. A wonderful display of power-packed hurling saw Wexford dominate the first half – a superiority not reflected on the scoreboard. With the final seconds of the game ticking away, Wexford held a one-point lead and looked to be winners – that is, until Kilkenny, from the very depths of defence, executed a movement that produced a remarkable equaliser. "We were like a team that hadn't won before. Even though I got nine or ten points I was very disappointed. We should have been putting Kilkenny away." Defeat in the replay was Wexford's lot. In 1993, Wexford undoubtedly had the ability and potential to have brought off a league and All-Ireland double, but the Fates ordained otherwise.

Fortunately, at parish level, there were many moments of rejoicing. A central figure in the Buffers Alley club was Tom's father Ger – "a fanatic about the game, he hurled himself in the early fifties. My mother helps neutralise things." Victory in eight county finals led to three Leinster club successes and one of those paved the way to an All-Ireland club victory. That was in 1989.

"We beat O'Donovan Rossa (Antrim) by 2:12 to 0:12. The atmosphere in the dressing-room was indescribable. In every corner you saw a friend. The club had achieved a lifelong ambition. My father predicted after the All-Ireland final defeat by Kilruane McDonaghs in 1986 that we would soon win a club title – that we'd have the best club team." That victory celebrated the "honour of the little village" – an honour that stirs all hearts.

The years were passing. Tom was in the autumn of his career. He had seen many a promising harvest blighted. Then came 1996 and Liam Griffin. Injury kept Tom out of the first-round game against Kilkenny until the second half was well under way. From then until the end of the championship he hurled with the passion and flair of a player rejuvenated. "'You're prepared to shed 500 beads of sweat to win an All-Ireland,' said Liam Griffin to me at a training session. 'I am,' I said, as I walked away. 'Tom,' he shouted. 'Make that 1,000 beads.'"

Tom became Wexford's most consistent forward. In the remaining games he was the county's leading scorer: 1:5 against Offaly in the Leinster final – three beauties (points) in the closing stages on a day when Wexford's hurling graph peaked in a thrilling and absorbing contest; 0:6 against Galway in a dour, mental and physically sapping semi-final encounter; 1:3 against Limerick in the All-Ireland final – it was the only goal of the game and a vital one it proved to be. It came from a ground stroke at a crucial time for Wexford, twenty minutes into the first half. It proved to be a winning score in Wexford's two-point win – 1:13 to 0:14.

Victory brought Tom a cherished All-Ireland medal and his outstanding hurling throughout 1996 brought him an All-Star award. Oh, and by the way, that goal he scored against Limerick subsequently attracted an added-value element. In appreciation of the role the goal played in Wexford's victory, the management of Murphy Flood's Hotel in Enniscorthy told Tom that for the rest of his life a free cup of coffee would be available to him at all times.

BILLY DOOLEY
OFFALY

Born: 1969
Interviewed: 1997

The Dooley brothers of Offaly hurling fame (left to right): Johnny, Joe and Billy.

"I started off in Clareen National School in 1982, where we won our first school final. After that I went to Birr Community School, where I hurled under-age with them.

"My first All-Ireland medal was won with the college when we beat North Mon. of Cork in the senior Colleges' final in Portlaoise in 1986. The same year, we won the minor hurling final with Offaly by beating Cork, and the next year we beat Tipperary in the final. Pat Joe Whelehan had a big influence on my hurling career. He trained us to the two minor finals, when I never thought I could get to play in All-Ireland finals. In 1989 we played Tipperary in the All-Ireland under-21 final and I feel we could have won that match. But we were beaten by two points.

307

"After that, I started on the senior panel. My first success with the senior team was in 1991, when we won the league final – Offaly's first and only one. It was 1994 before Offaly made the breakthrough again and we went on to win the All-Ireland. This was the highlight of my career to date. In 1995, we were beaten in the All-Ireland final by Clare, which was the most disappointing day of my life."

Billy Dooley comes from what is believed to be the smallest parish in Ireland. He also comes from a great hurling family, and the name Dooley will rank in hurling lore with the other great family names in the history of the game. His Uncle Joe played with Offaly in the fifties, while his grandfather, Jim Carroll, won an All-Ireland junior title with Offaly in 1929 with a win over Cork. His eldest brother, Joe, has played with Offaly seniors since 1984, winning All-Ireland titles in 1985 and 1994. Johnny, the youngest, has, like Billy, been with Offaly seniors since 1991. The senior successes of Johnny and Billy run hand-in-hand: an All-Ireland title in 1994, All-Star awards in 1994 and 1995, National League in 1991, Oireachtas in 1994, county titles in 1988, 1995 and 1996, and Leinster titles in 1994 and 1995. All three played for Offaly in the forward line in the successive All-Ireland finals of 1994 and 1995 – possibly a family record. They were joined by Seamus and Kieran when the club won the county title in 1996.

"Of course the All-Ireland final of 1994 against Limerick has to be memorable. We were lucky to be in the game at half time. We were down six points–could have been twelve; we were hurling bad. It all happened for us in the last five minutes." Well, it certainly did. Limerick were leading by five points. The score read Limerick 2:13, Offaly 1:11. The MacCarthy Cup seemed destined for the Shannonside – just a matter of concentrating and keeping it tight until the final whistle. Now, with five minutes to go, Billy Dooley was fouled to the right of the railway goal 21-yard line. Not an unduly threatening position really. Johnny Dooley stood over the ball, seemed set to take a point; then he lifted and struck low – not a bullet, but it beat defenders and goalkeeper for a green flag.

Thirty seconds later, the Limerick defence was caught flat-footed, as a ball from midfield ran ahead of Pat O'Connor, who pulled first time to despatch it for another green flag. Offaly one point up, Limerick in disarray; Offaly supporters suddenly delirious, Limerick followers stunned. A vapid performance was suddenly transformed, and more was to follow. In the space of ninety seconds, Billy sent over three glorious points, all with effortless ease from well out the field – target practice; manna from heaven. Not a drop of sweat was shed, either in the obtaining of possession or the execution of the scores. It was all unreal. "I feel the play got out of hand for Limerick: no one marking; everyone doing their own thing all over the field; it suited Offaly." Two other Offaly points gave the scoreboard at the final whistle a remarkable appearance: Offaly 3:16, Limerick 2:13.

All through the 1994 Hurling Championship, the Dooley clan was to the fore, and particularly so in the field of scoring. In the four games Offaly played, the Dooleys between them accounted for 6:41 of Offaly's total of 8:63.

Billy's next memorable game was the 1995 Leinster final against Kilkenny. Kilkenny were favourites. It will certainly live in my mind as one of the great games of hurling. Billy got five magnificent points that day. His performance earned him the Man of the Match award. When he scores, he makes it look easy; he is a master of his craft, an intelligent player, and he can read a game. That's Billy Dooley.

Billy Dooley

DAMIEN FITZHENRY
WEXFORD

Born: 1974
Interviewed: 2009

"I was born into a sporting-mad family of ten boys and five girls at the foot of the Blackstairs Mountains in a village called Kiltealy. It was not so hard for me, ever, to get anybody to play hurling or football with, as when you looked inside the door there was a team there waiting. I will attribute this to the reason that I ended up playing in goal. I was the youngest of the fifteen and when a goalkeeper was needed I would have no choice but to go in goal. I will always remember the two rusty barrels that we used as goalposts.

"My fondest school (FCJ Bunclody) memory was captaining the senior hurling team to Leinster 'B' success in my last year.

"We have had many great days in the Wexford jersey and 1996 will always bring a smile to the faces of Wexford people everywhere. We had a great team and a great management team, especially the charismatic Mr Liam Griffin. We had another nice Leinster victory in 1997 and had to wait again until 2004 for our next Leinster victory.

"Every day I pull on a Wexford jersey, I represent myself and my family who I owe everything to, especially my mam and dad, Nancy and Mark. My club Duffry Rovers means a lot to me and to see that name on the match programme every day is a real pleasure. And, finally, a special word to anyone that helped me along the way, probably too many to mention."

Damien is the baby of the Fitzhenry household. He arrived on 5 July 1974, the last of fifteen children born to Mark and Nancy (née Fortune). Damien, who played minor and under-21 for his county, first guarded the net for Wexford Seniors in 1993, having had as a role model goalkeeper Cork's Ger Cunningham whom he greatly admired. As one of the great goalkeepers of modern times, assured, eagle-eyed, inspiring, calm and composed, he has had a long and successful innings. On Sunday, 1 March 2009, Wexford played Antrim in the National League. It was Damien's 186th game for his native county – just one to go to equal Tony Doran's record of 187 games. Regrettably, Damien's honours list has not been in proportion to his outstanding performances – one All-Ireland title, three Leinster crowns, two richly deserved All-Stars and the honour of captaining the Wexford team in 2007.

One of my abiding memories of Damien centres on the Leinster final of 2004 against Offaly. In the opening moments of the game he was peppered with shots from all angles by the Offaly forwards. Undaunted, he blocked every one of them. He was truly magnificent. Offaly put one past him late in the second half but it wasn't enough. Wexford took the Leinster title on the score 2:12 to 1:11.

There are other memories too – his penalty and close-in free exploits. It was quarter-final day at Croke Park in 2001. Wexford and Limerick were serving up some delightful hurling. Time was ticking away and Limerick held a slender lead. Wexford won a 21-yard free in front of goal. Up came Damien. There was a delay as an injured player was attended to. Damien stood and waited – nonchalantly, unperturbed, displaying no sense of pressure. Now all was in readiness. In his own mind he had picked his spot. He bent, lifted, and struck and sunk the sliotar in the net at the top right-hand corner. Limerick defender, Mark Foley, threw his hurley to the ground in disgust. Game won, game lost. Wexford 4:10; Limerick 2:15.

Six years later, history repeated itself – this time in a quarter-final against Tipperary. Wexford won a close-in free to the right of the goal. A Tipperary defender further infringed and the referee moved the ball to the front of the goal. This was the cue for Damien to advance, bearing his pucking-out hurley. The Tipperary citadel fell. Wexford advanced to the All-Ireland semi-final.

In the 1996 championship, Damien left his goal on two occasions to dispatch the sliotar to the opposition's net. In the Leinster semi-final against Dublin towards the end of the first half, he got a vital goal to bring the score to 2:6 to 1:2, in Wexford's favour. Again, in the Leinster final against Offaly, he was called upon at a time when Wexford were under pressure in the first half. His shot was followed by the waving of the green flag and reduced Wexford's deficit to just one point – 1:4 to 1:5.

His brother Martin paid this tribute:

That he would become a top class inter-county hurler was never really a surprise. What was a surprise, however, is that he would do so as a goal-keeper. And a great goalkeeper he is – brave as a lion, able to read the game second to none, a great leader on the field – his greatest asset is his ability to be totally unaffected by the concession of a goal and he continues to man the posts as if nothing has happened – and finally his coolness under pressure.

Coming close to the end of his inter-county career, which in no small way has been extended by his teetotal lifestyle, I would like to thank Damien for the many great memories he has given our family over the past seventeen years playing in goal for Wexford.

No words of mine can do justice to my young brother's contribution to Wexford hurling, but I know he will probably be happy to paraphrase Othello and say "I did the county some service, enough of that" and move on to his next great love – horses. Hurling will miss him.

GARY KIRBY
LIMERICK

Born: 1967
Interviewed: 1997

"For me the greatest gift in life was when my mother and father gave me a hurley and ball. Since then, my life has always been around a game of hurling. I never won anything with the club until I was fifteen, but the enjoyment was everything.

"In 1984 – it was a year I'll never forget – everything seemed to go right for me, in that (1) I got picked to play for Limerick minors and ended up winning an All-Ireland, and (2) a dream had come true, in that I made the Patrickswell seniors and in the process played with my great-uncle Richard Bennis and went on to win the county.

"In 1986, I made my Limerick senior debut. Won an under-21 All-Ireland in 1987, but had my greatest disappointment in 1991, when we lost the All-Ireland club. The year ended on a high for me in that I won my first All-Star.

BRIAN LOHAN
CLARE

Born: 1971
Interviewed: 1997

"I was born into a hurling family in November 1971. My earliest memories of hurling started when I was bought a yellow plastic hurley when I was about four. It didn't take me long to graduate to the ash variety, saving the plastic stick for my brother Frank, who arrived three years after me in 1974.

"As I developed and reached the ages of nine and ten, the highlight of my week was training on a Tuesday, Wednesday and Thursday with my brother in Newmarket-on-Fergus. At that time, the clubs from Newmarket were coming towards the end of a very successful hurling period, winning Hurling Championships almost yearly. 1981 was the year in which my father won his eleventh or twelfth Senior Hurling Championship medal. On reflection, it strikes me now that my interest in training and hurling developed directly as a result of those nights inside in Newmarket.

"Wolfe Tone na Sionainne was beginning to blossom in the early eighties. There was a fantastic under-age structure in the club, which developed as a result of the tremendous effort and work done by the national school teachers. Gradually, Wolfe Tones started to become a force in Clare hurling, winning our first 'A' title in the early eighties to winning every 'A' title in hurling and football in 1988. The success at under-age level gradually matured to under-21, and later to the situation at present where we have in the past year won the county senior title combined with the Munster club.

"I struggled to make the county teams at under-age level. In 1992, when I made my inter-county debut in the Under-21 Championship, we lost the Munster final to Waterford. The following years of 1993 and 1994 were not much better on the county senior scene. In 1993, we were destroyed, ruthlessly so, by a Tipperary team. In 1994 we were well beaten by Limerick, probably the most disappointing performance by any Clare team which I've been associated with.

"In 1995, Clare won the All-Ireland. There was no magic formula which led to victory. We trained very hard. There was a fantastic work ethic within the team and the individuals associated with us."

The final whistle was the sound every Clare hurling ear had longed for for eighty-one years. They were now All-Ireland champions – Clare 1:13 Offaly 2:8.

Writing after the game in the *Irish Times*, Jimmy Barry Murphy commented: "I do remember being marked by a very good centre-back in the 1977 Munster final. His name was Gus Lohan. Yesterday his two sons Brian and Frank were brilliant. There is no other word to describe their performances."

Brian reminded me that his father played with Clare and his native Galway and won a variety of county hurling titles in an era spanning four decades, from the 1950s to the 1980s – and found time as well to play senior football for Monaghan and junior football for Clare – a career that took him into his early forties.

Dreams bothered many characters in the Old Testament. They feared the portents. So it was with Brian Lohan of Clare. On the Saturday night before the 1996 Munster semi-final against Limerick, he went to bed and in the course of the night had a dream in which he woke up on the Monday morning and reflected pleasingly on their victory over Limerick. It was a load off his mind. Then he woke up to realise that it was only Sunday morning and that the Limerick challenge still faced them. He was bothered

– not sure what way to interpret the dream; not sure what was at work in his subconscious. Well, at around five o'clock on Sunday evening he knew the reality. Clare, reigning All-Ireland champions and favourites in many quarters to retain the crown, led by 0:15 to 1:9 with five minutes remaining – and were looking good for victory. But missed opportunities by Clare and four remarkable points by Limerick from play snatched victory from the Banner men on the call of time. It was a nightmare ending. For Brian, the award of RTÉ Man of the Match was poor consolation.

In years to come, when many other games will have been confined to the limbo of forgotten things, Brian will still talk with vivid recollection and immense satisfaction of the 1994 Fitzgibbon Cup victory campaign. It will stand there, proudly, with other team and personal moments of glory:

"Victory in the Fitzgibbon Cup in 1994 – a competition that started in 1912 – was definitely one of my greatest moments in hurling. It was the University of Limerick's second title – the first in 1989. It was my last year in college. For three years we had played in the competition and won nothing. Then came 1994. We had a good team. We were physically strong, especially in the backs. We beat UCG, UCC and Waterford RTC in the final. All three games went to extra time. In the game against UCG, we got a goal in the last two minutes to beat them by one point. It was a fantastic game – had a few incidents. Weather conditions caused the game to be postponed from a Saturday to the following Wednesday. A huge crowd attended – fierce excitement. In the game against UCC, two sets of brothers were on opposite sides, the Maguires and ourselves. Victory in the final over Waterford RTC was reward for a dedicated training schedule. It went on from September to March – a huge mental and physical commitment."

Brian Lohan, holder of All-Ireland, provincial, All-Star, Fitzgibbon Cup, Railway Cup and club honours, was, according to Mícheál Ó Muircheartaigh: "no ordinary full-back and there have been numerous sightings of him racing to the corners, to the wings and betimes far outfield in his inimitable drive for possession. If a representative is ever needed to personify 'total hurling' it has to be Brian Lohan…His approach electrifies the atmosphere…adding a unique dimension."

SEÁN McMAHON
CLARE

Born: 1973
Interviewed: 2008

With his sons Eoghan (left), Cathal (in his arms) and Darragh in a Doora Barefield Jersey.

Seán McMahon was a spectator at the Munster final of 1993 between his native Clare and Tipperary at the Gaelic Grounds, Limerick. "It was the worst day I ever put down. I was on the terrace with some friends. Clare were being badly outplayed. Tipp. supporters were ragging us – half joking, half serious – saying it was only a training session for Tipp. Coming towards the end, my friends wanted to leave, but I wouldn't go – I wouldn't leave a match early ever." The final score was a merciless humiliation: 3:27 to 2:12 – a defeat more decisive than the final score might suggest.

Seán was twenty years of age when he was called to the senior panel in the autumn of 1993. "I was in UL [University of Limerick] at the time and there were no mobile phones so my father had to come to Limerick to tell me to be in Ballyline the following night for county training. I remember well feeling out of place, but Anthony Daly, sensing my unease, made me feel welcome and I always appreciated that.

"I grew up in a hurling atmosphere and my heroes were Joe Cooney, a fantastic player, Pete Finnerty and Tony Keady – all from Galway. In Clare it was Sean Stack – I only saw him towards the end, but I had heard so much about him." And the best of his playing days? "D.J. (Carey) was probably the best. Declan Ryan was the one I had the greatest battles with – a brilliant player, so big, a great hurler. I always admired Ken McGrath. The best corner-back, in fifteen years, I saw was Frank Lohan – he had the physique, pace and mental strength. His brother Brian was the best full-back."

Seán was centre half-back when Clare beat Tipperary by 2:11 to 0:13 in the Munster semi-final of 1994 – his championship debut. A county's pride was restored. Unfortunately, his hurling world fell apart again when Clare lost the Munster final to Limerick, 0:25 to 2:10. "There were seven points from play scored off myself and that was very disappointing. I learned a lot from that, but still it was a huge let down at the time." Drastic action was needed in Clare. In Sepember of that year, Ger Loughnane was called in as manager. A good league campaign ended with Clare losing the final to Kilkenny by 2:12 to 0:9. Following that result, some said Clare would never win anything. "But in the dressing-room, Ger said there was no one as good as Kilkenny and that we would win the Munster title."

On Sunday, 4 June, Clare faced Cork at the Gaelic Grounds. "I broke my collar bone as I went to clear a ball – that was in the last fifteen minutes. We had used all our subs so I couldn't go off. I went to corner-forward. I was now a one-handed hurler. Cork were two points up and very little time left when the ball came up to the Cork square. I pressurised the backs and forced them into clearing the ball over the sideline. Fergus Tuohy took the cut and Ollie Baker finished it to the net." Clare won by 2:13 to 3:9 and went on to beat Limerick 1:17 to 0:11 in the Munster final. "With my collar bone broken in the game against Cork I was lucky to make the Munster Final. Winning the All-Ireland afterwards was beyond our wildest dreams but it was amazing to be involved and to see what it did for the county."

"My greatest moment in all my hurling years was definitely the Munster final win of 1995. Growing up, my dream was about being in a Munster final – winning a Munster title. Croke Park and an All-Ireland were beyond my dreams. Things couldn't have been more right that day in Thurles. We were lucky with the players – a great blend. We were so determined that day. Davy Fitz. came down and got a goal from a penalty – we were a point up at half time. I remember we went six points up in the second half. But I was so scared Limerick would get a goal. Damien Quigley had hit the crossbar with a rasper in the first half and kicked a ball just wide of the posts in the second half. That's six points, you know. Then we went eight points up. I was still not accepting it. Soon we were nine up. Only then did I accept we would win."

The Clare half-back line that day was – Liam Doyle, Seán McMahon and Anthony Daly. It would represent the county for six years, 1995–2000 inclusive – one of the great half-back lines in the history of hurling.

During those years Seán McMahon grew in stature. He was superb at the heart of the Clare defence and gave displays that made him rank with the great centre half-backs of the game. So often, he was an inspiration to his colleagues and his points from long distance and far-out frees were McMahon specials.

The year 1995 opened the door to all kinds of honours for Seán – the first of three Munster titles, the first of two All-Ireland wins, the first of three All-Star awards. His outstanding displays of that year, as Clare accounted for Cork, Limerick, Galway and Offaly, saw him honoured with the Texaco Hurler of the Year Award.

In 1996, Seán won Railway Cup and Oireachtas medals and a few years later county titles and Munster club titles were added to Seán's list of honours. There was much to celebrate at St Joseph's Doora Barefield in 1999 when Rathnure were beaten in the All-Ireland club final by 2:14 to 0:8 – a game that, up to then, attracted the largest attendance, 40,106, to a club final.

Clare hurling and its players merited the seal of greatness in 1997. They accounted for the three superpowers of the game – Cork, Tipperary and Kilkenny.

"Proof that 1995 was no fluke. 1997 was the year − no question. It was our best combination. We were consistent and very good. If we had a failing it was not killing the opposition off."

Seán looks back on 1998 and 2005 with feelings of regret and disappointment at not winning All-Irelands in those years. The three games saga with Offaly in 1998 makes him wonder about the might-have-beens. And 2005, when Seán was captain, even more so: "In the semi-final against Cork we had hurled really well [but were] pipped by a point − a killer. I'd have bet the house that we'd have beaten Galway in the All- Ireland final − lost an All-Ireland in my eyes that year."

Seán McMahon, master hurler, prince of defenders, called it a day at county level after losing to Kilkenny 2:21 to 1:16 in the All-Ireland semi-final of 2006.

"I have enjoyed every minute of my hurling life and I feel very fortunate to have been able to play the greatest game in the world. Up the Banner!"

Seán McMahon.

GEORGE O'CONNOR
WEXFORD

Born: 1959
Interviewed: 1997

"1979 seems a long time ago now, but that was the first year I donned the Wexford jersey. It was against Offaly in the Oireachtas final. We were victorious that day, and little did I think on that day that it would be seventeen years later that we would walk the steps of the Hogan Stand once again.

"People sometimes ask how or why I kept going over those seventeen years. I suppose in the beginning it was an adventure, and the fact that Wexford were Leinster champions in 1976 and 1977 made expectations always high. Further to that, I suppose the love of the game was my incentive. To perform on the big stage was always an incentive thrill, coupled with the fact that I always enjoyed training and being part of the camaraderie of a team. My sincere belief that one day we would win was also a motivating factor. Throughout these years, while never achieving the ultimate, we were always able to compete with the best, which was very encouraging. In all the years of hurling and having played so many games and experienced so many defeats, 1996 was really a dream come true. It was an incredible year and one that no Wexford person will ever forget."

Sunday, 5 September 1996 turned out to be Thanksgiving Day for George. The final whistle, just before five o'clock, heralded a moment of prayer – prayer before celebration. We can only speculate about what silent words and thoughts passed through his mind, what thoughts, as he dropped to his knees on the sod of Croke Park, closed his eyes, and joined his hands in fervent prayer.

It had been a long career since that three-point Oireachtas final win over Offaly in 1979. A youthful George looked forward to hurling glory; he hoped to do better than his late father, Paddy, who captained a Wexford junior hurling team to Leinster honours in 1940. Many a spring promised an autumn harvest; but so many times a blight struck. Too often did the referee's final whistle spell nightmare, grief and disbelief. So many times in those seventeen years Wexford were as good as the best – kept the hurling flag flying; did honour to the game – yet they failed to reap a tangible reward.

Defeats sowed seeds of doubt in George's mind, especially as regards Croke Park, and as time passed he became a prisoner of those doubts. Yet he never abandoned hope. He felt that, given the breaks, combined with a disciplined approach and firm, positive management, and a proper mental outlook, Wexford could once again climb to the top of the hurling world.

The opportunity came in the person of Liam Griffin. "The opposition was studied in detail. A positive attitude was bred in every player."

On the pitch, George – who also played senior football for Wexford from 1978 to 1984 – cut a fine athletic figure. He was always very fit and mobile. He was conditioned to respond to physical demands by his daily work on the farm, and, as a consequence, the hardships associated with close physical exchanges on the field of play were taken by him in his stride.

In his displays, he combined flair and dash with the flamboyant and daring. He would soar into the air, oblivious of danger, to grab the sliotar with the left hand, a hand on which every finger has been broken at least once, where all the fingertips are damaged and bent: "My problem if an opponent pulls on the ball and I haven't protected the hand."

In the 1996 campaign George was as enthusiastic and committed as ever. He was happy to be part of the panel and play whatever role was required. To many of the players he was a father figure, looked up to and revered.

He played against Kilkenny and Dublin. Against Offaly, he came on in the closing stages; against Galway, he replaced his brother, John. On All-Ireland day against Limerick, Fate, unkind to Sean Flood – injured in the game against Galway – smiled on George, who was drafted from the substitutes to play at midfield. At thirty-seven years of age, it was a testing challenge for him but the experienced George was endowed with the physical and mental resilience for the occasion.

His All-Ireland medal at thirty-seven meant much more to George than if he had won it in his earlier years. At the celebration that night he savoured every moment, every detail, every smile and compliment. He wanted to be able to remember the occasion vividly in years to come and recall it clearly for family and friends. The privilege – which has eluded so many great hurlers – of winning an All-Ireland medal came George's way as the sun was setting and he took the stage for the last time. The final curtain came down in triumph amid a sea of purple and gold, and in that moment all the disappointments of a long career vanished from memory.

HUBERT RIGNEY
OFFALY

Born: 1971
Interviewed: 2002

"I was brought up, I suppose, in the thick of hurling tradition in the townland of Coolfin, Banagher, Co. Offaly. I grew up in the famed club St Rynagh's, who, by the time I was born, had made a name for themselves all around the country. I first played a competitive hurling match for St Rynagh's when I was eleven. My first hurling medal arrived when I was thirteen in a competition in Galway. We beat Portumna in that match. I would have been encouraged to keep up hurling by my father and older brother Kieran who, when I was under fourteen, was a selector. I have been fortunate to have been selected to play for my county at minor, under-21 and senior level.

"The highlight of my career would have to be All-Ireland day 1998 and the feeling when you have just won an All-Ireland title. The fact that I was captain made it all the more special in 1998."

Hubert Rigney was born in 1971 – son of Hubert and Philomena (née Gothery), a Galway lady from the parish of Tynagh. He was ten years old in 1981 as he watched on TV the men of the "faithful county" defeat Galway and take their first ever All-Ireland crown. Damien Martin, Pádraig Horan and Aidan Fogarty became his heroes.

Hubert won an All-Ireland minor title in 1989 when Offaly defeated Clare in the final. A year later, in the winter of 1990, he made his debut in the senior jersey of Offaly. "It was a league game against Derry on a rural pitch in Derry – a wet windy day. We beat them – not by much – and went on to win the league title – our first and only one to date."

From then on Hubert became a key figure in the Offaly defence. He has always played with a quiet authority – a style that is a reflection of his personality. Attention and adherence to the basics of the game and the execution of same with a simple and phlegmatic approach stand out as his forte.

He has played in many epic contests with Offaly. Among them must surely rank the Leinster final of 1995. It was, without doubt, the best game of the year and one of the great ones in the history of the game. Thunder and lightning and torrential rain presaged the drama of the game. This was hurling of rare splendour – fast, furious and first time; the stuff traditionalists love. Hubert was at the centre of the defence where he controlled the stout-hearted and energetic John Power – a defence that was phalanx-like in the face of every Kilkenny assault. A defence in which he joined with his colleagues in blocking, hooking, parrying, harassing, covering, batting and chasing with a spirit of no surrender. We witnessed a game for the gods.

The year 1998 dawned and the Hurling Championship began. It was a brave pundit who would have attempted a forecast. There was a strong field. In the end it proved to be Offaly's year. It was a long adventurous journey. It was a campaign in which they played eight games – the most any county ever had to play to capture the blue riband. "We were up and down. There were stages when we didn't know where we were. The pinnacle of the year was the final whistle on All-Ireland day – a very tight game. You need a bit of luck, no matter what." And the game he enjoyed most? "It has to be the third game against Clare in Thurles – it was unbelievable that day."

The campaign was not a tour-de-force performance of displays by Offaly – rather, an up-and-down graph. Their manager Babs Keating, dissatisfied with the Leinster final display against Kilkenny, departed the scene. He was replaced by Michael Bond, a Galway man. They played Kilkenny in a challenge two weeks later and lost by twenty points.

Tom Humphries wrote: "In Kilkenny, when they came off that evening having humiliated their most passionate enemies, they should have listened to the winds. That's all there was to hear. In the Offaly dressing-room it was quiet, too quiet. The boys of Summer were about to get serious."

We saw them in earnest in the third game against Clare in Thurles on Saturday 29 August – a day in which Hubert Rigney and his team demonstrated what they were really capable of; a day when we saw hurling of rip-roaring intensity, glorious pace and fierce passion; a day when aggression tested sportsmanship to the limits, and sportsmanship prevailed.

Writing on the game in the *Sunday Tribune*, Kevin Cashman had this to say: "Offaly's defence was probably tighter than it was even in the most Alcatraz days of its long experience. . . . Hubert Rigney had his best game ever at centre back. He was at the side of every colleague in the slightest difficulty. His striking was conciseness embodied, and *mirabile dictu*, he probably pucked more ball than Whelehan. Kevin Martin was tremendous too."

And so to the final against Kilkenny. Hubert and his men had a tentative start. They had luck when Brian Whelehan cleared a certain goal off the line and more luck when Stephen Byrne saved a rasper that had "goal" written all over it. Most importantly of all, though they had misfortune that turned to gold. A flu-stricken Brian Whelehan left the right half wing of the Offaly defence creaking. Michael Duignan moved from attack to defence to seal the gap. Brian Whelehan went to full-forward, proceeded to score 1:6 and emerged as Man of the Match.

As the game progressed, a superb Offaly defence marshalled around an increasingly effective Hubert Rigney, tightened their grip on proceedings and, like a collection of clams, sealed the road to goal.

A contest to savour ended Offaly 2:16, Kilkenny 1:13. Hubert Rigney had captained Offaly to their fourth All-Ireland success. It was easily Offaly's All-Ireland win of greatest splendour.

Hubert Rigney

MARTIN STOREY
WEXFORD

Born: 1964
Interviewed: 1997

"I grew up in the half-parish of the Ballagh, the other half being Oulart. From as long as I can remember, hurling played a very important part in my life. I am the youngest of eight children and started playing hurling at the age of six or five." Fast forward to 1996 and we found Martin Storey at the helm for Wexford. "My career was beginning to slip away from me and Wexford hurling was at a low ebb when a man called Liam Griffin took over as manager in 1994."

Martin was an inspiring captain and had a splendid season in 1996, which culminated in a well-deserved All-Star award, his second such honour. His leadership and experience had a settling and calming influence on his colleagues, especially the younger members of the panel. Martin probably had his best year ever in the purple-and-gold jersey, with speed and quick stick-work being the hallmark of his style as he strode with authority the terrain that a half-forward must strive to dominate if his team is to succeed.

As Martin held the MacCarthy Cup aloft in the Hogan Stand, success-starved Wexford fans gave vent to their feelings. He had much to reflect on in a campaign where Wexford had to battle with intensity. There was no easy game. Courage, character, fitness, endeavour, composure and concentration were all tested at different times to the very limits. For it was, as their trainer Liam Griffin said, a game for warriors – the Riverdance of sport. After the Leinster final, Liam Griffin said, "If we're going to win the All-Ireland I want to do it in a year when we beat Kilkenny, Dublin, Offaly, Galway and Limerick." He had his wish.

It had been a memorable campaign, and I wondered how Martin had perceived each of the five hurdles. "In the early stages of the game against Kilkenny I couldn't believe I was getting so much freedom. We led at half time by nine points to four, but before the last quarter Kilkenny had cut our lead to one point. The doubts come at you. You can get as used to losing as you can to winning; it can be very hard to get rid of doubts. Then Billy Byrne scored a great goal. It then clicked with me that we could win this one – Wexford 1:14, Kilkenny 0:14.

"Would you believe it, Dublin was the one team I was afraid of. I was nervous. We were expected to beat them. The final whistle was a relief: it was like getting out of jail.

"My one memory of the game against Offaly was the minute the final whistle went. It was the memory of the year for me. It sank in straight away: I was after winning something with Wexford. I had ten seconds to myself, and I thought to myself, Wexford will walk up the steps of the Hogan Stand today – not Kilkenny, not Dublin, not Offaly. It was a brilliant feeling. It gave me the greatest satisfaction. I have the ball from that game." The game was a classic: Wexford were rank outsiders, Offaly red-hot favourites. The game had everything, including a surprise result.

"In the game against Galway you could say we got out of the fire. The hurling at times was scrappy, because so much was at stake. The pace was so fast and furious you hadn't time to settle on the ball. What surprised me was the poor quality of the Galway free-taking. But, being a Wexfordman, I could understand!"

The path was now clear for an All-Ireland clash with Limerick, the first such meeting since 1918. "Both teams were very well prepared. We were calmer before the match, and it stood to us. It was always going to be a fifty-fifty game. At the beginning of the championship I would have settled for a Leinster title, but when we won that, we said we were going to win the All-Ireland. For me the whole day was special. It was nineteen years since Wexford hurled in September. I was captain. I was playing on the Limerick captain, Ciarán Carey, with whom I was friendly down the years.

"The first five balls or so that came my way, Ciarán got all of them. He was hurling much better than me. I could feel my head sinking. How could I encourage the team if I wasn't producing the goods myself? On one occasion I went to chase Ciarán and tripped over myself. I pointed to Damien [Fitzhenry] to send me a high one. He waved his hand saying no, I'd missed too many. Then he sent me one. I caught it and got a free. My attitude changed."

The final whistle saw Wexford capture their sixth All-Ireland crown: a three-point win over Kilkenny; six points to spare over Dublin; an eight-point defeat of Offaly; Galway headed by three points; a two-point win over Limerick. Unlike defeat – and especially after so many of them – the realisation of victory sank in very slowly. "I found it awful hard to grasp it. At times I found it hard to believe. I woke up the morning after the game in the hotel and saw the cup beside me near the bed. Jesus, I thought to myself, we're after winning it!" *An rud is annamh is iontach!*

Martin Storey

2000—

ANDY COMERFORD
KILKENNY

Born: 1972
Interviewed: 2002

Andy in his year of captaincy (2002), with the spoils of victory. (Photo courtesy of his mother Kathleen.)

"My father manufacturing a hurl for me from a flooring board was my intro to hurling. From there to the school in St John's, I served my hurling apprenticeship. Although unsuccessful, it was a good education – hurling education, that is.

"From there I went to St Kieran's College, where success was bred into players. A great period but the education suffered – unfortunately, mother. I met players there who I would have the honour of winning All-Irelands with in later years. Graduation to Kilkenny Seniors was easy after a hurling upbringing like that.

"My biggest thrill in hurling has to have been winning the senior county final with my brothers Martin and Jimmy and my friends who hurled with me throughout the lean periods with O'Loughlin's and St John's."

It was around 5.00 p.m. on the afternoon of Sunday, 8 September 2002. Referee Aodhán Mac Suibhne of Dublin blew the final whistle in Croke Park to bring to an end an absorbing All-Ireland hurling final between Clare and Kilkenny.

The scoreboard was a source of joy and elation to every Kilkenny supporter in the official attendance of 76,254.

Andy Comerford, Kilkenny's twenty-second successful captain had guided the Noresiders to their twenty-seventh All-Ireland crown. Earlier in the year he had led them to a tenth National League success.

There was a glow of modest triumph and satisfaction in Andy Comerford's face as he held aloft the MacCarthy Cup to exultant Kilkenny followers. Later in the dressing room he exhorted his colleagues to celebrate victory with pride and dignity. "Don't spoil this great victory by doing rash things now or some weeks or months down the line. We have gained the respect of the entire hurling world so let's not blow it."

This big, rangy man of 6'2" and turning the scales fit at 13½ st. was born in London in 1972 where he spent the first seven years of his life and "never caught a hurley".

Back in Ireland, he developed his hurling skills at under-age level with his club, O'Loughlin-Gaels, in Kilkenny City.

At St Kieran's College, his hurling talents won him a place on the college senior team and he won successive All-Ireland titles in 1989 and 1990.

In the early 1990s, Andy emigrated to England. Hurling remained a major part of his recreation. He played his hurling with Brother Pearse's Club and practised at Ruislip and, on occasion, at Ealing soccer pitch. "In London the hurling was tough."

Andy won an All-Ireland senior "B" medal with London – place of his birth – in 1995, following victories over New York and Wicklow.

Back in Ireland, Andy won his place on the Kilkenny senior team. He made his debut against Dublin in the championship of 1997, lost the All-Ireland finals of 1998 and 1999 to Offaly and Cork respectively, but won the All-Ireland contest of 2000 when Kilkenny gave a display of precision and power-packed hurling to record a fine victory over Offaly.

Andy is a player in the mould of a Frank Cummins rather than that of a John Fenton. When he moved well at midfield – his favourite position – Kilkenny's performance was enhanced.

As captain, Andy had that essential gift of being a great leader and inspirational captain both prior to a game and on the field of play. He was also a wonderful motivator and brings a spirit of total commitment to the task on hand.

He operated at midfield like a hungry forager. His style was determined, tenacious and speedy of delivery. It was exceedingly difficult to outshine Andy because of his capacity to disrupt play. He had a great engine and his high energy levels enabled him to instinctively fall back towards defence or advance forward as the tide of battle demands. You found him at the main action with remarkable regularity.

In the All-Ireland final of 2002, Andy led a Kilkenny hurling outfit that was fine tuned and trained to the ounce by their manager Brian Cody, and were majestic and awesome in almost everything they did.

Andy will always look back on 2002 with great pride, and the honour and privilege of being captain will gather added value and nostalgic glory as the years speed on; as will the sharing of the glory with his brother Martin who played at full-forward that day.

Diarmuid O'Flynn, writing in the *Irish Examiner*, summed matters up well in his Monday morning report on the game:

The thunder and lightning All-Ireland final of 1939, Kilkenny and Cork, has gone into the annals of GAA history. The Cats won that one too, but yesterday, in the new magnificence that is Croke Park, they blew up a storm all on their own. Thunder at the back, lightning up front, the cyclonic force that is Captain Comerford with Lyng alongside at midfield, an immense Kilkenny team took what has been probably the most physical force ever in hurling and blitzed them off the park . . .The thunder, the lightning, but on this year, it all came up from the pitch. Split the heavens above, tore the Banner apart.

It was a privilege to have been there.

BRENDAN CUMMINS
TIPPERARY

Born: 1975
Interviewed: 2008

"I would like to reflect on 2001 as it was the year for my biggest achievements: to win league, All-Ireland, All-Star and be part of a squad that were undefeated in every game played that year.

"The journey to this started in 1999 when Nicky English took over as manager. He had Ken Hogan and Jack Bergin as selectors with him. The training started in November that year and was totally physical, all running – getting up at 6.00 a.m. and heading to the Devil's Bit outside Templemore more times than I care to remember. We won the league that year but Clare beat us in the first round of the championship so that was the end of our year.

"We met again in November 2000 to start the process again. The training changed slightly as it was decided that there was no game played on the side of a mountain and so we would have to change our style to win. The training changed to more speed work with shorter runs and the intensity had increased. The game was changing so we had to adapt. We were beaten in the Munster final in 2000 by Cork, and three weeks later Galway beat us in the quarter-final in Croker by three points. This was one of the lowest points in my career. So much effort for no reward. We formed a circle in the dressing-room after the game and made the promise to each other that the following year 'Liam' would be in the middle. A meeting was held in Thurles in December of that year, to plan for 2001. We all had gained enough experience over the previous year – it was now time to win something. The training was a mix of the previous two years. I can remember thinking that I had never trained so hard and made as many sacrifices – the team all felt the same.

"The league went well again; we were winning all the close games. We beat Clare in the final in Limerick. Things went well for me on the day; always great to contribute to a win, especially a final. The Cup was put to one side, there was a bigger prize.

"We went back down to Cork to play Clare. This time we won by one point. Players collapsed after the game – the heat and the relief that we had gotten over the hump. Clare were going well – we had beaten them. In the Munster final we beat Limerick – hottest day of the Summer. Two-point win this time. When the whistle blew the sense of achievement was great but we all knew this was still only a stepping stone to the bigger prize.

"We had six weeks off before Wexford and this was nearly our undoing. When we arrived in Croker for the semi we were nearly caught. This was the worst I have ever felt in the goals. I was very nervous on the day. Wexford got three goals and we escaped with a draw.

"The replay the following Saturday, we won easily in the end. We had gotten our wake-up call. I felt like myself again in goal.

"The final was a huge occasion. We headed to Dublin the day before with a band at the train station. I had played in the 1997 final but was too young to appreciate the importance of it all. This could be the last final I would ever play in. It was to be enjoyed but had to be won. The feeling leaving the dressing-room heading for the tunnel and the wall of noise hitting the field was like nothing I had ever experienced. All work had been done since 1999 – we were ready. The parade and meeting the President was to be enjoyed but I was looking forward to getting the game going.

"The end came when we were three points up and Pat O'Connor signalled to me I had the last puck out. I can remember delaying it. I wanted that moment to last forever. One more hit and the job was done. In the dressing-room after the game we formed the circle and 'Liam' was in the middle.

"I want to recognise the contribution my family has made to that day and my hurling career. My wife Pamela, who has always been very understanding. There are new beginnings now with the arrival of my son Paul on 17 Jan (2008). I have a few years left in the game – hopefully more highs to come."

Brendan, an only child, was born to John and Ann (née O'Donoghue) on 11 May 1975. He grew up in football territory in South Tipperary and, until his minor days, football would have been his number one game. This, no doubt, was influenced by the fact that his father had played at county level for Tipperary and was chosen in the 1960s to play for Munster in the Railway Cup competition.

When Brendan settled down to playing both hurling and football, his proficiency took him to the highest level in both games. He played in goal for the county senior hurling team and at centre half-forward for the senior football team. He is acutely aware that a goalkeeper represents the last line of defence for a team.

Some hurling supporters remember the "soft" ones that go in. They tend not to fade from memory. I recalled for Brendan the succession of marvellous saves he made in the All-Ireland semi-final of 2003 against Kilkenny.

Reporting on the game in the *Irish Independent*, Martin Breheny had this to say: "The winning margin (3:18 to 0:15) would have been far higher were it not for the remarkable defiance of Cummins who produced at least six truly amazing saves."

Brendan has given wonderful service to his county since he became its established senior custodian in 1995. Between the posts – agile, ever-alert, composed and athletic – he is at all times in tune with his defenders: "I live with my backs – we set out a plan and stick to it."

Since I met Brendan in the early days of Spring 2008 he has added to his All-Star awards of 2000, 2001 and 2003 and won a second All-Ireland medal following an epic contest with Kilkenny in 2010.

KEN McGRATH
WATERFORD

Born: 1978
Interviewed: 2009

Ken and his father Pat putting the finishing touches to hurleys in the kitchen. (Photo courtesy of Ken McGrath.)

"My earliest hurling memories are chasing my father around Mount Sion's pitch – I'd say I was around four or five. My father played for Waterford and Mount Sion for most of the seventies and eighties, and myself and my older brother Roy would watch him train any chance we could.

"To us in the house my father was our hero. He had played for Waterford for years without much success but he was still talked about as a great player in hurling circles. Mount Sion offered more hope and he won seven county medals and a Munster club medal.

"We all started off playing for Mount Sion, myself and my three brothers Roy, Eoin and Pat. I was playing well enough and I was asked up to the

SEÁN ÓG Ó hAILPÍN
CORK

Born: 1977
Interviewed: 2008

"Tosnaíonn turas fada le coischéim amháin. I remember landing into Cork on a miserable February day in 1988, having spent the Christmas in Rotuma when Mum said her final goodbyes to her family. That was a tough day for her and her emotions showed it too. After the initial few weeks and shock of settling into our new life in Cork, hurling came to my rescue. I joined the nearest hurling club from our house in Fair Hill, Na Piarsaigh H & F Club, and never looked back since. I became part of a community and the northside people accepted their new adopted son. I started to make friends but there was one more obstacle I still had to overcome – [I] had to master this beautiful ancient game of hurling. Having been part of the 1994 victorious Harty Cup team with 'The Mon.', this gave me huge confidence of taking my hurling to the ultimate level – inter-county. I played two years' minor for Cork where I won an All-Ireland in 1995 under the guidance of the former Cork great Jimmy Barry Murphy. Next up was the three years I played for the Cork under-21s where we landed

two All-Irelands in 1997 and 1998. Great achievements, but you soon realise after spending years in Cork that its about winning senior All-Ireland medals. My first break came in 1996 when I was called into the Cork senior hurling squad by then Manager Jimmy Barry Murphy. A dream was realised when I made my debut in Senior Championship hurling when I came on as a sub against Limerick that year.

"Hurling came at a time in my life when my morale was low after leaving Australia. I was heartbroken leaving Sydney. Hurling and its demands have developed me from a boy to a man. Without the game I would definitely have not turned out to be the rounded, groomed person that I am today. I thank the game for that. I thank the sport for introducing me to values such as determination, commitment, honesty, will to win, dedication and respect – values that I have brought to other aspects of my life. But most of all I thank the game for the endless friends, players and people that I have met. Hurling community is unique. *Mar a deireann an seanfhocal – An rud is annamh, is iontach.*"

In the Pacific Ocean, on a line of east longitude close to the International Date Line and about 12° south of the Equator, lies a Fijian Island called Rotuma. It was there that Seán Óg – the eldest of a family of four boys, Seán Óg, Setanta, Aisake, Teu, and two girls, Sarote and Etaoin – was born on 22 May 1977. The social structure on the island, under seven chiefs, was tribal.

Seán Óg's mother, Emeli, was Fijian; her ancestors were Polynesian – seafaring people, warriors of tremendous strength and physical endurance. Emeli was taught at school by two Irish missionary priests, Fr Maguire, now enjoying his eternal reward, and Fr Johnson.

His father, Seán, hailed from Rosslea, in Co. Fermanagh. In the early 1970s he headed for Scotland in search of work and from there to Australia. While there, he and a few friends decided to take a holiday in Fiji. The receptionist in the hotel where they stayed was Emeli. The rest is a little piece of history.

Seán Óg was only two years old when the family moved to Sydney on the east coast of Australia. He remembers getting up with his father at midnight to listen to the All-Ireland final broadcasts. Jimmy Barry Murphy became a hero – the name appealed to him. Little did he realise how closely their futures would be linked. He took to his young heart the Kerry footballers, influenced by the fact that his grandmother, Peggy O'Sullivan, came from Kilgarvan.

Success on the Gaelic fields came Seán Óg's way quickly – a National League medal in 1998, followed by All-Ireland titles in 1999, 2004 and 2005. As a dual player, Seán Óg lined out at full-back for Cork in the 1999 Football Championship. The team was successful in Munster but lost to Meath in the All-Ireland final 1:11 to 1:8. Earlier that year, he won a National League medal with a win over Dublin and a Railway Cup medal following victory over Connaught.

Seán Óg has collected three All-Star awards. In 2004 there was no doubting the outstanding hurling man of the season. He received the Hurler of the Year award from three sources – Texaco, Vodafone and GPA. He was also named as RTÉ Sports Person of the Year.

His versatility as a sportsman was in evidence in 2004 and 2005 when he was selected to play against Australia in the Compromise Rules Football games.

There were joyful celebrations in the Ó hAilpín household in 2004 after Seán Óg, Setanta and Aisake – three giants of 6'2", 6'5" and 6'6" respectively – won the Cork County senior hurling title with Na Piarsaigh.

Seán Óg has been a wonderful ambassador for our games. His sportsmanship on the pitch has been impeccable, his commitment total – a truly superb role model for youth.

The man is physically very strong and fiercely committed. He won't be shouldered off his feet. There is tremendous strength in his body and hips – the kind of strength we associate with rugby players from the part of the world where he was born. This is the strength of the warriors that were his mother's ancestors.

Seán Óg is more than an ambassador for our games. He makes one feel proud as he speaks in our native language – one of three languages spoken in the Ó h-Ailpín household. I have particularly in mind his speech in Semple Stadium in 2005 after he had captained Cork to a Munster crown – a speech for which he thanks Brother Jack Beausang, his Irish teacher at North Mon.

Our very pleasant meeting drew to a close and we prepared to go our separate ways. *"Go mbeirimíd beo ar an am seo arís,"* arsa Seán Óg, agus sinn *ag fágaint slán le céile. Maith thú, a Sheáin.*

Seán Óg.

HENRY SHEFFLIN
KILKENNY

Born: 1979
Interviewed: 2009

"My earliest memory of hurling would be of myself and my younger brother Paul getting two squash rackets, a tennis ball and heading out to the squash court behind my father's public house in Ballyhale. There we would play a hurling match between us until one of us started crying and went running in to my mother. (I must say this was normally Paul!).

"In those early days I was in the heartland of hurling. My club Bally-hale Shamrocks was contesting county titles each year and were the most successful club around at that time. This is where I developed the love for the game.

"From the mad world of the pub I moved up the 100 yards to my local national school. This is where I came across Joe Dunphy who developed so many hurlers for Ballyhale and Kilkenny.

"From there I went to the other heartland of hurling in Kilkenny – St
Kieran's College. Both my older brothers had gone there so I kept up
the tradition. I must add that I suffered a bit here as I was not up to the
standard of a lot of the other kids and was well down the pecking order
in hurling teams. But it did teach me to work hard and by the time I had
left Kieran's, I felt I had done this – with an All-Ireland College's medal
to boot.

"I have been very lucky to come from (a) a club like Ballyhale and (b) a
county like Kilkenny. Yes, I have had success to date but what I take more
pleasure out of is the friends and enjoyment I have got out of all those
years. People often ask me, "What was your best achievement?" Winning
my first club county final in 2006. Full stop.

"I would like to say a special word of thanks to all who have helped
me in the numerous ways over the years in my hurling endeavours: to Joe
Dunphy, Brian Cody (greatest manager ever), the Shefflin family and my
wife Deirdre O'Sullivan and her family. There are a lot more people but
too many to name."

The name Shefflin intrigued me. I had never come across it in GAA lore
or, indeed, anywhere else for that matter. I wondered if it was of Norman
origin, given Kilkenny's strong Norman links. I probed and discovered
that Henry's great grandfather emigrated from Carrickmacross, Co.
Monaghan towards the end of the nineteenth century. He left Ireland as
Shevlin; when he returned he was Shefflin.

Henry is one of a family of seven, four boys and three girls, born to
Henry and May (née Fitzgerald) on 11 Jan 1979. Henry Snr spent a few
years in England and played with Warwickshire in the All-Ireland Junior
Hurling final of 1965 against Roscommon at Dr Hyde Park. They lost by
two points, 3:10 to 2:11. On the Roscommon team was Gerry O'Malley
of football fame. The Warwickshire team was trained by Paddy Phelan, a
Kilkenny man, one of the great wing-backs of hurling, who excelled for
Kilkenny in the 1930s. Henry was home to stay in 1965. He played with
the local club – no honours came his way. However, his brother Denis
captained Ballyhale Shamrocks to their first county title in 1978.

On the Fitzgerald side (definitely Norman), Henry's uncle, the late
Monsignor Paul, played minor for Kilkenny, while a cousin, also Paul,
played at senior level and also played for Leinster in the Railway Cup.
So, as the saying goes, there was hurling in the blood. Henry's three

brothers John, Tommy and Paul all wore the county jersey at under-21 level. Tommy won an under-21 All-Ireland medal in 1990 and John won a minor title the same year.

Talent and artistry are manifested in a variety of ways. In the case of Henry Shefflin, this was done through the medium of hurling. He has proved to be one of the great exponents of the game and when he retires his name will reside in the company of the all-time greats, where a place awaits him.

Henry made his county senior debut in 1999 just as the door opened on another golden era for Kilkenny that has rivalled, and may yet surpass, the one of the early days of the twentieth century.

Henry has played a major role in the glorious days that began following a one point defeat by Cork, 0-13 to 0-12, in the All-Ireland final of 1999. Throughout his career, he has been a prolific scorer, a consistently high performer, an inspirational colleague. Just picture him on the pitch – tall, slim and athletic: 6'2" and turning the scales some pounds short of 14 st, full of speed, stamina and skill, with a huge work rate and driven by a never-say-die spirit.

He has received much praise: Nicky English of Tipperary hurling fame said of him that he "adds perspiration to inspiration and raises the team's tempo." "King Henry" was how one sports editor chose to head his article. "The best I've seen" was Brian Cody's assessment. "Supernal" wrote journalist Kevin Cashman.

Henry, during his playing days to date, has won every honour in the game, including Hurler of the Year Awards, All Stars, National Leagues, All-Ireland club and seven All-Ireland titles. He was captain of the county team that won the All-Ireland in 2007. It has been the kind of return that most hurlers, including some of the great ones, could only dream of. Henry knows he has been fortunate and privileged to have come on the hurling scene at a time when his club and county were reigning supreme.

So, with so many trophies, medals and awards to his name, was there – could there have been – a disappointing moment? "Yes, there was. It was the 2005 county final against James Stephens. I played very poorly. I missed chances. We lost. I had never won a county final – I began to feel we could never win one. I felt bad."

Homer had nodded. But not for long. Henry was back with a venge-
ance in 2006 to play a great championship and score ten points against the
O'Loughlin Gaels in the county final.

A further glow was added to Henry's achievements when the final whistle blew on the All-Ireland final of 2011. He won his eighth All-Ireland
medal and joined the illustrious ranks of Christy Ring (Cork) and John
Doyle (Tipperary). So, also, did his team mates Noel Hickey and Eddie
Brennan.